LIVING WITH A GIFTED CHILD

LIVING WITH A GIFTED CHILD

by

Frieda Painter

With an Intelligence Test devised by
Dr. L. F. Lowenstein, MA, Dip. Psych, PhD
Assisted by Pat Thorne, BSc

SOUVENIR PRESS

Photoset in Great Britain by
Rowland Phototypesetting Ltd,
Bury St Edmunds, Suffolk
Printed in Great Britain by
Mackays of Chatham Ltd, Kent

Contents

Illustrations

Figures

Tables

Introduction

Perhaps you have a very clever boy or girl – or a baby who takes an unusual amount of interest in what is going on around him? You probably start wondering whether your child is gifted and how you can get some idea as to how bright or talented he really is.*

This book will help you find out. Then, if you think your child really is exceptional in some way, it will tell you how to get confirmation from someone outside the family. You will probably also begin to wonder what you ought to do to make sure that your boy or girl has the best opportunities – and you will start to become conscious of the extra responsibilities that rearing a gifted child imposes on parents and the sort of difficulties which may arise. This book will help you in these ways as well. It also gives you some simple tests to use in order to find out whether you are justified in thinking your child is exceptional. If the results show that you are, it will tell you how to obtain objective evidence by arranging for an educational psychologist to give your child an IQ test.

If your child is exceptionally bright, knowing in advance the difficulties you might meet and how to avoid them will help you do the best for him. An understanding of the reasons why problems may arise, and of the form they may take, will place you in a much stronger position for tackling them should the need occur. So Chapter 1 explains some of the root causes of difficulties in bringing up a gifted or very bright child. Chapter 2 describes the experiences of several boys and girls and illustrates the sort of thing that can happen if preventive measures are not taken. The questions as to why and how gifted children are different from others are complicated. One way of trying to answer them is to look at what the IQ is and how

---

* Whatever is said about boys in this book applies equally to girls.

IQ tests are devised. In Chapter 3 an attempt is made at answering these questions as simply as possible; a test is included so that parents can get a rough estimate of their child's IQ.

You will want to know, too, what positive options are open to you so that not only will you be able to avoid difficulties but also be in a position to take steps to aid your child's growth and development. So the subsequent chapters look at the sort of things you can do at home, whether your boy or girl is still at the pre-school stage or has already started attending a primary or secondary school. You will also want to know the sort of toys and games to choose in order to stimulate his learning without cutting across what the school is trying to do.

Which school to send your son or daughter to is a major decision. It will affect his or her whole future life. It is not only a question of which schools are more efficient than others and of knowing what to look for when deciding which is best – it is also necessary to know which school is most likely to be the most suitable for the educational needs of your particular child, taking into account his or her temperament, personality and intellectual ability. A later chapter explains the ways in which schools differ, the differences between private and state education, the extent of the choice that you have and your rights under the law.

As your son or daughter passes through secondary school, the time comes when decisions have to be made regarding the subjects in which to specialise and those to be dropped. The choices made will depend largely on what he wants his future career to be. But the issue is more complicated than this, since, during the years between their pre-O level course and the time when, as young adults, they want to take up some particular study in higher education geared to a specific occupation, many boys and girls change their views as to what they want to do as adults. Chapter 8 sets out some of the essential points to take into consideration when a youngster is deciding on his future career. It describes how to find out how various occupations differ from each other, with the aim of helping parents and adolescents to make the right choices about future careers while they are still in school.

At the same time, the chapter supplies information for those who did choose the wrong options at O level stage, and seeks to show them how they can still obtain the sort of job in which they believe they can make the greatest contribution and achieve most satisfaction.

1 The Problem

Why are gifted children a problem to so many parents –
and to many teachers as well? It might have been expected
that to have a gifted boy or girl in the family, or in a school
class, would be a source of unalloyed pride and pleasure for
the child's parents and for the school. Sometimes this is so,
but often it is a cause of worry in the home and an
embarrassment for teachers. It seems amazing that this
should so frequently be the case, but unfortunately there
is no doubt that serious difficulties often arise. It is in
order to try and help those parents who have the responsibility of bringing up a gifted child to avoid the pitfalls, that
some of the reasons for this situation will now be examined.

What are the most usual difficulties and problems? As
everyone knows, all children differ from each other. Even
brothers and sisters within the same family are often very
different with regard to temperaments, personalities and
interests, and this is even more true in a school where
about thirty children may be brought together in the same
classroom at any one time. In spite of the natural differences between them, all children have to learn certain
patterns of behaviour and, at the same time, be given
opportunities to develop their own individuality.

The essential things that a child must learn derive from
the fact that man lives in a society. If he did not, his life
would be 'nasty, brutish and short', as Thomas Hobbes
recognised in the seventeenth century. The individual
gains to an inestimable extent from living with other
people, but has at the same time to accept some limitation
on his freedom of action. The benefits and restrictions of
living in a society are found in every aspect of life, starting
in the family, where the young child first learns that he
cannot have everything he wants. Other constraints on an
individual's actions are found when he enters the wider

world of school, and subsequently the world of work when he becomes a young adult. Yet in spite of the limitations which inevitably affect a youngster's actions and with which he is forced to comply, there are always opportunities for boys and girls to develop their own individual personalities and interests. This is not to say that everyone has the same chance of achieving self-fulfilment. In fact it is here that we find the root causes of the difficulties and problems that come with the rearing and education of gifted children. Although a variety of choices is open to the individual, at different stages in a child's development these are limited by constraints on his actions – which are due to his stage of physical growth and the prohibitions on certain types of behaviour imposed by the family and the community. For most children these limitations may be annoying and irritating and lead to the occasional flare-up of temper, but the resentment is usually fairly superficial and short-lived. For gifted and very bright children the situation is often more serious.

We all know how children of the same age can vary in size. Although most five-year-olds will be about the same height, some will be shorter and some taller than the average – and one or two children may be very much shorter or very much taller than the rest. In the same way nearly all seven-year-olds are bigger than most five-year-olds, but occasionally a very tall five-year-old will be the same height as most of the children two years older, or, most unusually, even taller than they are. That most children conform to an average in their physical development but that a few are different are very well known facts. Nearly all mothers will have been at some time or other into a shop to buy their child a T-shirt and have been asked by the shop assistant, 'How old is he?', in order that she may fetch the right size. In fact, most manufacturers of children's clothes mark the sizes in years. Some mothers of children who are particularly big or small for their age have come to recognise that they must buy a garment marked, say, size 8 or 9 years, or 6 or 5 years, as the case may be, when the actual age of their boy or girl is seven. If a child is especially large or small for his age, as a rule, the abnormality does not cause any great difficulty: in spite of the child's age, his or her physical size can easily be seen and so articles of clothing can be bought that are a good fit.

There are great differences, too, in children's mental development but, unlike the physical variations, these frequently give rise to misunderstandings and difficulties. Differences between different children's intellectual capabilities cannot be seen as in the case of physical growth. It is true that it is not difficult to recognise, among a group of children of the same age, that some are more advanced than others. At the same time, it is very difficult to say *how* much more able a boy or girl may be compared with the rest of his age group. The differences between children's height or weight can be measured with a ruler and a pair of scales – there is no comparable, easy and precise way of measuring variations between children's mental abilities or the extent to which they are talented in some particular way.

The fact that gifted and very intelligent children are mentally advanced for their age holds out promise of great achievements and benefits in the future, but it is also the source of two kinds of difficulty.

The nature of the first sort of difficulty is indicated by the way in which a psychologist once described a highly gifted six-year-old boy: 'He has a man's mind in a boy's body.' While the other cases of very bright and gifted children may not be as extreme as this one was, the description does point clearly to an important cause of frustration and temper tantrums in many intellectually advanced children. A baby in his pram who is mentally alert may want to reach out to something he sees – perhaps a brightly coloured flower in the garden – but although he stretches forward he has not yet developed the physical ability to get out of his pram and go to it, so he points and starts to cry. The same sort of thing happens with older children too. A boy or girl may be quick to see how to do something but has not yet developed the necessary manual dexterity. One of the commonest things found with gifted children is bad handwriting. The reason is, of course, that their thoughts run on so rapidly that they cannot write them down quickly enough; untidy and poorly formed letters are the result and quite often words are missed out, too. Able teenagers, also, often become impatient to leave school and to enter into adult life, either by going to some institution of higher education or by starting work.

This first group of difficulties comes from within and results from the child's mental growth rate being out of step with his physical development. The second set of difficulties arises from circumstances outside the child himself, and derives from the fact that in important ways the gifted individual is different from most children of his own age. Although every child is unique, the majority of normal boys and girls conform, broadly speaking, to similar patterns of development. From this results a general framework of expectations, held both by the adults and the main body of children who have the same cultural and socio-economic background, as to what is acceptable behaviour on the part of individual children belonging to their group. It is usually when the gifted child begins to meet a wider circle of people outside those in his immediate family and friends that problems begin to arise. It will probably not be until he goes to school – whether infant school at the age of five, or a nursery class or pre-school playgroup – that he may begin to feel the effects of the expectations of the outside world.

Playgroup and nursery school
Playgroup leaders and nursery school teachers are used to meeting three- and four-year-olds. These kindly people make a point of welcoming the new little boy or girl into their group and are at pains to make him or her feel at home. When a mother takes her little one along on the first day they will take her round so that she can see what the children are doing, and she will then be shown the place where her child is to put his or her coat. When the mother has gone, the person in charge will take the newcomer over to some of the other children and introduce him, and he will then be invited to join in with what the other children are doing.

For the new child everything is strange and new. There are far more people than he has seen before and, compared with what he is used to, much more activity. There are many brightly coloured pictures and materials about the room, and children busily doing things and talking to each other. Children react differently, whether gifted or not, when they first find themselves in a new environment. Some children are shy and others are little extroverts: it depends on the child's personality, and gifted children vary as much as others in this respect. A gifted boy or girl who is very advanced mentally compared with others of the same age may be timid and very quiet and retiring, or very lively and bouncing into everything, or somewhere in between these two extremes. Whatever their personalities, most gifted children (in some cases after a short settling-in period) like the exciting new environment which a playgroup, nursery class or infant school presents. This is because of the care those in charge take to make all children feel at home and that they belong to the group, and because new surroundings present them with many opportunities to learn about new things. All young children want to know about their surroundings, but as a rule gifted children are even keener than others to find out about how things are made, what you can do with them and how they work. They want to try things out and to experiment, and they usually find new and original ways of using ordinary things.

After an interval of some months, or in some cases only a few weeks, the parents of a gifted child may notice some change of attitude on the part of their son or daughter. The child's early enthusiasm for going to the playgroup or nursery class may fade away and gradually be replaced by a disinclination to attend, although the other children in the group seem to be quite happy. And despite the fact that, when they first join the pre-school group, gifted and exceptionally intellectually able children find everything interesting, they soon master the facilities and learning materials available and are ready for a fresh challenge. The following example of a gifted four-year-old illustrates the point.

Tracey started attending a local nursery school every morning when she was three and half, although children were not usually admitted until they were about four. This little girl was very excited about going to the nursery school, settled down very quickly and got on well with the other children. As well as having exciting toys to play with such as a large Wendy house and a shining-bright and very realistic-looking car big enough to seat four children, there were simple books for the children to look at and they did a little writing, drawing, colouring and cutting out. Tracey continued happily enough for two terms but with the third term her enthusiasm began to wane. A week or two later the teacher in charge sent for Tracey's mother and told her that 'Tracey had finished with nursery school'. She went on to explain that Tracey no longer had any interest in playing and working with the other children and that all she wanted to do was to be with the grown-ups and help them set out the chairs and do other similar jobs. The nursery teacher said Tracey was ready for school.

At the time Tracey was still only four and half and it was almost unheard of for the school to accept a child under the age of five. However, on the recommendation of the nursery school teacher the head of a nearby school agreed to admit Tracey the following term when she would be nearly four and three quarters. When Tracey heard the news she ran around the house singing, 'I'm going to big school. I'm going to big school.' When the time came, Tracey started as arranged, settled down immediately and applied herself with zest to her schoolwork. For the time being, at least, she was again progressing well.

Schools
Schools divide children up by age and to a lesser extent according to their sex. The pupils attending a school must be formed into groups – usually classes or forms – for most activities. The simplest and most obvious basis on which to divide the children is their age. This is because, as is well known, the level of development of, say, a class of thirty eleven-year-olds will be on average more advanced both physically and mentally than a similar group aged ten. The key words here are 'on average'. There is no doubt that it would be very unusual to find a class of ten-year-olds with a greater average height than that of a group of eleven-year-olds who were attending the same school. At the same time, it would also be very unlikely if, when the heights of the same children were considered individually, there were not an overlap between some of the taller ten-year-olds and the shorter eleven-year-olds. In fact, the tallest ten-year-old might well be found to be taller than

most of those in a class of twelve-year-olds, or the shortest ten-year-old shorter than the *average* height of children in a class of nine-year-olds.

Although schools seek to treat children as individuals, they do so within the framework of the school class. At the beginning of a school year when there is a new intake of perhaps fifty, a hundred or even more children, the teachers have not yet had an opportunity to get to know the newcomers as individuals, and there is usually an underlying assumption on the teachers' part that the children coming in who are of approximately the same age will be, broadly speaking, at the same stage of physical and mental development. However, given the natural differences in the physical development of those making up the new intake, an individual boy's or girl's size will affect to some extent his or her school life, in spite of the school staff endeavouring to treat everyone fairly and so – as teachers usually see it – equally.

There are two main ways in which a child's physical development may affect his school progress: the first is in sport, and the second is in the attitude of the other children.

Most children in primary schools, and particularly at secondary level, enjoy one or more forms of physical activity – team games, gymnastics, swimming, running, and so on. Generally speaking, fat children will be less successful at these activities – although occasionally they make good goalkeepers. When a youngster is not particularly good at some activity he will tend to avoid doing it, and lack of practice will then make him even less successful than his physical development could have allowed. On the other hand, agile children will tend to achieve relatively high levels of performance in various physical activities. And being very tall or very short is an advantage in some circumstances but not in others.

Pupils who are successful at sport and similar activities are held in high regard in most schools. The teachers generally exude a benign approval towards those youngsters whose abilities as footballers, tennis players, and so on win them a place in school teams. As for the main body of the children, they too usually show admiration for the most able on the games field or in the swimming pool. The approbration of staff and pupils alike encourages the self-esteem of those on whom it is bestowed. The popularity that children naturally good at sport enjoy encourages them to spend more time on it, and so their standards of performance rise still further. Natural aptitude and the human environment work together to realise to the full the sporty child's capabilities.

Perhaps unexpectedly, giving a great deal of attention to some sport or other does not as a rule have a detrimental effect upon a boy's or girl's classwork. This is probably partly because of the beneficial psychological effects of being popular with the other children, and of the generally favourable attitudes of the staff, who often appear to assume, probably unconsciously, that those children with a good physique who are able at physical activities will also be good at classwork. In fact, this very expectation tends to make the supposition, at least to some extent, a reality. When a child is expected to do well by those in authority, the assumption is likely to increase his confidence in improving his performance and so, within limits, his actual standard of academic achievement is raised. Providing the demands of the adult world are not excessive, reasonably high expectations of a child's scholastic performance by parents and teachers, and popularity among the peer group, are likely to promote healthy psychological development in the boy or girl. However, in the case of gifted children, this is not enough to ensure that their academic and creative abilities will be developed to the full. This point must be emphasised and will be discussed more fully later.

There are, of course, many bright and gifted children who are not particularly good at any form of sport. For such youngsters school life is often much more difficult. As a general rule, being the quickest at classwork and in reaching the right answers is often more likely to lead to hostility from the other children, rather than popularity. More surprisingly, a boy who has the answers almost before the teacher has asked the questions, or who has gone on on his own to the next chapter in the textbook before the rest of the class is ready to do so, may well be the subject for some caustic remark from the teacher rather than of praise for good work.

The academically gifted child may become the butt of other children, be called a 'big-head' or 'know-all' or some similarly degrading term, and may be the object of bullying and physical assault from bigger boys. Far from coming to the defence of the unfortunate gifted boy or girl, the majority of the class will probably watch with amusement or join in with the bantering. Much of this sort of teasing and baiting will go on out of the teacher's hearing – in the playground, during break times and on the school buses, and, in secondary schools, in the lesson-change interval between one teacher leaving and another coming into the formroom. When the staff do overhear such remarks or detect some surreptitious needling of a gifted boy or girl while their class is actually in progress, they will, of course, take steps to stop it. However, sometimes the measures taken by teachers in such circumstances seem to be half-hearted – perhaps they have a secret feeling that the 'little upstart really has asked for it'.

There are occasions when there seems to be a certain empathy between the teacher and the children against a gifted pupil. This may be illustrated by an instance re-counted by a highly gifted sixteen-year-old boy about an experience during his first year in a secondary school. Derek's father was a scientist. *The Times* and the scientific journal *Nature* were both delivered to the house. Derek was in the habit of picking up both and reading those parts that interested him. While reading an article in *Nature* he had found a section which he could not understand, so during a physics lesson at school he raised his hand and put his question to the teacher in antici-pation of receiving an explanation. Unfortunately the boy was not taken seriously. The master, presumably assum-ing that Derek was just trying to attract attention to himself, replied sarcastically and then turned to the rest of the class for general approval of the rebuff he had given to the presumptuous twelve-year-old. Derek, of course, who had genuinely wanted to know the answer and had thought the teacher was the proper person to ask, was extremely upset by the incident, and this and other simi-lar happenings led to him becoming very disillusioned. When he recounted this experience four years later he said that, while he had been able to put up with the boredom of the class and even the teasing of the other boys, he could no longer bear it when the teacher and the pupils joined forces against him. He felt he could no longer continue in the class, or for that matter in the school; the situation reached a crisis and he developed school phobia. Although attempts were made by social workers to place him in another school, these failed, and for most of the time he was given home tutors until he reached the legal school-leaving age. Once he was sixteen the authorities lost interest in his case.

So far we have looked at two groups of gifted children – those who are very good at some form of sport with the result that they are usually fairly popular, and those whose main interest is in some form of academic work and who tend to be nicknamed by the other children as 'little professor', 'brains', or worse. What is most important to a gifted boy or girl in school is maintaining reasonable social relationships with other members of their class, since they spend nearly all their time in the company of this set of children. In most cases being on good terms with teachers is of secondary importance. Nor are the gifted usually particularly concerned with their levels of attain-ment in classwork – it is generally, for them, very easy and they know that, should the need arise, with a little effort they will easily be able to bring their work up to the expected level. There are other gifted children, besides those who are exceptionally good at sport, who find one of a number of different ways of adjusting to being a member of an ordinary school class. The method any particular child adopts in solving the problems he faces in school depends largely on his personality.

Gifted pupils may achieve social acceptance by the other children when, from the children's point of view, they appear to be benefiting the whole class. One approach used by some gifted children who are extroverts is to apply their intellectual ability to become the classroom comics and so keep the rest of the class amused with quick wit or funny behaviour. The role of classroom clown will usually win popularity with the other children at both primary and secondary level. Where the teacher is inexperienced or weak, the gifted boy or girl who acts in this way may combine clowning with 'teacher-baiting' and throw the

class into fits of laughter. Needless to say, such activities may build up great hostility in the teacher concerned and possibly in other members of staff as well.

Another approach may be used by gifted pupils who lack the ability to amuse. These individuals may make a bid for social acceptance by the peer group by daring challenges to the teacher's and/or the school's authority, and so win a following among the other children, who relish the teacher's discomfiture without themselves having to take the risks of reprimand and punishment. Still another way is by being useful to the dominant pupil in the group, the unofficial classroom leader, or to several dominant children. One thing which the gifted boy or girl can do easily is classwork – something that for most of the other children requires a considerable amount of effort and time, and many, if not most of them, have other things they would prefer to do such as playing or watching football or tennis, watching TV or listening to pop music. It follows that if the gifted child does the homework, and where possible the classwork, for some of the other children, he becomes an acceptable member of the peer group.

The following example illustrates how this sort of thing can happen. A friendship grew up between two primary school boys, Buck and Jonathan. Buck was a strong, tough boy who could knock down anyone else in his class who challenged him – as such, he became the peer group leader. Buck's intellectual ability was only about average and in any case he had no great interest in 'book work'. The other boy, Jonathan, in the same class, was highly intelligent and very sensitive, and although not particularly good at sport he found the classwork easy. Buck found it convenient to get Jonathan to do his schoolwork for him, or at least to provide him with the answers which he could just copy out. In return Buck gave Jonathan his 'protection' – none of the other children were allowed to tease Jonathan or to molest him in any way. It was a partnership which both boys found very satisfactory. However, the relationship was broken when they were transferred to different secondary schools. Now the gifted boy became vulnerable; he was baited by the other children and jeered at for his sensitivity, while the school staff apparently failed to recognise, or at least to value, his exceptional intellectual ability. His friend Buck held his own in another school, as before, with his fists. When his schoolwork fell below an acceptable standard, he was provided with extra help from the teaching staff.

Gifted pupils who are inclined to be introverted may choose merely to keep a low profile and to conceal their intellectual abilities from both the peer group and the staff. Gifted and able children, unlike their less able contemporaries at the other end of the ability continuum, are able to conceal their capabilities from their teachers, and occasionally from their parents as well, and to pass through school without their intellectual abilities or talents being recognised. These children may be called the 'covert' gifted. The ablest pupils in our schools have at least two incentives to behave in this way. First, just because they are children the things they want to do with their time may be quite different from those which adults wish and expect them to do: for instance, they may want to spend a large part of their time on their own particular hobbies. Second, as has been shown above, the most usual attitude of the other children in the class and in many cases of the teachers as well, discourages the display of exceptional learning ability and of unexpectedly advanced knowledge.

The concealment of the exceptional mental abilities they possess is a characteristic of gifted children that has long been known: Jean-Jacques Rousseau in *Emile* (first published in 1762), referring to the childhood of Cato and the Abbé de Condillac – two boys who were to become outstanding men – says that, 'As a child, the young Cato was taken for an idiot by his parents; he was obstinate and silent, and that was all they perceived in him', while the Abbé was 'reckoned a fool by his family'. It is almost certainly true that this device is adopted by a higher proportion of gifted and very able children in our society than ever before, on account of the spirit of egalitarianism that prevails. A comparable outlook is also found among teachers. Eric Ogilvie* began researching the views of primary school teachers in 1970 with a grant from the

*Ogilvie, Eric, *Gifted Children in Primary Schools* (Schools' Council/Macmillan, 1975), p. 112, Table 5.3 B.2(iv).

Schools' Council. One of his findings was that a majority (53 per cent) of the teachers in his study believed there was anti-intellectualism in the schools. A quarter of this sample of teachers 'emphatically' agreed that this was the case. It is probable that this is one of the reasons why many gifted pupils do not fulfil their educational potential.

Exceptional children
Under the 1944 Education Act, local education authorities have a legal obligation to meet the needs of mentally or physically handicapped children by making special educational arrangements within the framework of the general educational provision made for all children. The authorities are also required to ascertain which pupils suffer from disabilities. In 1945 eleven categories of children were defined as being those for whom the education authorities had to make specific provision either in ordinary or special schools. The types of children covered were the blind and partially sighted, the deaf and partially deaf, those with delicate health, the diabetic, physically handicapped, epileptic, those with speech defects, the maladjusted and the educationally subnormal. The categories for whom special provision *must* be made still covers all these groups, but in 1981 a new Education Act extended the scope of special educational provision to cover all children with learning difficulties. Formerly grammar school places were available for able children but today, apart from the very limited help given to bright pupils under the Assisted Places Scheme (see p. 214) and places in the few remaining grammar schools, the extra facilities made available specifically to benefit exceptionally clever children are minimal. At the same time, local education authorities are legally obliged to make special arrangements for all their mentally subnormal pupils.

The contrast between the attention paid to the special needs of other exceptional children and the manner in which the special requirements of intellectually gifted children are met, could not be greater. Special educational provision has been made since 1945 for the roughly 10 per cent of the school population considered to be educationally subnormal. The Warnock Report, published in 1978, says* that in 1945 it was estimated that in urban areas about 1–2 per cent of the school population needed to be educated in special schools and the remaining 8–9 per cent should be provided for in ordinary schools, where 'They should be taught in small groups, in attractive accommodation and by sympathetic teachers.' During the following years the number of special school places for educationally subnormal pupils increased, and the same report says†, 'Of 16,159 places provided between 1945 and the end of 1955, 68 per cent were for ESN pupils, 14 per cent for the physically handicapped and 7 per cent for the maladjusted.' In addition, child guidance centres were set up in each local education authority area, staffed by educational psychologists and other professional people, to identify those children in need of extra teaching. New courses were provided by teacher-training establishments – colleges of education – to provide teachers specially qualified to teach mentally retarded pupils and children who were backward for other reasons.

Bright, very able and gifted children do not enjoy the sort of extra consideration that is made available for less able pupils – the fast learners are not treated on equal terms with the slow learners. Her Majesty's Inspectors, in their report published in 1978 by the Department of Education and Science, found this to be the case in their survey of English primary schools. Over half the classes of nine- and eleven-year-olds which they visited withdrew groups of less able children for extra teaching, while less than one in ten of the classes of eleven-year-olds had special groups for the exceptionally able children – in the case of the nine-year-olds, less than one class in twenty. The comparison was even worse with regard to the number of individual children taken out of class for special attention. Of the classes of eleven-year-olds inspected,

* *Special Educational Needs:* Report of the Committee of Enquiry into the Education of Handicapped Children and Young People. Chairman: Mrs H. M. Warnock. Presented to Parliament by the Secretary of State for Education and Science, the Secretary of State for Scotland and the Secretary of State for Wales by Command of Her Majesty, May 1978. CMN 7212 HMSO (The Warnock Report), p. 21.
† Ibid., p. 22.

over twenty times more were found to give individual special teaching to less able children than to exceptionally able pupils*; as for the nine-year-olds, the percentage of classes from which the slow learners were withdrawn for remedial work was over fifty times greater than similar withdrawals of very bright or gifted children to do new, more advanced, work.

A similar situation holds in the great majority of secondary schools. Most comprehensive schools have a separate remedial department where backward pupils can be helped in small groups, or individually, if their schoolwork is below the average level for their age group; and usually the staff who teach these educationally subnormal children have been on special training courses for the purpose.

There is no doubt that the parents of very bright and gifted children at both the primary and secondary stages are usually justified in thinking that their children are receiving insufficient encouragement and stimulation at school with their academic work. Providing children turn out work which can be graded as 'good' for their age group, teachers are usually satisfied. Consideration is rarely given to whether a child's work is 'good enough' relative to his capabilities. In local education authority schools there is generally a feeling of the urgency and importance of bringing backward pupils' work up to scratch, but as far as the exceptionally able children are concerned, providing they are keeping up with the general level of work in the class and are not behavioural problems, no need is usually seen to raise the level of their work in accordance with the level of their ability. It is for the parents, then, of such pupils to take steps to see that their children enjoy the same opportunities for the full development of their abilities as do virtually all other groups of children.

A word of caution must be added here. Many children do not have any specific exceptional ability either physical or mental, but this does not mean that they will not grow up to be capable young adults, well adjusted to the world in

---

* Department of Education and Science 1978. *Primary Education in England – A Survey* by HM Inspectors of Schools, HMSO 1979, p. 33, Table 17.

which they live. It is not easy to know whether a child is doing the best he can when the work produced does not reach the standard that parents and teachers might have expected and hoped for; or whether the child is not putting sufficient effort into his schoolwork through lack of interest in it; or whether he is deliberately underachieving in order to fit in with other children in the class. To press for more from a child who is already doing his best can only be damaging: it can lead to a stressful situation with tension between parents and child – or perhaps between teacher and child. Where this happens the boy's or girl's own self-confidence may be undermined and a feeling of resentment may be generated against the parents, teachers and the adult world in general.

This book aims to make it easier for you to decide whether your son or daughter is working satisfactorily relative to his or her capabilities. The next chapter describes a number of gifted boys and girls, the sort of problems they presented to their parents and teachers, how these were resolved and whether the results could be viewed as satisfactory or not. Chapter 3 sets out certain tests which will help you decide whether your child is about average or is advanced for his or her age, and whether you need to do anything further about it.

What do parents aim at when they are bringing up their children? Few would disagree that the decisions parents take and their consequent actions are intended to benefit their sons and daughters. There is still the question, though, of what we actually mean by the word 'benefit'. Is it that our children should be good at their schoolwork, take examinations and gain qualifications, and, at the end, obtain a good job? Most parents probably do want these things and, generally speaking, they are likely to be beneficial to their children. However, they are not the only things in life, and even when they are obtained there may sometimes be discord between parents and their grown-up children. Probably our aim should be that, when children have grown up, both the young adults themselves and their parents should be satisfied with the achievements of their schooling and out-of-school experiences. If a fairly bright child, who is trying hard to please his mother and father and is producing work of a standard beyond which he cannot go, is pressed to do better still, it may lead to the child having a mental breakdown. On the other hand, if an exceptionally able child underachieves to such an extent in his schoolwork that, when the time comes, he is unable to obtain the paper qualifications necessary for him to enter some desired form of higher education, he may turn on his parents and say, 'Why didn't you make me work harder?' It is to help parents of very bright, intellectually gifted and talented children to make the right choices and to take the appropriate actions, that this book has been written.

2 Some Gifted Children

It may help parents gain a clearer idea as to whether their boy or girl, in comparison with most children of the same age, is very bright or gifted, if the stories of a number of gifted children of different ages are described. It may also help parents to see the sort of problems that can arise when there is a gifted child in the family. In some of the cases outlined the child has developed smoothly; in other instances difficulties have arisen for which no satisfactory solutions were found.

There are a number of factors which have some bearing on whether exceptional intellectual or any other outstanding ability (for instance in sport or the arts) that a child may possess comes to fruition in adulthood. The main ones are probably the child's own personality and motivation, the social and cultural environment into which he is born, the attitudes and behaviour of the parents, the type and ethos of the school attended – and chance happenings. These elements are not independent of each other: for instance, the child's personality and motivation will be affected, though not completely altered, by the other circumstances. There is no doubt that the actions of parents and of the schools to which children are sent are major influences, and probably the dominant ones, in their future lives. But these are not the only factors, and it may sometimes be through no fault of the parents if a boy or girl does not grow up to fulfil his or her childhood potential in adult life.

Gifted toddlers
The younger a child is, the less time there has been for his giftedness to develop. All children go through the same main stages of development, but a gifted child goes through them more quickly, at least in some respects, than is normal. If a baby seems to be much more advanced

than other babies of the same age it may be a sign of giftedness, but it is not necessarily so, for there is a tendency for babies to develop first in one way and then in another. For instance, one baby may get one or two teeth earlier than usual, while another child begins to crawl sooner than most others. Yet there can be indications of giftedness in babies of only a year or eighteen months.

Jeremy was such a child. From the time he was about six months old he demanded constant attention from his mother or some other member of the family. If he was not kept constantly amused, he would scream and cause such a disturbance that someone would go over to play with him. He belonged to what was to become a fairly large family. He had an older brother, a sister who was born when he was fifteen months old, both parents, and a grandmother who lived not far away. The new sister was a 'good' baby, so although a new baby usually has the main attention, at least for a time, Jeremy continued to demand and receive the lion's share of his mother's time; even when a fourth baby came along, a new brother this time, Jeremy continued to dominate the family circle and to be the focus of attention.

Before he could walk and while he was still in his pram, when Jeremy saw something in the room he wanted he would screech in fury because he could not reach it. His mental growth had already outstripped his physical development, causing him extreme frustration. In spite of this, Jeremy developed well, benefiting from the constant attention he received in response to his demands. As a result the other three children had rather less than their fair share of their mother's time. Although they realised it later on, Jeremy's parents did not know then that they had a gifted child. If they had known, what steps could they have taken to prevent the needs of their other children being overshadowed and receiving insufficient attention? No doubt they would have been able to keep him occupied by giving him some of the intriguing educational toys described in Chapter 4.

In another case, a health visitor identified a gifted baby when she was calling upon a mother who had just given birth to a second child. The mother was suffering from post-natal depression, which was worsened by the ceaseless demands of her older child, at that time a baby not much over a year old. The child cried and shrieked continuously when the mother did not give him her full attention. As she had no one to help her, she could not do this with a new baby needing a considerable amount of her time. Worst of all, the older child, John, needed very little sleep; he was awake late into the evening, again early in the morning and usually once or twice during the night as well, crying and shrieking for no apparent reason and preventing his parents from getting enough sleep. The mother became increasingly distraught and was approaching a breakdown. The health visitor gave the older baby a number of tests which showed that he was very advanced for his age, and then told his mother that she thought he was 'gifted'.

Once it had been recognised that John was a gifted baby, it was possible to alleviate the situation. The main cause of John's bad behaviour was seen to be extreme frustration, as his intellectual development had far outstripped his physical control. The toys John had been given were the usual ones, such as a bunny rabbit and a rattle composed of a coloured plastic ball at the end of a handle. The source of his frustration was that while he could see things he wanted to touch or pull, he could not reach them since he was in his cot or pram; at the same time, there was little he could do with the toys he was given other than hurl them out. Once the cause of the problem was recognised by the health visitor, she took positive steps to find out what could be done. She found out that John needed different sorts of toys – ones that he would find challenging and stimulating and which would hold his interest. She explained this to John's parents and talked over with them how they could satisfy the child's needs. The father was an electrician, so he was able to make a game with coloured lights for him to play with, and the mother bought him educational toys said by the makers to be for children aged two to five years. During the months that followed and as he became a toddler, John continued to be very demanding of attention from his mother who, with her younger child to look after as well, was at times at her wits' end as to what to do. Then she remembered that she had stored away some of the teaching materials she had used when she taught in an infant school before her marriage. She got out some simple jigsaw puzzles and other things that she had used, and these kept John occupied for some of the time. The most important acquisition was a typewriter, which the father adapted with an electric battery and complex circuits so that banging on the keys brought on various combinations of coloured lights. John was allowed to have it in his bedroom. If he woke up during the night or early in the morning he occupied himself with this and other gadgets and did not wake up the rest of the family. When he was two and a half his mother took him to a day nursery for two half-days a week, and as he gradually became interested in more and more things the pressures on his mother lessened.

Frustration is commonly experienced, too, by gifted three- and four-year-olds. By this age many can recognise complex relationships and have as much, or even more, understanding as some adults. Several incidents which happened when Susan was between three and three and a half will illustrate this point. It was summer and the family were away on holiday. It was a fine, sunny day, and at the resort where they were staying one of the places of interest was a cave. The parents, grandmother and Susan went in. As soon as they were through the entrance there was a sharp change in the temperature and there were small pools of water on the ground. The grandmother said, 'Isn't it funny, it's wet in here', to which Susan retorted immediately, 'That's because the sun can't reach in here.' The three adults were so surprised at the spontaneity and the accuracy of the prompt reply that they were unable to say anything other than, rather weakly, 'Oh.'

Susan had shown that she had understood that warmth came from the sun (temperature change), that this warmth caused puddles to dry up (evaporation) and that in a different situation where the sun's rays were cut off the ground would not dry – that is, she was able to make an analogous deduction. A power of reasoning at this level is not generally found among three-year-olds, but is not unusual with gifted children of this age.

Two other incidents which happened about the same time will serve to illustrate the sort of situations which often arise with a young gifted child. The first happened on the same holiday as the one recounted above. Susan was staying with her mother in a bed-and-breakfast house. There was another mother there with a son of seven and another boy of the same age who was a friend. In the sitting-room one day the two boys started a game of Happy Families with the mother. Susan watched with keen interest and was desperate to join in, but she could not read the cards (she was only just three) and so the other family were hesitant about allowing her to join in. Eventually they agreed to let her try and she was dealt a hand. She soon mastered the differences between the cards and played with them as an equal – although she was four years younger than they were! This shows how quickly a gifted child can learn when highly motivated to do so.

The second incident illustrates the acute frustration which may be experienced by a young gifted child. One day when they were back home again Susan's mother overheard the child say, greatly agitated, to her aunt, '. . . but my Daddy said so', then the aunt's brusque reply, brushing aside the child's objections and taking no notice of what Susan had said. The mother, who knew that the child was right when she told her aunt that her father objected to a particular practice, went into the kitchen and put the matter right. The episode shows the sort of frustration a gifted child suffers when, knowing that she is right, she is brushed aside by adults because 'she is only a child'.

Frustration was the main cause, too, of Peter's temper tantrums, which started when he went to nursery school at the age of three and continued when he went to an infant school. Peter's mother says he was a good baby and although he did not need much sleep he was usually able to amuse himself in his cot without disturbing anyone else. His favourite entertainment when he was in his cot was inventing words, and doubling numbers mentally *ad infinitum*. He was never bored with his own company.

Later Peter displayed temper tantrums at home and at school. He became intensely frustrated when his parents could not understand his needs or answer his questions, so much so that he would gnaw the furniture and bite and scratch himself. In the infant school he was not understood by the class teacher: she merely thought that he was retarded and when his extreme frustration found its outlet in a tantrum, she put him on a chair outside the classroom.

Intellectually gifted children are rarely as advanced in their emotional and physical maturity as in their reasoning ability. All the same, although not nearly as far ahead as in their cognitive development, they are often more advanced than the majority of other children of the same age in these respects as well. However, some gifted children may lag behind the norm for their age group in certain other ways, as was the case with Peter. Younger boys and girls did up the buttons of his coat and the laces of his shoes for him. Emotionally Peter was immature for his age. He was extremely sensitive to criticism and could not bear to be laughed at by the other children.

In most respects Peter was typical of children with very high IQs. As might be expected, he learned to read and write very quickly – yet he was slow with regard to the actual amount of writing he did since he set a very high standard for himself. He always strove after perfection and would not write at all if he could not find the right words to express exactly what he wished to say. His drawings, too, contained a great deal of detail and were meticulously executed. Peter was able to concentrate for very long periods on anything in which he was particularly interested – such as tracing mazes and solving puzzles – and on countries and languages which were his own inventions. As he grew older his interest in solving problems continued. He always looked for a hidden meaning, often discounting the obvious answer, and explored all other ways to a possible solution, seeking a second meaning and perhaps even a third. Peter usually ignored the apparent answer as not worth mentioning, and as a result people often considered him to be mentally slow.

The sort of social relationships gifted children make depends partly upon their personality. Some are 'loners' as was Peter. When he was at the infant school, and later, he had very little interest in the other children which, when it is remembered how much more advanced he was in his mental development (at the age of six he was mentally roughly on a par with ten- or eleven-year-olds), was not surprising. He did not like the noise and boisterousness of the other children. At break time in the playground he used to just walk slowly round on his own, picking up bits of stone, wood and glass which attracted his attention. When he was seven he was physically attacked by the other children, presumably because he was 'different', and his neck was twisted. This traumatic experience had a great effect upon both Peter and his parents. The incident was probably partly the result of Peter's general unpopularity, which was perhaps exacerbated by his strong dislike of all forms of physical activity, particularly swimming.

Peter's intense dislike of going into water led to another very upsetting experience. The school made him go to the swimming baths with the rest of the class. Once there the teacher wanted him to get used to the water and to learn to swim. But Peter would not go in, so, in an attempt to get him to overcome his dislike of the water, the teacher threw him in. The result was the opposite to what the teacher had intended. Peter's dislike of water turned to acute fear. These two happenings – the attack by the other children and the rough treatment he received from the teacher at the swimming baths – led his parents to decide that another school must be found for him. Peter was taken away from the primary school and sent to the junior department of a private school, where there was an easygoing approach which was compatible with his personality. No attempt was made at the new school to make him go swimming or do sport, and to a large extent he was allowed to follow his own inclinations as far as his academic work was concerned.

Gifted children in junior schools
Children are aged seven when they enter junior schools, unless they are transferred below the normal age. It is among gifted children of eight to nine that difficulties have most frequently arisen: the children are less easy to handle at home and at school than when they were younger. Many parents have written asking for help with the problems and difficulties they face, and the examples given below illustrate the sort of situations that occur.

Parents often complain that their boys and girls are bored with the work they are given to do in primary schools. This is not surprising since the primary school curriculum has not been designed to cater for the needs of exceptionally able children. Most of the gifted are avid readers and have built up a wide general knowledge from books designed for older children or even for adults, which they have obtained in school, on their parents' bookshelves or from public libraries. One mother writes that her son 'is just nine' and that already 'he has displayed signs of boredom with his schoolwork'. In the case of another boy the parent writes that, although he is in the first-year juniors, 'the school says he is being given second-year work'. She goes on to say that her son's 'complaint is one of boredom and of having to wait for the slow members in his class'. He has exceptional intellectual ability and is especially interested in mathematics, but he is also an all-rounder, has played the piano for three years and 'has a passion for all sports'.

Boredom is often linked with underachievement in schoolwork, and many parents express worries about how their children are developing. The parents of a nine-year-old were very concerned about their son, of whom a psychologist had said he had a very high IQ. The parents, psychologist and the school all knew that Roger could do good work, but what he produced was usually of very poor quality. The boy's excuse for this was that he was 'bored'. Certainly what he was given to do failed to hold his interest and stimulate his learning. A similar story is told by another parent of his eight-year-old girl. In spite of the fact that the junior school had put her up into a class higher than normal for her age group, her father says that although his daughter seems fairly happy there are times when she complains bitterly of boredom. There is, too, he says, the question of what she will do in the coming two years, as she is already in a class of mixed third- and fourth-year juniors.

Objective test scores can give a measure of the underachievement occurring in the case of a particular boy or girl. In Joanna's case it was her class-teacher who believed her to be a gifted child who was underachieving. Joanna was the youngest in a family of four, and her eldest brother Alan had been recognised as gifted for some time. His bad behaviour had led to so many problems at school that the head teacher asked the parents to go and see her. When they did so it emerged that serious difficulties were also arising at home. After some discussion it was agreed that the boy should be referred to the child guidance clinic. Conversations with the parents revealed that even before the school had felt it necessary to take action about Alan's behaviour, he was already the centre of attention in the family. When Alan and his parents started attending the clinic and an investigation was begun into the causes of his disruptive behaviour, the parents' attention centered even more on Alan and his needs, so that they became to a large extent oblivious to the requirements of their other children, and in particular to the needs of their youngest child, Joanna. This little girl of six did not misbehave either at home or at school. She played happily enough with her younger brother and older sister and kept herself occupied with the toys that were around the house; and it seemed that she did not particularly need, or seek, her mother's attention. At the infant school Joanna's class teacher noticed that the child seemed very quick in her verbal responses and actions, especially when she was talking to or playing with the other children. At the same time the standard of Joanna's schoolwork varied greatly from very good one day to very poor the next, and frequently she seemed to be day-dreaming and paying little attention to her work.

The teacher arranged for Joanna to be one of three bright children to be given a test of mental ability. The test to be used was made up of four short sections and the children would have only three minutes on each to see how many of a set of puzzles they could solve. All three children were given examples to work through, and to make quite sure they would know how to do the test questions they were told the answers to the examples. The children were then given the test. When their work was marked it was found that Joanna's results were most extraordinary. She made no attempt to answer any of the first set of puzzles, merely sitting with the paper in front of her and doing nothing, so her score was nil. When the second set of puzzles was started, she applied herself – and she did the same for the last two sets. Her total score for the three sets she attempted was 22; the second child, who was of the same age and who had been chosen by the teacher as one of the brightest in the class, scored only 16 on the four sets

(11 on the three sets Joanna worked – exactly half her score), while the third child scored only a total of 14 in spite of being a year older than the other two. Joanna was undoubtedly a gifted child.

It is interesting to speculate why Joanna made no attempt to solve the first set of puzzles. It seems likely that she was so accustomed to schoolwork being (for her) very easy and uninteresting that she did not apply herself, and that it was only when she discovered that the puzzles were in fact difficult and represented a challenge that she gave her full attention to solving them. The test which the three children were given was a well recognised group psychological test designed for children between the ages of five and eleven. The maximum score on this test is 48. Joanna had scored 22 at the age of only six!

There are other cases, too, which show the failure of primary schools to provide adequately for very able and gifted children. Even when exceptionally able children are recognised by teachers and the need to give them a more stimulating curriculum is appreciated, the schools themselves are handicapped in their attempts to make adequate provision for fast-learning pupils by a lack of resources, both human and material. There is a shortage of teacher time and expertise, and a dearth of books, audio-visual and visual aids and computer programmes geared to the educational requirements of children whose mental abilities are two or three years in advance of those of the majority of pupils in their age groups. One parent writes that his eight-year-old son appears to have under-achieved consistently and that the boy 'is bored by what he sees as the unnecessary repetition (for him) for the benefit of the rest of the class'. The mother of another boy of the same age says she believes he has been thwarted by the type of education he has been receiving. She reports that the boy's class teacher describes him as 'very bright but erratic', as apparently from time to time he just refuses to do any work. In the mother's opinion the child is bored, frustrated and depressed, and she is very concerned about his future schooling. In a further case, this time in a rural area, the parents of a ten-year-old boy say that they are encountering great difficulties with their son. The head of the school is reported to have told them that 'he doesn't

know what to do with Michael for another year'. There is
no other school in the vicinity to which the boy can be sent.
A third mother inquires what she can do to help her
eight-year-old who already has a reading age of fourteen
plus.

It is not surprising if some of the clever children who
are forced to spend their days in classes where they are
learning nothing, or very little, find an outlet for their
frustration in bad behaviour. When this happens, it is
naturally a great worry to the parents. Three cases, this
time of girls, will illustrate the sort of thing that occurs.
The first relates to a nine-year-old with a reading age of
thirteen years. The mother is a single parent and no
matter how she tries to control the girl 'she persists in
doing as she pleases'. In the second case, a girl of eight, the
bad behaviour occurs at school. She is able to do the work
set by the teacher far more quickly than the other children, and 'when she has finished, just will not sit still'.
How unreasonable to expect her to do so! The third girl
was ten when her mother described her as having behavioural and social problems. The teacher, the parent
says, told her that her daughter was 'a very bright child,
make no mistake about it'. Nevertheless, her daughter's
work was deteriorating seriously, she had no friends
among the other children and she was extremely unhappy.

The social effects of being a gifted child in a junior school
class of children of average ability worries a number of
parents. One father writes to say that his seven-year-old
son has already learnt to camouflage his true ability as a
means of protecting himself from the other children.
Another parent says her very able eight-year-old daughter is shy and lacks confidence: she is the oldest in her
school class and lacks competition. Lastly, among this set
of able and gifted junior school children, a father writes to
say he wants his daughter to be able to mix with other
children of similarly high ability of her own age. As it is,
she is in a class where the children are on average two
years older and she finds no difficulty with the work.

Gifted children in secondary schools
Many parents think, or hope, that once their son or daughter transfers to a secondary school, the problems arising

from being very bright or gifted will be solved automatically. Unfortunately, this is wishful thinking. The problems may change their form but they do not go away – in fact, with the onset of adolescence they may become worse.

Although at secondary stage most children are taught by subject specialists, whether they are in a middle school or in a school catering for the eleven-to-sixteen or eleven-to-eighteen age range, the level of work is still frequently not high enough to stimulate very able pupils. One mother of an eleven-year-old daughter with a very high IQ attending a middle school reports that 'she is not having the attention required' and that 'she is frequently bored by lessons repeating what she already knows'. Another parent writes that she has been told by her son's school that although he is very talented he is totally unmotivated in his work. It seems that the teaching has failed to engage his interest. In a third case, the parent says that although her daughter of twelve has shown considerable ability for some years in imaginative writing, has a vivid imagination, good vocabulary and powers of expression, in her view the school is failing to provide the stimulation and opportunity for these abilities to be developed. However, she has not raised the matter with the teachers as she has felt there might be some adverse reaction on her daughter. In yet another case the mother says she has a boy and a girl of eleven and twelve at a comprehensive school, but although the school seems good of its kind, it is clear that the potential possessed by neither child is being utilised or stimulated.

The experiences of many very able pupils in secondary schools is illustrated by Jeffrey's story. The boy's parents arranged for him to be tested by an experienced educational psychologist. Jeffrey was tested on the Wechsler Intelligence Scale for Children – Revised (WISC-R), the most commonly used children's IQ test at the present time. He gained a score of between 130 and 135 on the full scale, which for mental ability placed him well within the top 2 per cent of children of his age. With such a high level of intellectual ability, it would not be unreasonable to predict that he would later gain an honours degree at Oxbridge. Yet in spite of his capabilities, the failure of his secondary school to meet his educational needs makes it unlikely that he will achieve this sort of academic success. At the age of thirteen Jeffrey's school reports showed a predominance of Cs; he was in the lower set for French where his term grade was D, while for mathematics his term grade and examination grade were both Es; the only indications of his true level of ability were an A grade for his geography examination and a B in each case for music, art and physical education.

Jeffrey's mother strove continuously to find a way whereby his ability would be recognised by his teachers and her son provided with suitably demanding and stimulating work, but without success. She approached, in addition to the headmaster, the chairman of the board of governors and one of the assistant-officers at her local education offices.

There is no doubt that the situation which faces the parents of gifted secondary school pupils is extremely difficult, and in the case of Jeffrey's parents none of the options open to them apparently offered a solution. In addition to their son's lack of scholastic progress, the parents claimed there was poor discipline in the classes, which had a bad effect on the boy's behaviour since he joined in with the general rowdiness of the other children. The parents thought of keeping Jeffrey out of school and trying to educate him themselves, but they decided they would find this too difficult to do. They then considered moving to another town so that Jeffrey would attend a different school, but when they discussed the practicalities of doing this they found that it would be too expensive. As far as I know, their case remained unresolved. There seems to be a distinct possibility that Jeffrey will become a frustrated underachieving young adult and possibly a clever delinquent.

Some gifted children do make good progress in comprehensive schools. The progress of two boys whom I tested when they were both aged nine contrasts sharply with Jeffrey's experiences. Both boys were fortunate with regard to the infant schools they attended. One, whom we shall call John, was among the first children to attend a new school. At the time it opened it did not have its full quota of infants, so each child had more individual attention than would otherwise have been the case. In addition, the head teacher's policy was to group the children by ability and not by age, so John was well ahead when he transferred to an unusually good junior school where the head encouraged the very bright to achieve as much as they could intellectually as well as in other respects. The other boy, for present purposes named Ben, was equally fortunate at another infant school. In Ben's school the head teacher encouraged all the children to produce work of the highest quality, and since she applied this approach to the very clever and advanced infants as well as to the more average ones, no ceiling was placed on the level of work the children were encouraged to do. In Ben's case the result was that his work, too, was well in advance of his age group when he transferred to the same junior school as John. The junior school head continued the encouragement and stimulation which the two boys had received in their infant schools; he allowed them to skip one of the junior school years and to transfer to a secondary comprehensive school at ten-plus instead of at the usual age of eleven-plus.

The all-round development of both boys, now in their third year at the secondary school, is thoroughly satisfactory. In spite of being a year younger than the other pupils, John came third in his year in mathematics. As a result he is now in the 'fast' group and will take O level maths in the fourth year – that is, when he is only fourteen. He was also first in German and had good marks in all his other subjects. John gets on well with the other children, likes swimming but is not interested in playing football. Out of school he spends a lot of time on his bike; at other times he likes to play chess, cards and board-games and to solve puzzles. Like the majority of gifted children, he is an avid reader.

Ben's progress has also been very satisfactory and his mother says that, although she was doubtful at the time about her son going up a year as she did not want to pressurise him, she is sure now that it was the right thing for him. Looking back to when Ben was younger, his mother says he was always an avid reader; he would study a particular subject, say trains, and then when he had got to know all he wanted to know about them, he would move on to another topic, perhaps cricket, and would do the same with that. Even when Ben was very small he could grasp the meaning of words without having them explained to him, and in this and other ways he was quite different from his younger sister. Left free to follow his own inclinations, Ben has always chosen the company of children older than himself, or of adults. He is not particularly interested in mixing with the other children in his class and his mother says he is 'a bit of a loner'. Nevertheless, although not forming close friendships with them he gets on with them well enough and helps them with their schoolwork when they are having difficulties with it. Ben is good at sport but not outstanding – he belongs to the school chess club and the computer club and helps with the various fund-raising activities to collect money for charities. Although, as has already been said, he is a year under age in his year group, his academic performance is quite exceptional. In his last school report he had an A for every subject except sport, where he had a B. His yearhead's and headmaster's comments at the bottom were: 'I have rarely seen reports of such all-round high quality' and 'An outstanding report'.

Four case studies
The examples which have been given so far have concentrated on gifted children's progress in school, and particularly on progress in classwork. This aspect of the school career is, of course, very important because of its effects on the opportunities open to them when they become adults. It would be wrong to pretend that happenings in school are not a major contributory factor in a child's future life style. Besides determining whether or not he will gain access to a large range of occupations in the professions, industry and commerce, they will affect his general outlook and will, to some extent at least, influence the sort of opinions he will hold on contemporary affairs when he becomes a young adult. Things that happen in school will also probably be reflected in an individual's social relationships; his experiences there are a factor in the development of his personality, and they may contribute to a 'chip on the shoulder' at a later stage.

Nonetheless, it must be emphasised that the length of time a child spends in school is relatively short. The hours at school are sandwiched for most children between the times when they are at home in the early morning and evening. The days spent at school are interspersed by weekends and school holidays, which are also usually spent at home. Five years usually elapse before children start school, and in most cases, within eleven or twelve years after that they have left. Consequently, a great deal of a child's learning takes place out of school, and failure with formal learning does not preclude an individual from establishing very satisfactory social relationships as an adult, nor may he or she be debarred from many interesting and remunerative occupations. A formal education is less important in the fields of sport and entertainment and for some forms of self-employment. However, even in these fields success may be more difficult to come by without it.

In the next few pages we look at the interaction of home and school and the different effects of specific incidents on four gifted children, two boys and two girls, of primary school age. Then we trace the long-term development of two contrasting gifted boys, from their early childhood until they are young adults.

Rowena   When she was nine Rowena did not seem to be making sufficient progress with her schoolwork. She appeared to her parents and her teachers to be an intelligent girl, but she often seemed to be unhappy, unsure of herself and easily upset. She also had difficulty getting to sleep at night. For these reasons it was decided that she should be referred to the local child guidance clinic to try to find the cause of the trouble and to rectify it.

When Rowena attended the clinic with her parents she was seen by an educational psychologist who was at pains to reassure her and put her at her ease. Once Rowena had relaxed, the psychologist asked her if she would try her hand at finding the answers to some puzzle questions, which she agreed to do. The questions and problems she was set were in fact those comprising the Wechsler Intelligence Test for Children (WISC). Rowena's score gave her an IQ of 138 – a score so high that among a large number of unselected children of the same age, less than 2 per cent might be expected to achieve it.

Later the psychologist considered other aspects of Rowena's development – first her level of attainment in school subjects and then her personality characteristics. The psychologist tested Rowena's reading ability and number work and found that the child was over two years ahead of the average standard attained in both subjects by the majority of her age group. As regards her personality, the tests showed that she was rather introverted, neurotic and very imaginative. These taken together led her to terrify herself by building up pictures of awful things happening – like, perhaps, one of her parents being killed in a road accident.

As a result of talking to Rowena and testing her, the psychologist thought that although her schoolwork was well above the average for her age group, her score in the IQ test suggested that she was capable of doing considerably better. She recommended to the parents that Rowena should go to a different school, one where the work would be sufficiently academically demanding for a highly intelligent child like Rowena to be interested and stimulated. She also suggested that it should be one where there was good discipline and where the general control was firm without being repressive. By surrounding the child in this way with an atmosphere of security, her fears could be gradually allayed.

The parents decided to follow the advice the psychologist had given them and searched around for a suitable school. Finally, they found an independent school which they felt would fit the bill, and Rowena started there at the beginning of the following term. After a year she went back to the child guidance clinic and was seen again by the same psychologist. She worked another set of tests of the same type as before. The psychologist found that the child had made excellent progress in the meantime. With the more favourable school environment Rowena's IQ score had risen by four points to 142 (very superior intelligence). Her mathematics score, too, had risen more than proportionately, although this was not the case with reading. The psychologist concluded her report by saying that Rowena seemed very happy in her new school and had settled down well, and she noted too that the previous problems the child had been having at home had also largely been overcome. She concluded that the prospects for Rowena's future were good.

Joan   Being the child of a single-parent family was one of the circumstances which contributed to Joan's later difficulties. She had no father and the relationship between the mother and daughter had always been abnormally close. Joan's school referred her to the local school psychological service because of her behaviour – she did not mix with the other children and took very little part in school activities outside the classroom. She did not belong to the after-school clubs or help in preparations for the school bazaar, and she never willingly played netball or other sports – she was definitely a loner. The standard of her classroom work, too, was only average or below.

Joan was taken along by her mother to see the school psychologist, who concentrated to start with on making the child feel at ease. Once she had relaxed and the psychologist had won her cooperation, she tested her on the Wechsler Intelligence Scale for Children. The result showed that Joan possessed very superior intelligence, scoring an IQ of 139 on the full scale. Less than one child in a hundred unselected children of the same age is expected to gain a score as high as that. Other tests showed that she tended to have an extrovert personality. At the same time she tended to be neurotic and on occasion was moody and depressed and felt a sense of frustration. Her mental stress sometimes affected her physically, so that she felt sick or her pulse rate increased sharply. After investigating her case thoroughly, the psychologist attributed Joan's mental disturbance to two main factors: first, having only one parent and second, her very high intelligence.

In her recommendations the psychologist advised that Joan should be moved to a school with a high academic standard. It was not possible to change the one-parent situation, but it was felt that if Joan was placed in an intellectually more demanding school, she would expend more of her intellectual ability on the work with which she was presented and at the same time was likely to be among peers with whom she would have more in common. In these two ways her over-strong dependence on her mother would be weakened and a more normal and healthy development would be encouraged. Fortunately, the mother was in a position to afford the fees at a suitable independent school, and after she had been there a year Joan's report showed that both her relationships with her peer group and the standard of her schoolwork were improving.

Mark   Mark was first tested by a psychologist privately when he was seven, as his mother believed him to be highly intelligent and wanted him to be moved up a year in the preparatory school that he was attending at the time. Mark was also tested on the Wechsler Intelligence Scale for Children, scoring an IQ of 148 on the full scale. This very high result supported Mark's mother's view that he was highly intelligent. Unfortunately, the family had suffered a series of misfortunes resulting in a crisis. Mark's father had been made redundant by his firm and had found it impossible to find a similar job. Eventually, the father was forced to accept the offer of a lower-grade managerial appointment than he had held previously, in the North West of England and at a greatly reduced salary. The family were forced to sell their house in Surrey and to move to Lancashire. Mark had to leave his school, and as there was no suitable private school near his new home and since in any case the family would have found it a struggle to pay fees in their changed circumstances, he was sent to the nearby LEA primary school. At the new school he was uncommunicative and uncooperative, and towards the end of his second year the head teacher suggested to his parents that he should be referred to the local child guidance clinic. The parents reluctantly accepted this course.

Mark was given the WISC IQ test at the clinic by an educational psychologist. The results showed a very marked discrepancy in Mark's score in the two parts of the test: his IQ on the verbal scale was the same as it had been three years before in Surrey, at 146, but his non-verbal (performance) IQ, which formerly had been the slightly higher of the two scores, had dropped dramatically by thirty-four points. The psychologist explained to the parents that this large drop in Mark's performance in the non-verbal part of the IQ test was likely to have been caused, at least in part, by the emotional disturbance and frustrations he had experienced as a result of the family's move to the North West, and in particular, his having to leave his school and the children with whom he had been friends. The psychologist found it different to suggest ways in which the child could be helped, other than that the parents should try to help him to make friends at school by encouraging him to invite other children to his home, and that they should take him on visits to places of interest as often as possible.

By the end of another term these measures had led to no improvement. Mark's parents managed to obtain some financial assistance from a relative and he was sent to a private school as a weekly border. After the first term he settled down in the new school. He gradually became happier and his work started to improve.

George George was a rather quiet, shy boy of nine. He was unhappy at school, and possibly also at home; he felt unsure of himself, was usually on the defensive when he was criticised, and worried a great deal about his school-work. He magnified what to anyone else would have been quite minor difficulties into major problems. The tensions he experienced were probably the main reasons for him frequently wetting himself and for his difficulty in getting to sleep at night.

George was a very clever boy. He was first given an intelligence test when he was seven as part of a general medical investigation into why he was apparently unable to control his bladder. The result showed him to be of very high intelligence and he scored a WISC verbal IQ of 131, non-verbal 148, and so a full-scale IQ of 143. However, he was showing nothing like this ability in his ordinary schoolwork. His reading age, for instance, was only two years ahead of the average for his age group, whereas with such exceptional mental ability (only about one child in a thousand is expected to gain such a high score) George might have been expected to be four years or more ahead.

George's mother was dissatisfied with his progress. She was both worried and annoyed at the large number of 'accidents' he had as a result of failing to control himself; she was also displeased at the relatively poor level of his schoolwork and was critical of both his teachers and his school generally. In order to correct the trouble with his bladder, a number of visits to the local hospital were necessary, which George always found very upsetting. As for his schoolwork, his mother attempted to make up for what she considered to be inadequate teaching at the independent school he attended by giving him extra work to do at home. She found that he made mistakes with reading even comparatively easy books, that he was poor at creative writing, and that in her opinion he was being taught mathematics badly. The parents also complained to the head of George's school, and as a result his teachers tried to improve the level of his work and criticised him sharply for failing to make sufficient effort. Matters were brought to a head when it was found that George was responsible for the theft of money from other children's coats in the cloakroom. The school head sent for George's parents and told them that if he stole again he would have to leave the school; George himself was sent for by the head and was sharply reprimanded in her office. He was told that he would not be allowed to go into the cloakroom at break time for the rest of the term.

The mother went back to the psychologist who had seen George two years before, and the boy was given further tests. They showed that his IQ had dropped by nine points and that his level of attainment in school subjects was also lower than it had been when he was aged seven. The boy told the psychologist that he did not like any of the work in the classroom, that he was unhappy at school and that the only thing he liked during the week was the swimming lesson. The psychologist recommended that George should move to a smaller school, rather more flexible in its approach, where he would be given more opportunity to follow his own inclinations and where a set amount of work would not be demanded in a given time. The psychologist also recommended that the mother should stop giving additional teaching at home. Since George was a highly intelligent child he would easily and rapidly be able to master the schoolwork normally expected, once the pressures on him at school and at home were relaxed. In George's case, because of his quiet ways and rather shy personality, high parental and teacher expectations had been self-defeating. They had led to the boy being under stess, which was actually hampering his learning and development.

George's mother accepted the psychologist's advice and the boy gradually settled down in his new school. A reduction in the stress he had suffered, together with the fact that he was growing older, saw the gradual disappearance of his old problems. His work, and his general psychological adjustment at school and at home, improved steadily during his later school-years. George gained university entrance, took a degree in science and subsequently obtained a satisfying job.

Mark and George were both highly gifted boys, but their characters and their problems were quite different and so the ways in which their parents could help them most were also very different.

Mark had suffered a traumatic experience through no fault on his part – nor was there any suggestion that he was in any way to blame – through a misfortune which had befallen his family. Formerly he had been fairly well adjusted to his surroundings at school and in the neighbourhood, in spite of being considerably more intelligent than the other children with whom he mixed. However, the move to the North West meant not only that he had to leave the school and children with whom he was familiar, but he was disturbed too by the obvious distress of his mother and the continually worried expression on his father's face; he also had had to contend in his new primary school with an educational approach that was very different from the one to which he was accustomed in his former independent school.

Any child undergoing Mark's experiences would probably have been disturbed by them – but in his case there was the added dimension that he was intellectually highly gifted, which exacerbated the situation. His abnormal degree of mental awareness, his vivid imagination, his great sensitivity, his more adult outlook compared with that of most children of ten made him particularly vulnerable. An additional factor contributing to his unhappiness and maladjustment was the greater gap between his own mental ability and that of most of the other children in his new class, compared with that between himself and his contemporaries in his former school. The parents were most likely to help their son by finding, if at all possible, a different school in their new neighbourhood, similar to his former school. Another way of helping Mark was for his parents to find families in the new district whose children also had unusually high mental ability and similar interests to his own, with whom he could become friends. Third, in this case the boy would have benefited from intellectual stimulation and opportunities for more advanced learning at home to compensate for the shortcomings of the primary school.

In George's case the courses of parental action which would probably have done most to aid his development were almost the direct opposite to those needed to benefit Mark. The chief reason for this were the very different causes of the acute mental stress under which he suffered, and the nature of his personality. Although quite and rather retiring, in normal circumstances George was able to get on with other children fairly well. His mother's pressure on him to do better, her complaints to the school about his 'unsatisfactory' progress, and the resultant pressure on him from his teachers, all had the reverse effects to what was intended. They set up in George severe internal stresses: he wanted to please his mother and the school, but the more he tried the more anxious he became and the more unsuccessful in his attempts to satisfy them. Because he was mentally very advanced for his age, the work that his mother gave him to do bored him. No matter how hard he tried he could not keep his attention on it – so he made mistakes – and then he was in trouble again. George was helped by all pressure, as far as was possible, being taken off him, particularly by his mother. Following the psychologist's suggestions, she looked for what was good in the things George did well. She made a point of showing appreciation of these, praising where she could and ignoring, as far as possible, his weaknesses and his mistakes in order to help build up her son's self-confidence. The stress he suffered was reduced and he became able to use his energies and abnormally high mental abilities constructively. Both his general development and his school-work benefited as a result.

The cases of Mark and George demonstrate that there is no simple answer to the question, 'What shall I do to help my gifted child?' Undoubtedly, George's mother thought she had acted in his best interests, but she had failed to understand him and so her actions had had completely the wrong effect. It might help, particularly with able and gifted children, if parents tried to see things through their children's eyes, and if they sought to recognise not only the similarities but also the ways in which their children's characters differ from their own, especially with regard to strengths and weaknesses. There is at least one advantage in dealing with the very able and gifted compared with other children: their advanced intellectual ability makes it possible to reason with them in a more adult manner. At the same time, it should be appreciated that such children are quick to realise when they are being fobbed off with an excuse and not being told the truth.

Two gifted children's progress from early childhood to university

Important incidents in the lives of a number of gifted children while they were at school, as well as adverse experiences which took place in both school and home with damaging effects, have been used as examples of the sort of difficulties that may arise with the exceptionally able. An account of the long-term growth and progress of two children provides a broader view of the vicissitudes that can occur during the development of highly gifted individuals.

Julian Julian's parents were both of superior intelligence, as measured on the Wechsler Adult Intelligence Test. He was the elder of two children and was born into a fairly poverty-stricken environment. The parents had emigrated to Australia and had found it difficult to settle and 'find their feet'. They lived in very humble surroundings and the father was frequently out of a job. He had not, at that time, completed his own education and was attending university in the evenings. Both parents were cultured in their interests and neither drank nor smoked, preferring instead to spend their evenings reading or, when finances allowed, going to cinemas or theatres.

Julian's mental ability was assessed at frequent intervals during his childhood. This was possible because the family was very friendly with a psychologist who was interested in the child from an early age, and who advised that regular testing might produce information which could help in directing him on the right course throughout his life. Julian is now in his early thirties, having graduated with honours from a leading university. He is working as a journalist for a large newspaper and also as a researcher for a television company. This gifted man is over six feet tall and very attractive both physically and in his personality. He has an air of assurance, and is tolerant and friendly towards all with whom he comes in contact. He frequently plays rugby and participates in a number of other sports. He is a keen reader and is beginning to write short stories.

As a child the boy was assessed on a number of tests, but most reliance was placed on the Wechsler Intelligence Test for Children and on the Stanford Binet (revised form). It is interesting to compare the results of the two tests. While the Stanford Binet is based more on academic learning, the WISC – which provides, as we have seen, two intellectual assessments, verbal and non-verbal – is a better indicator of 'potential' intelligence. The IQ results from these two well recognised intelligence tests which were given to Julian at intervals between the ages of five years six months and thirteen years one month are shown in Figure 1.

The variation in the IQ scores that Julian gained illustrates the fact that, although intelligence tests are valuable instruments for measuring a child's mental ability, they do not give the kind of exact result that may be obtained by using a ruler for his height or scales for his weight. The reasons for this lack of precision are, first, that such tests can only *sample* the testee's mental abilities and, although they are designed to cover a wide range of different abilities such as memory, perception of likenesses or differences between objects, and verbal ability, the testee's response is limited by the form of the questions. Second, the number of correct answers depends upon the individual's degree of willingness to solve the problems set, or on whether or not he is feeling well, in

Figure 1 :

Julian's IQ test scores on the Wechsler Intelligence Scale for Children and the Stanford-Binet Intelligence Scale

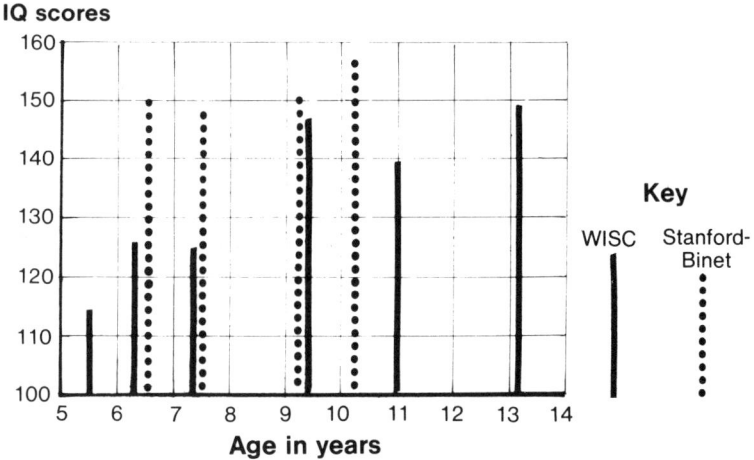

IQ scores

Age in years

Key

WISC   Stanford-Binet

addition to numerous other extraneous factors. Thirdly, there is a statistical reason why a child's IQ results vary. This is known as 'regression to the mean'. It is a difficult concept to explain but an attempt will be made to do so by the use of analogies.

Suppose a secondary school has 100 eleven year-olds. Most of the children will be about the same height, but one or two will probably be much shorter and one or two much taller than the majority. If the children's heights are plotted on a 'frequency diagram', (that is, a diagram showing the number of children of each height) and the points are joined up, the result will be a curve rather like that made by a cocked hat.

Figure 2 shows the approximate shape to be expected. If for the same group of children we examine how far away they live from the school, we shall probably find that most of them live at about the same distance, but that a few live very near the school and one or two live a long way from it. Although it is possible, it is unlikely that the two tallest children in the group will also be those who live nearest to the school. The two things are not connected so it is more

Figure 2 :

The way in which a set of children's test scores are distributed about the average

Frequency of test scores

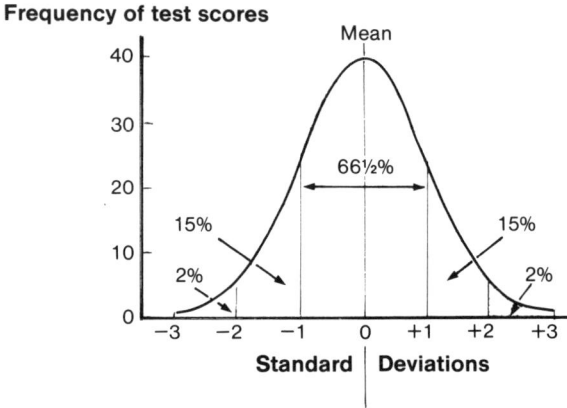

likely that the two tallest children will live an average distance away from the school for no other reason than that there are more children in the whole group who do so; so there is a greater chance that they will be one of these than that they will be one of those who live nearest to, or furthest away from, the school. This phenomenon is what statisticians call 'regression to the mean' (that is, to the average.) So it is with IQ and other tests. To the extent that chance has partly contributed to a child gaining an exceptionally high score when tested on a particular occasion, it is unlikely that chance effects will also operate to give another very high (or low) score on a second occasion.

Of course, it is only the chance effects that will influence a boy's or girl's score in this way – for instance, when a child just happens to know the answer to a particular question; if the youngster is truly highly intelligent then the result will be as high (or even higher) on the second test as on the first. Also, if the same sort of abilities are called into play as, say, when a child is tested for reading and general knowledge, it will probably be found that a boy or girl who is outstanding at the one will also be exceptionally good at the other. At the same time, it is unlikely that the test scores will show the youngster to be exceptional to exactly the same degree for both subjects.

The importance of a high IQ score stems from the fact that only a very small percentage of people possess the outstanding mental ability which it represents. The simplest way of showing *how* exceptional a child is, is to give the size of the percentage of others in the population with the same level of ability. The 'standard deviation' is a device used by statisticians which makes it possible to do just this and to show *how* exceptional a child's test score, or IQ, is compared with the scores or IQs gained by other children. In this way, parents, psychologists and teachers can judge whether a child is gifted or very bright. The standard deviation is a measure of the extent to which a set of test scores are spread out. A simple example of how it is calculated is given in the footnote below.* Although a

* The function of a standard deviation is probably most easily understood by an example of how it differs for two contrasting distributions and a simple explanation of how it is calculated.

For instance, suppose you have the following two sets of seven numbers:

Set A 10, 9, 9, 8, 8, 7, 5 = a total of 56. There are 7 items so the average number is 56 ÷ 7 = 8
Set B 16, 11, 9, 8, 6, 4, 2 = also a total of 56. Again there are 7 items so the average number is 56 ÷ 7 = 8

The average for both sets of figures has been found by adding up the numbers in a set and dividing by the number of items. The average number for both sets is 8 but *Set B* obviously includes some higher and lower numbers compared with *Set A*. The STANDARD DEVIATION is the average size of the differences of the individual items from the average number which in both sets is 8. The differences of the individual numbers from 8 for *Set A* are: +2, +1, +1, 0, 0, −1, −3. To avoid positive and negative differences cancelling each other out, each difference is squared and then added up. This total is then divided by the number of items, in this case 7. Then, because we squared the differences from the average of 8 to start with, we take the square root of the dividend.

So we have: $2^2 + 1^1 + 1^2 + 0 + 0 - 1^2 - 3^2$
= 4 + 1 + 1 + 0 + 0 + 1 + 9 = 16. 16 is now divided by the number of items, 7, and the square root of the result is found. The answer is 1.5 and this is the standard deviation for this distribution.

For *Set B* the differences of the items from mean 8 are: 8, 3, 1, 0, −2, −4, −6; squared these are 64 + 9 + 1 + 0 + 4 + 16 + 36 which add up to 130. Dividing by 7, the number of items, and taking the square root, we have 4.3 which is the standard deviation. As was to be expected, it is very much bigger for *Set B* than for *Set A*.

normally distributed set of scores may be spread out more widely compared with another (say, 22–64, and 18–75) the number of standard deviations from the mean score will be the same for the same *percentage* of the items in the distribution in each case. (The difference in the spread of the scores is taken account of by the *size* of the standard deviation itself.) So, if in two tests only one child obtained the score 64, and one child (possibly the same individual) gained a score of 75, the boy's or girl's score in both cases would be more than two standard deviations from the mean which would place it in the top 2 per cent. It is easy to see the levels of achievement in this simple example where top marks have been taken, but it would not have been so easy to see how well the boy or girl had done compared with the other children if the child's results had been, say, 61 and 69. With these scores, depending upon how the whole set of marks was spread about the mean, the boy or girl might still be found to come within the top 2 per cent in the two sets of results. Figure 2 shows the percentages of a set of scores which fall within one, two and three standard deviations from the mean. Providing the standard deviation and the average score are known, whether a set of scores is widely spread out or close together, it is possible to know whether a boy's or girl's test result is in the top 10, 5, or 2 per cent and so on, and to compare the result with those from other children.

An important feature of the standard deviation is that it makes it possible to estimate, say, how an IQ score given by a test on WISC corresponds to an IQ result from a test with the Stanford-Binet. The WISC has a standard deviation of 15 so that children who score an IQ of 130 or above can be said to have an IQ of two standard deviations (2 × 15), or more, above the average (IQ 100). Theoretically, at least, although not necessarily in practice, in a random group of children of the same age, the child with an IQ of 130 or above will be in the top 2 per cent (see Figure 2). This means the boy or girl may be expected to be one of the two cleverest children in a random group of 100 children of the same age. Of course, in practice there may be three or four children with a similarly high IQ, since the cleverest children are not spread evenly between schools. The Stanford-Binet Intelligence Scale has a higher standard deviation than the WISC, 20 instead of 15. This means that to have an IQ two standard deviations above the mean and so to be among the top 2 per cent, a boy or girl needs to score an IQ of at least 140 (100 + (2 × 20)). So test results on the Stanford-Binet give a higher numerical value for an equivalent level of ability compared with WISC. This is partly the explanation of the differences in the IQ scores. On the other hand, the first two causes of variation in IQ scores are a child's family and his school environment, both of which affect to some extent his or her ability to answer at least some of the verbal questions included in an IQ test. In addition, unhappy and disturbing experiences can reduce an individual's powers of concentration and his desire to put effort into finding the right answers to problem questions. Hence, even on the *same* IQ test, a child's score may be found to have dropped when he is re-tested after a period of time. This was found to be the case with Mark – his IQ score on the WISC non-verbal scale at the age of seven was 148, but after the unhappy experiences he had been through three years later, and when in addition he was in an unsuitable school, his non-verbal WISC IQ had dropped to 116.

Daniel The second example demonstrating the long-term development of a gifted child is that of Daniel. Despite high promise of intellectual ability, this boy failed to fulfil expectations during his subsequent education. There are a number of possible explanations, including Daniel's personality. There was also the fact that his home background was not entirely stable, and there were deficiencies in his relationship with his mother. Daniel was a child who needed encouragement from his mother, but because of her own personality she was unable to fulfil his need.

Daniel's mental abilities were tested on a number of occasions during his childhood. The results obtained are set out in Figure 3. He was first tested on the Merral-Palmer Scale when he was two and a half, which showed him to have a mental age of three years nine months, equivalent to an IQ of approximately 150. Later, at the age of three on the Stanford-Binet Intelligence Scale and a year later, at four on the Wechsler Pre-School Primary

Figure 3: Daniel's IQ test scores and reading ages at different ages

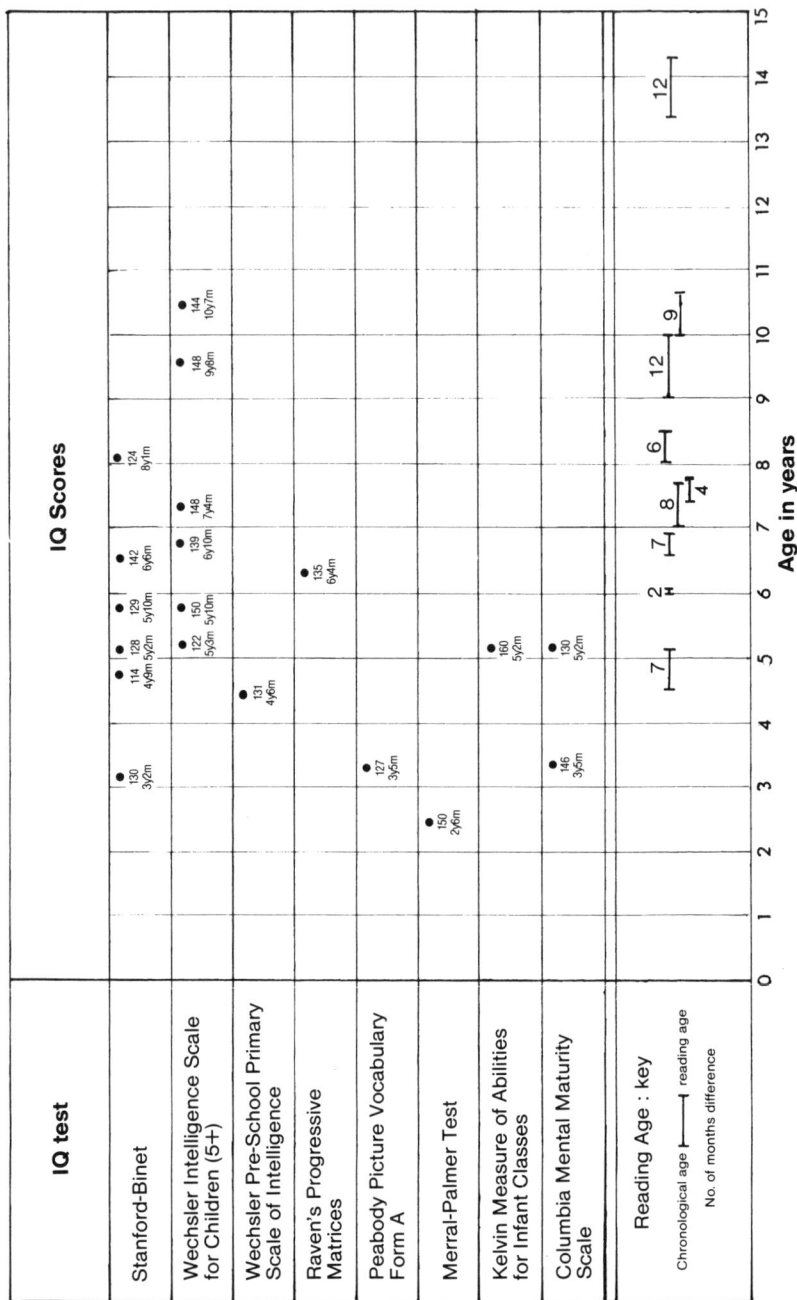

IQ Scores

IQ test	Data points (score / age)
Stanford-Binet	130 3y2m; 114 4y9m; 128 5y2m; 129 5y10m; 142 6y6m; 124 8y1m
Wechsler Intelligence Scale for Children (5+)	122 5y3m; 150 5y10m; 139 6y10m; 148 7y4m; 148 9y8m; 144 10y7m
Wechsler Pre-School Primary Scale of Intelligence	131 4y6m
Raven's Progressive Matrices	135 6y4m
Peabody Picture Vocabulary Form A	127 3y5m
Merral-Palmer Test	150 2y6m
Kelvin Measure of Abilities for Infant Classes	160 5y2m
Columbia Mental Maturity Scale	146 3y5m; 130 5y2m

Reading Age : key
Chronological age |———| reading age
No. of months difference

Reading Age data: 7 (5y); 2 (6y); 7, 8, 4 (7-8y); 6 (8y); 12, 9 (10y); 12 (14y)

Age in years (0–15)

Scales of Intelligence, his results gave him an IQ of 130 and 131 respectively. These two results are very close to each other, but there were sharp differences in the level of ability indicated by the scores he gained subsequently on the Stanford-Binet, Wechsler and other tests over a period of eight of his childhood years.

Although at first sight there appear to be enormous differences in Daniel's IQ scores, the results do provide useful information. If we take children scoring in the top 2 per cent for their age group as being in the gifted category – this is the definition of giftedness adopted by some local education authorities – then in twelve tests out of nineteen Daniel is shown to be gifted; while his scores in eight tests show him to be within the top 1 per cent, which may be described as being highly gifted. There is, too, a consistent pattern to be seen in the results. Daniel's first score when he was only two and a half years old was equivalent to an IQ of approximately 150; he gained an IQ of 144 on the WISC when he was just over ten and a half years old. During the intervening years he scored 146 on the Columbia Mental Maturity Scale when he was three, and on the Wechsler test 150, 148 and 144 at the ages of five, seven and nine respectively. The high scores are probably the most reliable since the lower scores could merely reflect an unco-operative mood at the time of testing.

There are reasons, too, for believing that the high IQ scores that Daniel achieved throughout his childhood more truly reflect the level of his intellectual ability than do the lower results. Providing the IQ tests are properly administered, it is very nearly impossible for a testee to come upon the right answer to a question by chance. On the other hand, a child may not want to bother to try to find the right answer to a problem; he may be poorly motivated to do a test on any given occasion for any number of reasons – physical discomfort, annoyance at having to do the test when he wanted to do something else (perhaps play football), a feeling of anger after a recent argument with someone, and so on. But when scoring a child's performance on an intelligence test it is not possible to make allowance for *why* a child does not give a correct answer, as the test would no longer be objective but would reflect, at least in part, the subjective views of the psychologist giving the test. Accordingly, a boy's or girl's IQ score is determined only by the number of correct answers given. It may well have been that on the occasions when Daniel gained his lowest IQ scores of 114 and 122 it was because he was disinclined to do the test.

We have seen that when Daniel was two and a half years old the Merral-Palmer test showed his mental age to be three years and nine months. Eight years later, the difference between Daniel's chronological and mental ages had increased to about five years – that is, when he was ten and a half years old he had the intellectual capacity (but not the knowledge) of an average fifteen-and-a-half-year-old. If, in order to take account of the lower scores, an IQ of 135 is taken as a typical result, Daniel would still have had a mental age three and a half years greater than his chronological age at ten and a half.

As for his scholastic attainment, the picture is very different. His reading age was tested nine times during his school career, but on none of these occasions was his reading ability shown to be more than a year ahead of the norm for his age group. One test, when he was six, showed his reading age to be only two months above the expected level for his age. There is no doubt that Daniel did not achieve the level which might have been expected for a boy with his mental capabilities. Reading is a basic skill which enters into most school subjects, so the standard reached is a good indicator of a child's general progress (or lack of it) in schoolwork. Although Daniel's schoolwork kept up to the average level achieved by the other children, he was underachieving.

There are many possible answers as to why Daniel underachieved at school. Most probably it was as a result of a combination of interacting factors which may be grouped as follows:

1   home influences, including the attitude and behaviour of his parents, and particularly of his mother;
2   inadequacies in the schools he attended and in their curricula, and lack of stimulation from the teachers and other pupils he came into contact with within these institutions;
3   outside his home and school(s), the general egalitarian

views held by most people in the wider society, be it village, town or country, to which Daniel's family belonged;

4 the aptitudes, inclinations and personality tendencies which Daniel himself brought to the environment in which he grew up.

As an adolescent, Daniel was moody and very anxious about what other people, particularly those of his own age, thought of him. His actions were often rash and without forethought. He developed an interest in girls at an early age, which led to him spending a great deal of his time on recreational activities and parties. He neglected his schoolwork either because it bored him, or because he spent a disproportionate amount of his time on social activities, or for both reasons. His O and A level examination results were poor except for mathematics, so he was offered a place only at one of the lesser known universities.

The stories of these two boys contrast with one another. The outcomes, too, differ markedly as they became young adults. Most people would view Julian as having become very successful, and Daniel as unsuccessful. Probably, too, the two young men themselves would agree with this conclusion.

These two long-term cases show that while ability is generally a necessary attribute for entrance into high status and highly paid jobs in adulthood, it is not sufficient in itself. The boy's (or girl's) own motivation and personality may not be strong enough. The effects of the other factors already mentioned, too, may result in relatively low A levels and subsequent poor success in higher education, despite the gifted child's very high potential ability.

It is hoped that the cases outlined in this chapter will help other parents gain a better understanding of their own child, thus enabling them to be better equipped to make decisions during his or her upbringing. The various examples above show that there are great differences in personality and temperament between gifted children, which means, for instance, that while one particular school may be the best choice for one gifted child, a totally different sort will suit another. A parent who is worried about some aspect of the development of his own child may find a parallel in one of the stories recounted above, which will make the main issues in the situation clearer and so the decision easier to make. Parents will often find it helpful, too, to look back into their own childhood and to try to imagine how they would have felt in a similar situation to the one in which their child is placed. But most important – although comparing similar experiences in this way can be helpful, it must not be forgotten that no two children nor two sets of circumstances are ever exactly the same, and equally careful consideration must be given to the differences between cases.

3   Is Your Child Gifted?

1   Types of giftedness

Who are the gifted? Many parents ask themselves the question, 'If my child is gifted, how would I know?'

There is no simple answer to this question, but parents can certainly be helped when deciding whether their boy or girl is probably gifted or not. First, though, we must make it clear what we mean here by the words 'gifted', 'bright', 'talented' and 'creative'. We must also mention those children who are outstanding in sport.

Although most of us know what we mean when we use these words – and generally our interpretation is much the same as that of most other people – it is important to know which children are to be included in one or more of these categories, and why. This is because the most usual reason for wanting to know the level of a child's ability is to see that others outside the family – teachers, perhaps social workers, the local education authority, and for the older children, careers advisers – recognise that the child has some exceptional ability. These people may need to be convinced, and they must be persuaded to take the child's abilities into account in connection with his schooling, social needs, higher education and career prospects. For this reason we will start by giving practical, every-day definitions of the four terms we have used.

The 'gifted'
The term 'gifted' as used here refers to intellectually exceptionally able children. This means those youngsters who:

1   score an IQ of 130 or above on the Wechsler Intelligence Scale for Children, or the Scale for Adults, or a

correspondingly high level on another well recognised intelligence test;

2 obtain a standardised score* of 130 or above on an English or mathematics attainment test such as produced by the National Foundation of Educational Research (NFER);

3 are the winners or runners-up in national or regional competitions in essay-writing, mathematics, engineering or some other branch of technology, or design.

There are some other gifted children, too, besides those who satisfy one or more of these criteria: those who have outstanding talent in music or the arts, or who are original thinkers and are creatively gifted, or have exceptional ability in some type of sport. These gifted children are considered briefly in later sections of this chapter (see pages 73–5).

Let us consider two points discussed in Chapter 1. First, it is a matter of common experience and universal acceptance that children develop physically and mentally as they grow older, at least up to adolescence. Second, it is generally accepted that the level of children's mental abilities tends to settle around an average according to their age. The term 'gifted' can be used to indicate the possession of intellectual ability so exceptional that, unlike the majority of children, the child concerned will not find adequate facilities to develop his abilities satisfac-

---

* The score which a child gains when given an NFER attainment test only takes account of the number of correct answers he has given and makes no allowance for his age. This is known as a 'raw score'. For instance, if the test comprises 45 questions and a boy answers 30 correctly, his raw score will be 30. In order to take account of how old children are so that the attainments of boys and girls of different ages can be compared, the raw scores are converted into 'standardised scores'. Tables of 'Standardised Scores' are provided by test publishers. These give, for children of different ages by monthly intervals over a period of one or two years, the mean (average) raw score gained by a group of children at each of the 12 or 24 ages as 100. Children who gain a raw score above the mean will have a standardised score above 100, and vice versa. The NFER Standardised Scores tables are drawn up with a standard deviation of 15, so that a standardised score of 130 or above indicates a child's achievement on the test used as being within the top 2 per cent.

torily in most ordinary schools. Of course, schools do vary in what they have to offer, so that it may be that school A is suitable for a particular gifted boy or girl, whereas school B is not. 'Gifted' here means possessing exceptional intellectual ability such that the normal school curriculum is inadequate as regards both the level and the speed at which progress is made with academic work in the ordinary classroom.

Taking this definition of giftedness, some children will be considered gifted in one set of circumstances but not in another, or during a particular period in their childhood but not at other times. Although this definition may be considered less satisfactory than one which is cut and dried – say, achieving more than a given IQ score on a well recognised intelligence test – flexibility has the advantage of being able to relate to the needs of exceptionally able children. The important point is that if there is a gap between the learning capabilities of an outstandingly clever child and the standard of work, appropriate for nearly all the children in the class, that the school expects, it is unlikely that the clever child will make much progress.

As was shown in the last chapter, an individual's IQ score may vary for a number of reasons, and it would be wrong to say that a child was not gifted merely because on a single occasion he or she failed to reach a particular IQ score. Second, there is variation in the level of a child's IQ *relative* to the average for a school class. The general level of ability of the children, and the expectations of the teaching staff, vary from place to place and from school to school, so that the average IQ level among one group of children might be 95 whereas elsewhere it might be 115. This gap of twenty IQ points, indicating a large difference in the intellectual capabilities of the two sets of children, might mean that the education provided for a very clever boy or girl would be inadequate in the first school but satisfactory in the second.

So far nothing has been said here about how great the difference should be between a child to be considered gifted and one of average ability. Again, it is difficult to give an exact figure, since all sorts of other factors are relevant, such as a clever child's personality and motivation, the attitudes of the school's head and its other teachers. Nevertheless, it can be said with a fair degree of certainty that all those pupils in the top 2 per cent and probably those in the top 5 per cent of intellectual ability need to be provided with more demanding work than is given to the main group of pupils. The reasonableness of this conclusion may be appreciated when it is remembered that, in most schools at both primary and secondary level, about 10–20 per cent of the main pupil body receives extra educational provision on account of some mental or physical disability.

It may be that it is only in one area of the curriculum that the classwork is too elementary and the pace too slow to meet the intellectual needs of the very clever boy or girl. That is, a child may be gifted in only one aspect of the school curriculum. For instance, a child of six or seven who is still in the infant school may read story-books and other material fluently when at home but when at school be obliged to read only simple books which are part of the class teacher's reading scheme. In some cases a gifted reader can become so bored with the books he is told to read at school and so frustrated with the slow pace at which the teacher takes the class through the reading scheme, that he performs very poorly on the work set. I know of a seven-year-old girl who was a gifted reader but was not exceptional in other ways, and who was said by her teacher to be making good progress in all her school-work *except* in reading, in which she was backward. A similar problem may arise with mathematics.

A parallel situation may be found with boys and girls attending secondary schools. For instance, a pupil may be gifted just in science or perhaps in English or some other subject, but if the teacher concerned does not recognise the fact the individual may become so bored and frustrated that, far from the teacher thinking the youngster is a star pupil, he is said to lack ability in the particular subject.

Bright children

Most of what has been said about 'gifted' children applies also to 'bright' ones. Like the gifted, bright pupils may be so much more able than the majority of their classmates, and the circumstances in the classroom may be such, that they, too, are insufficiently extended by most of the school-work they are given. The intellectual ability of bright children is not as exceptional as that of gifted pupils, so there is less likelihood that they will be undersupplied with stimulation and learning opportunities during their school day; but this does not mean that the intellectual environment in schools is generally adequate for most able pupils – only that it is even less likely to be satisfactory for gifted ones. Also, there is a far larger number of bright than of gifted children in the school population as a whole. These two points will now be looked at in further detail.

As regards the probability that bright children enjoy a suitably stimulating learning environment in most primary schools, the reader may be assisted in judging this for himself from Table 1. The findings of a survey carried out by Her Majesty's Inspectors of Schools of a national sample of 542 primary schools in England were published by the Department of Education and Science in 1978.* The Inspectors examined the extent to which the work performed by children aged seven, nine and eleven in 1,127 school classes matched what might be expected according to the children's levels of ability. The class teachers were asked to identify, within their own classes, three groups: the more able (this group would include the bright children), those of average ability and the less able children.

The schoolwork of each of the three groups of children was compared separately by the Inspectors with the standard of work they considered could reasonably be expected in view of the three levels of ability. The HMIs set out their findings in three tables, one each for the 'more able', 'average' and 'less able' groups of children. The data given in Table 1 and Figure 4 have been extracted from the HMI tables. As may be seen for both the classes of nine- and eleven-year-olds, the mismatch between the children's ability and the level of work produced was greatest for the more able children in all eleven subjects. That is to say, there was more under-achievement by the able children than by either of the other two groups. The situation was similar with the classes of seven-year-olds. The match between the capabilities and the level of scholastic attain-

---

* See Table 1, p. 70, source note.

Table 1 The match found between ability and performance in classes of nine-year-olds*

Percentages of classes where match satisfactory	More able groups	Average groups	Less able groups
94–85		reading	reading
84–75		mathematics	mathematics and writing
74–65		physical education	spoken language physical education & music
64–55	reading physical education	spoken language music	history
54–45	mathematics music	history	geography

44–35	writing spoken language	geography art & craft	art & craft science (observational)
34–25		science (observational)	science (experimental)
24–20	art & craft, history, geography, science (observational)	science (experimental)	
14–10	science (experimental)		

* *Source*: 'Primary Education in England: A survey by HM Inspectors of Schools', pp. 86 and 87, Tables 30, 31 and 32, Department of Education and Science, Her Majesty's Stationery Office, 1978.

Figure 4 : The match found between ability and performance in classes of eleven-year-olds

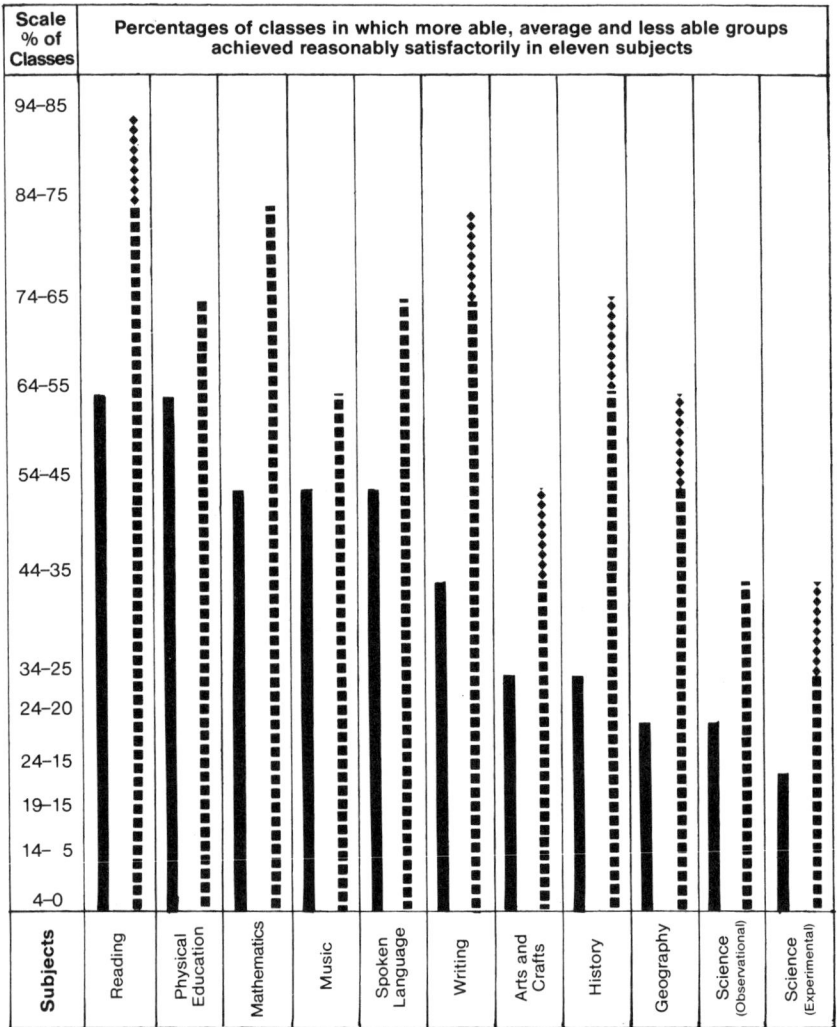

Scale % of Classes	Percentages of classes in which more able, average and less able groups achieved reasonably satisfactorily in eleven subjects
94–85	
84–75	
74–65	
64–55	
54–45	
44–35	
34–25	
24–20	
24–15	
19–15	
14– 5	
4–0	

Subjects: Reading, Physical Education, Mathematics, Music, Spoken Language, Writing, Arts and Crafts, History, Geography, Science (Observational), Science (Experimental)

Source:
As for Table 1

Key

More able   Average and less able   Less able

ment was closest for the groups of less able children for all the subjects taught and for the three age groups. Hence most bright children were not doing as well in their schoolwork as might have been expected.

As has been said above (p. 67), the level of work in schools varies from one to another, so although there may be a likelihood that many schools are not making adequate provision for their bright pupils, it is possible that the reader's own child is receiving adequate stimulation and is developing satisfactorily.

Talented children

The term 'talented' is taken here to mean those children possessing exceptional ability in one of the arts or in music. Recognition that a child is talented in a particular way can be fully established only by someone who is a specialist in the field.

The circumstances in which a child possessing a specific talent is recognised are often quite different from those in which intellectually bright and gifted pupils are ident-ified. The main reason for this is that most primary schools do not have specialist musicians, dancers or artists on their staffs. On the other hand, it is not unusual for the parents of a child with a specific talent to be professionally qualified in the same field – thus they are able to recognise exceptional ability in their children in their own or in a related field. There are, too, parents who have an intuitive feeling for, and understanding of, a particular art form. Although in these instances confirmation by an outside specialist of a child's talent is required, the affinity and empathy between parent and child is such that a mother or father is often shown to be right in their estimation of their child's capabilities.

Parents who are not professionally qualified in the relevant activity but who nevertheless believe that their child is particularly talented in some direction, can get this confirmed in various ways. For instance, a child may be awarded a prize or be highly commended for his or her performance at a festival of music or dance, or for a piece of artistic work. Ordinary public examinations such as those for the Royal Academy of Music, or of Dancing, can also serve to confirm a child's exceptional talent.

Creatively gifted children

'Creativity' is an ill defined word, but usually it implies originality in some constructive way. This ability is not one that can be easily separated off from others, and there may be an overlap between a child's creative ability and a specific talent or exceptional academic ability. A person who 'has music in him', or a dancer for whom dancing is the way in which she most naturally expresses her inner feelings, or an artist whose perception of the world is revealed through painting or sculpture, are probably all creatively gifted individuals.

Children who are creatively gifted perceive things differently from others, and it is their novel view of some aspect of life that is the source of originality in their activities and work. When children's creativity is not channelled constructively it is often wasted. An absence of opportunities to express themselves in their own way can lead to intense feelings of frustration, with detrimental effects both on the children themselves and on others with whom they are in contact at home or school.

When creatively gifted children cannot find an outlet for their originality in their schoolwork – that is, when they become bored with what is uninspiring and largely routine work – the result can be unfortunate for all concerned. Such children often do not conform and behave in the usual manner, and their quick wit and awkward questions can be a thorn in the side of unimaginative, although otherwise competent, teachers. The conflicts which may arise from such explosive situations often start with a teacher taking disciplinary measures against a creatively gifted boy or girl – measures which, in their turn, breed resentment in the child. A clever non-conforming boy who is a natural comedian, a mimic or unusually perceptive of a teacher's weaknesses, can undermine his or her authority with the whole class. The outcome of such conflicts is nearly always damaging to the child's future educational progress and may end with his expulsion.

Such a sequence of events is, of course, extremely worrying to parents. If, however, the basis of the conflict is understood, and it is appreciated that little or no blame is to be attached to the child but, on the contrary, that the source of the trouble has been the failure of adults and of the school system to recognise and cater for an imaginative child's originality, it becomes easier to find a remedy. When serious conflicts of this sort have become acute, it is usually better for the boy or girl to leave the school and to make a fresh start somewhere else. Should this course be adopted, it is important when selecting a new environment for the child that care is taken to find surroundings where his creative gifts will be appreciated and fostered. Just to find a new school will not be a solution, if the attitudes of the staff and the schoolwork are similar to those in the previous school.

Children who excel at sport

Some boys and girls have an exceptional aptitude for and interest in sport, and these children are fortunate indeed.

There is, of course, a great variety of activities under the general heading of 'sport', which may be as different from each other as football, tennis, swimming, running and snooker. Nonetheless, sports have certain common characteristics. First, they are all competitive; second, people in general, both children and adults, accept it as natural that sport should be competitive. This contrasts sharply with the widely held contemporary view among teachers that classwork should not be competitive, and the frequent antagonism towards an intellectually gifted child on the part of other pupils in the same school group. The clever child is contemptuously called 'swot', 'know-all', 'teacher's pet' and 'clever guy' by the other children in the same class. The opposite happens with sport. When a child with exceptional ability, say, as a swimmer, wins a competition, she is congratulated by the other children and encouraged by the swimming instructor who, in addition, often goes on to give the youngster extra coaching so that she can take part in other higher-level competitions. More often than not, encouragement, stimulation, coaching and facilities are available to help any boy or girl with sporting potential to improve his or her performance. The child's progress is checked only when, with the passage of time, he or she wishes to do other things and loses interest, or when the limits of the child's capabilities in the particular sport have been reached.

2   Identifying children with exceptional ability

The high frequency of competitions makes the children whose gifts are in some form of sport the easiest to recognise, since an individual's performance is compared directly with that of others. Competitions are held more rarely in the fields of music, art, dance and drama, but when they are, they too assist in the recognition of a particular talent. Auditions and public examinations are other means of identifying children with exceptional ability. The identification of creativity in children is a complex subject which cannot be explored in depth here, but it is likely that some of the children seen as having some other kind of exceptional ability will also be creatively gifted.

Of the categories of exceptional children mentioned in the first part of this chapter, there remains to be discussed only the means of recognising the intellectually gifted. These children, as has been shown in Chapters 1 and 2, may hide their abilities for a variety of reasons: the desire not to be unpopular with the other pupils is the most likely motive for concealment, and another is lack of interest in work that is too elementary to stimulate them. In order to help parents decide whether their boy or girl does possess exceptional intellectual ability that is not being shown in schoolwork, a simple intelligence test is provided with this book (pp. 105–28). It must be emphasised, though, that this test can only give parents a very rough idea of their child's IQ level. It can, however, help them decide whether it is likely that their child is receiving insufficient stimulation in his schoolwork, and whether it would be advisable to arrange for his IQ to be assessed by an educational psychologist.

Parents who decide on this course may set about arranging for their child's assessment in two ways. He or she may be referred to one of the local education authority's psychologists, or the parents may ask an educational psychologist to assess him or her privately for a fee.

LEA assessment centres
All local education authorities are legally bound to maintain assessment centres where the problems and needs of

less able, backward and maladjusted children can be investigated. Some authorities refer to this aspect of their work as being carried out by a 'school psychological service', but other education departments speak of 'child guidance centres'. In spite of the difference in terminology, both of these establishments are staffed by psychologists, have access to a psychiatrist and social workers, and do much the same work.

When a child is referred to an educational psychologist, he will use various objective psychological tests to discover the level of the child's intellectual ability and his personality type. The psychologist then examines the report sent by the school regarding the level of the child's schoolwork, participation in school life, general classroom behaviour and details of any particular problem which has arisen while the child has been in school. Once the case has been fully investigated, suggestions are made to the child's parents and teachers as to how his problems can be overcome, and how they can help to promote his healthy mental development.

Usually children are only referred to the authority's psychologist by the head of a school, after permission has been given by the parents for the investigation to proceed. And it is very rare indeed, if not unknown, for a school to suggest to a parent, in the absence of any other problems, that a child's IQ should be assessed in order to ensure that the schoolwork he is given is sufficiently stimulating. Teachers often ask for a youngster to be seen by the school psychologist because he is behind with his work in comparison with the expected level for the class, but not because the child might be intellectually gifted. The most usual reason for a teacher to want to refer a child is because there has been a behaviour problem in school. The boy or girl may have been disruptive in class or aggressive during break time, or perhaps was thought to have stolen something from another pupil. Alternatively, the child may have withdrawn into himself and refused to mix with the other children.

It is fairly safe to say that a very bright or gifted child, who experiences a great deal of frustration on account of the slow pace of the class and a lack of companionship in school from children of a like intellectual level, will only succeed in drawing attention to his situation by behaving in one of the ways set out above or by throwing a temper tantrum. The truth of this is illustrated by those youngsters known to be highly gifted who make a point of pleasing their parents and teachers by producing work of the kind expected although they know themselves they are not learning anything at school, and about whom the adult world then says, 'Oh, he's obviously quite happy at school. He's getting on well with his work.' Another comment frequently made by teachers is, 'She is very well behaved and working well. But she is not the best in the class and is obviously not as clever as she was thought to be.' Even when a child's bad behaviour has led to him being seen by an educational psychologist and an IQ test has shown him to be intellectually gifted, the psychologist and teachers may still judge that the bad behaviour merely indicates emotional immaturity, and the fact that the child is suffering severe frustration due to an unsuitable school environment may be overlooked or discounted.

Once parents and head (or the senior member of staff in a secondary school) have agreed on a referral, the head will forward an application to the child guidance clinic for the boy or girl to be seen. At this stage there may be some weeks' delay, for there is probably a waiting list of children requiring attention. Eventually the parent will be asked to take the boy or girl along to the clinic, and once there, the psychologist will want to interview the mother and father in order to obtain background information regarding what has led up to the child's problems, before testing the child for about forty-five minutes, sometimes longer. Afterwards the psychologist will usually see the parents again and will tell them, in very general terms, what his or her findings have been, and recommend ways in which the child might be helped. Although an intelligence test will have been given to the youngster, it is normal practice not to tell the parents their child's IQ score. Precise results from the testing, including the child's IQ score, are, however, sent to the head of the child's school, together with details of the findings on personality characteristics and the psychologist's recommendations.

It is extremely rare for a school head to allow a parent to

see the psychologist's report. As for any action which may be taken as a result of it, this varies from school to school. In practice it may be that the report will make little difference to what happens to the child in school, unless there were serious behaviour problems such as those already mentioned: disrupting classes, refusal to attend school, stealing, or physical attacks on other children or on a teacher.

There are several reasons why this should be so. First, it is very unusual for either the LEA or the government to allocate to schools any money for the sole purpose of providing specialist teachers and extra teaching materials and books in order to cater for the particular requirements of fast-learning and intellectually exceptionally able children below the age of sixteen years. (Above the age of sixteen, provision for intellectually able children is made in sixth forms and in other forms of higher education including the universities.) Hence, if a school is to make special provision to meet the needs of the gifted, it must take the money out of its general school fund. As we have seen, the situation is quite different with regard to mentally retarded and physically handicapped children, and for those considered to be maladjusted. These pupils belong to those categories of children which, under various Education Acts, are classified as being in need of 'special education' (the gifted and talented are not included under the Acts). For all those children who are mentally or physically handicapped and so require special educational provision, spending from public funds averages about three and a half times the funding per child for normal (including gifted) children.* Hence, even where a head does want to make some extra provision for a gifted child, it is probable that for financial reasons it will be impossible to do so.

Second, a psychologist's recommendations may not be acted upon by a school because of a lack of conviction that implementation of the recommendations is necessary or desirable. The members of the different professions concerned are not always in agreement as to whether any

* Department of Education and Science Financial Information Unit, *Handbook of Unit Costs 1980–81*, Tables 2, 3 and 4.

action should be taken, and if so, what that action should be. The psychologist's report may suggest that a boy or girl should be moved up into a higher age group or be given extra work to do, neither of which measures involves the school in extra expense. But putting a child among older children because of his or her exceptional intellectual ability is viewed with disfavour in most schools. This is almost certainly largely due to a lack of understanding among teachers of the ways in which the gifted differ from most other children.

Teachers are invited to attend numerous training courses on the special needs of slow learners, of the physically handicapped and of children belonging to ethnic minority groups, but there is an almost complete absence of similar courses on the needs of bright and gifted pupils. For instance, the 'Programme of Short Courses: April 1983 to March 1984' issued by the Department of Education and Science includes eleven courses concerning children coming within those categories requiring special educational provision or who belong to ethnic minority groups, but there is not one course on the needs and problems associated with intellectually gifted or very bright children at either the primary or secondary stages. Hence, quite naturally, a common assumption among teachers is that such pupils will progress quite satisfactorily on their own and that they do not need any extra help. It also explains why teachers often find it difficult to understand the stress that so many gifted children experience and the difficulties with which their parents are faced.

If a parent believes a child is not being catered for adequately at school on account of high intellectual ability, or for any other reason, then an interview should be sought with the school head (not the class teacher or form tutor). There will rarely be any difficulty in arranging an appointment to see the head, but it is as well to be prepared when making the appointment for the school secretary's question: 'Can you tell me what it is about, please?' It is advisable not to go into details but to give a simple answer such as, 'I am concerned about Ben. He has not been sleeping well and seems to be worrying over something.' It is most inadvisable to tell the secretary or any other member of the school staff that you believe your child is gifted and that the work he is being given in school is inadequate. Even if this is true, and it may well be, it is a matter to approach with great delicacy and in a face-to-face conversation with the head.

If a parent says to a teacher that a boy or girl is not being taught appropriately, this amounts to saying to a professional person that he or she is not doing his job properly. There are few professional people, whether in teaching or other occupations, who can accept such criticism with equanimity. An abrupt approach of this sort would probably lead to resentment and perhaps antagonism on the part of the head towards the parent concerned. Although it would be most unusual for a teacher to 'take it out' on a child because of anger towards a parent, such a situation would almost certainly make it less likely that suitable steps would be taken to meet your son's or daughter's needs, and might even lead to undesirable repercussions.

It is a parent's duty to take action if he or she believes that a child's development is being harmed by the situation in which the youngster is placed in school. All that is intended here is to warn parents of the dangers of the wrong approach to teachers. Exactly how to tackle a problem must depend on the circumstances, but some general guidance can be given.

First, as has already been suggested, it is advisable to ask for an appointment to see the senior member of staff. The appropriate person is usually the head in the case of a primary school, the head of lower school for pupils in the first three years of secondary school, and the deputy head or head for youngsters in the upper forms of secondary schools. These may not be the exact titles of the senior staff in your child's school, since there is some variation from one geographical area to another, but the essential point is that you as the parent should obtain an interview with a senior member of the staff. Do not try to discuss any matter of major importance during the course of a parent-teacher evening. Teachers have to talk to many parents on these occasions, and they cannot spend much time on the problems associated with one child since they will be keeping other parents waiting.

When the interview takes place it is usually preferable for the parent to begin by describing some disturbing aspect of the gifted child's behaviour either at home or at school. Behaviour is a safe subject with which to open the discussion. After all, if a boy or girl is not happy at school and finds the work he or she is given boring, it is to be expected that some sort of undesirable reaction will have resulted from the frustrations the child has experienced. During the course of the exchange of views the topic of bad behaviour can then be led carefully on to why the bad behaviour has arisen, the child's schoolwork, capabilities and so on. From this point it is relatively easy to move on to what can be done about it all, the need for the child to be given more stimulating work and the possible ways of doing this.

Since parents are rarely allowed to see a local education authority's psychologist's report to the school on their child, they usually have little evidence with which to support a claim that the education provided in a class, which apparently successfully meets the needs of some twenty-nine other children of the same age, is not sufficiently advanced to meet the needs of their gifted son or daughter. Even though this may in fact be the situation, it is embarrassing for parents to have to express this view to teachers who consider that, as they are the ones who are professionally qualified, it is for them to judge the educational requirements of their pupils. The teachers often form the opinion that the parents are just trying to 'push' the boy or girl and that this is detrimental to the child's true interests. Some teachers do not express this view openly to parents, although others do. Either way, parents may be left with a feeling of helplessness and hopelessness as to how they can obtain the sort of educational provision they are convinced their child requires in order to promote his or her present and future well-being.

The main weakness in the parents' case is, as we have seen, that the test evidence obtained by the LEA's educational psychologists is withheld from them. An account of the advanced work that the child does at home is often largely disbelieved by the school and considered to be an exaggeration or wishful thinking on the part of the parents. Very often, as has been said, a gifted boy or girl does not produce work of a high standard at school and, perhaps not unnaturally, most teachers judge the ability of their pupils by the work they produce for them. What then are parents to do?

If a parent is seriously worried about his or her child's welfare, consulting an educational psychologist is undoubtedly the best course of action. The youngster may be having difficulty in getting to sleep at night and, when sleep does come, is having nightmares or is wetting the bed, while during the day there may be temper tantrums and other kinds of disturbing behaviour, which, either singly or in combination, may be a sign of mental stress. If a parent is meeting problems of this sort, it is important that the school is informed and that some measure is taken to identify the cause and find a remedy. When told of the difficulties that have been arising, the head or other senior teacher may recommend anyway that the boy or girl be referred to the LEA's educational psychologist. As we have said, the parent's permission is required before this step can be taken. And if the suggestion for referral does not come from the school, then the parent has a golden opportunity to ask the head or the senior teacher concerned to request it.

If a head teacher does not want to refer a child to the school psychological service or child guidance clinic, parents can contact an educational psychologist direct. Some authorities give the address and telephone number of the *school psychological service* (or child guidance clinic) in the telephone directory among the list of services provided by their education or health department. Alternatively, you may be able to obtain the number from your local council office. If you cannot make direct contact in this way and the head of your child's school does not want to make a referral, you can ask your family doctor to write a letter to the authority's school psychological service with a request for your boy or girl to be seen. If you live in or near north-west London, you may like to contact the Tavistock Clinic which is a part of the National Health Service. The clinic has several departments, including one for children and another for adolescents. The children's department investigates all types of psychological problems which a child may experience in school or in the

family. Parents may phone for an appointment, or they
can ask their family doctor, a social worker or their child's
school to make a referral.

Independent assessment of a child's IQ

The alternative way of obtaining an assessment of your
child's IQ is to approach a qualified educational psychologist yourself.

If you should adopt this course you will have to pay a fee
of between £50 and £150 (in 1983); the amount charged
will vary according to the amount of time the case requires. For instance, although sometimes it is merely a
matter of testing a boy's or girl's intellectual ability in
order to help persuade the school authorities to see that a
child is given more demanding work, many cases are more
complex. If the youngster is showing signs of stress, then
the psychologist will need to try to find out the cause. It is
possible that anxiety in a gifted child is the result of other
factors at home or at school, in addition to boredom with
schoolwork. Where this is so the psychologist will probably give a personality test, will spend time talking to the
child and the parents, and possibly will also visit the
school in order to see the head and class teacher (year head
and form tutor in secondary schools). The time taken to
give a child an IQ test is usually about forty-five minutes
to an hour. After that, the psychologist must make up a
record card and calculate the final IQ score from the points
gained on the individual test questions. Professional expertise is required to interpret the child's responses so as
to reveal his particular strengths and weaknesses in mental development. Finally, the psychologist writes up a
report of his or her findings and recommendations. All
this, of course, takes a considerable amount of time. The
charges made do vary substantially from one psychologist
to another, so parents should obtain a clear statement of
what they will be before making final arrangements for
their child to be tested.

Parents should also confirm that the psychologist will
give them a written report of his findings, which will
specify, among other things, the name of the intelligence
scale used, the child's chronological and mental ages on
the date of testing, the IQ, full details of the results of all

tests given, and the psychologist's recommendations, in the light of the findings, for the child's future education. The psychologist may give only the IQ percentile level, and while it is useful to have this it is less precise that the IQ score, and parents should insist that they are given this as well. Most educational psychologists are in the habit of not giving the full results to parents. It is, of course, precisely these details which parents need, and if the psychologist is not prepared to give them on paper it is advisable to find someone else to undertake the testing. In any case, it is desirable to approach two, or possibly three, psychologists whenever private testing is required. Parents can then compare the service offered. This includes the fees to be charged, the promptness with which the boy or girl will be seen, and whether the psychologist will visit the child at home (the preferable alternative) or whether he or she must be taken to the consulting-room.

Finding an educational psychologist

Considerations to take into account here are the degree of experience a psychologist has had in testing and assessing intellectually able and gifted children; how far away is his consulting-room, if this is where the testing is to take place; and third, whether there is likely to be any delay before your child can be tested. It must be remembered that the great majority of educational psychologists who undertake private testing are employed by the local education authorities, usually carrying out their private work in a different area from their full-time employment. Although the training of psychologists prepares them for work with individuals of every level of ability, the fact that under a number of Education Acts there is a legal obligation for education departments to assess and provide for the needs of educationally subnormal children means that most of their day-to-day experience is likely to have been with less able children. Another point to consider is whether you would prefer to approach a young psychologist who has recently completed training, or someone who has had ten to twenty years' experience of testing children, visiting schools and talking to teachers. It may be an advantage, too, if the person you consult has brought up his or her own children, particularly if among them there was one who was very bright or gifted. If the psychologist has also experienced as a parent some of the difficulties with which you are faced, it may help him or her to understand your problems and worries. Another point to think about is whether your child is likely to respond better to a man or a woman in a one-to-one face-to-face test situation.

Once you have decided on the sort of person you are looking for, the next step is to find the names of some psychologists. Several courses of action are open to you. You may write to the British Psychological Society for names of psychologists who would be willing to test your child privately. Second, you can ring up or write to the psychological department of a local education authority *other than your own* stressing that you want a private assessment and that you do not live in the area adminis- tered by their authority. It is not considered ethical for psychologists to charge fees in the area in which their employers provide a free school psychological service. Third, you may approach the psychologist who has devised the intelligence test for the use of parents that is contained in this book. Dr Lowenstein has had a long-term interest in and great experience of the needs of bright and gifted children and of the problems which may arise. Lastly, you may like to consult the National Association for Gifted Children.

LEA or private testing?

If parents obtain a referral to a local education authority psychologist, they will not have to pay a fee. Their son or daughter will probably be put on a waiting list and there may be a delay of some weeks before the child is seen. The parents will almost certainly not be given full details of the test results when the head teacher talks to them about the psychologist's findings and recommendations. The head may say something like this: 'Yes, the psychologist has found him to be quite bright and has suggested it would be useful for him to be given some extra maths. Unfortunately, it will be very difficult for us to do any- thing about it as we are so short-staffed.' Even where the psychologist's report has shown a child to have an IQ of over 130 and to be in the top 2 per cent of the ability range for his age group, it would not be unusual to find a head making this sort of comment to parents.

All the same, it is nearly always worthwhile for parents whose child is attending an LEA school to try, in the first instance, to have their child assessed through the school by the authority's psychologist. There are several reasons for this. First, it might work – it does sometimes and you might be lucky. If you are, your child will be tested by a competent person at no cost to yourself, you will be told your child's IQ score, the results of any other assessments regarding his personality and problems, and the recommendations that have been made in order to assist his future development. You will then be given an opportunity to talk these over with the school head and you will decide together the best way of implementing the recommendations and of helping your child. Of course, it is very rare for it to happen like this – but there is enough of a chance that the outcome will lead to the school taking measures to meet your child's needs for it to be worth a try. Most teachers genuinely have the interests of *all* their pupils at heart, including the bright and gifted ones. If they fail to appreciate the needs of such children, it is in most cases because they have had no opportunity to attend courses on the characteristics of such pupils, and do not understand them. It is quite possible that the school will take some positive steps to meet your child's requirements even though they will not confirm to you that he is very bright or gifted. The class teacher in a primary school, or a subject teacher in a secondary school, may be asked by the head to provide your child with more demanding work. It is unlikely where this does happen that you will be told about it, and if you find out at all, it will almost certainly be from your child. Unfortunately, even if the head does make the request to a teacher, there is no certainty that he or she will continue to provide the extra work after a couple of weeks.

If, having consulted an educational psychologist privately, you have discovered that your child's IQ is high, say 130 to 135 on the WISC, you now have documentary evidence that your child's intellectual ability is exceptional. Broadly speaking, it may be said that he or she is one of the two children in a hundred who are expected to gain such a high IQ score among children of the same age and over the country as a whole. Under most definitions, such a score places your son or daughter in the gifted category. And if the IQ score is about 124 to 129 the child may be considered to be bright or very bright. You are now on stronger ground when you ask the school to give him or her more demanding work to do.

In spite of having objective information from a qualified psychologist as to the level of your child's ability, it is still necessary to approach the school tactfully and to take care that you do not give the teachers the impression that you are telling them that they are not doing their job properly. They may not be willing to accept the psychologist's findings if these conflict with their own views of your child's ability. Even if the school does agree that you have a gifted child who requires more stimulating work to do, there may not be the staff and facilities, as mentioned earlier, to enable the teachers to make extra provision for him, although it is probable that, given the will, the school could go some way to meeting your child's special needs. The point here is that even when you have a supporting report from your own psychologist, the solution to your child's educational problems will not follow automatically – although you are, of course, in a better position than you were before to press for steps to be taken. If, in spite of having written confirmation from a qualified psychologist that your child is gifted or very bright, you do not obtain satisfaction from the school, you are in a good position to take the matter up with your local education office. It may even be sufficient just to state to the head teacher your intention of doing so since, with the prospect of the dispute moving outside the school, he or she may decide after all to make an extra effort to find a way of providing more adequately for your son or daughter.

Approaching your local education authority
If you know that your child's schooling continues to be inadequate, it is your responsibility as a parent to take all the steps within your power to remedy the situation. If the approach to the school has failed, then the next step is the education office. It is advisable to make a number of copies of the psychologist's report to use in support of your case.

Local education departments are organised in various ways. In the case of a very large authority, there are usually district or area education officers coming under the Chief Education Officer or Director of Education. Where this is the case, parents should ask for an appointment with the area or district education officer. When this interview takes place, it is useful to give him a copy of the psychologist's report, and it may be that some satisfactory arrangement for your child will be agreed.

If the outcome is not to your satisfaction, the next step is to arrange an interview with your authority's Adviser for Primary Education if your child is in a primary school, or with the Chief Adviser – sometimes they are called Inspector – if your child attends a secondary school. A few authorities now have an adviser, part of whose job is 'special responsibility for gifted pupils'. These officials are usually based in the authority's central administrative offices and the receptionist will tell you the precise titles under which they are known, and whether there is an adviser or assistant education officer with special responsibility for gifted children.

It is usually quite easy to arrange an interview with someone in a senior position at the LEA's offices. The procedure is to ask the secretary of the person you wish to see for an appointment. She may ask you what you want to see the official about, to which you can reply briefly that problems have arisen with regard to your child's schooling. She will probably ask you the name of the school and then fix the appointment. If you do not receive satisfaction at this stage you can ask to see the Director or Chief Education Officer. Although this official may not meet parents, you will probably be able to meet his deputy.

By this point you will have worked through the hierarchy of your local education authority. There really are no short cuts, for if one stage is missed out, the more senior official will merely refer you back to the person responsible at the lower level. If the educational facilities provided for your child have not improved to your satisfaction within a reasonable time after your talk with the officials at the education department, it is time to turn in other directions.

Some parents will feel that they have a sufficiently

strong case to justify a request to their Member of Parliament to intervene with the education authorities on their behalf. Most MPs hold 'surgeries' in their constituencies where they meet constituents and discuss any difficulties they may be faced with in dealing, among other things, with local or national government bodies. A second option open to parents is to write to the Secretary of State for Education and Science. When making approaches of this sort it is desirable to keep the complaint as succinct as possible. It should include the following:

1   your child's name, date of birth, sex, and the name of the school attended;
2   a *brief* statement outlining why you are dissatisfied with the schooling being received and the associated problems;
3   a *brief* account of the action you have taken and the outcomes of the interviews you have had with the head of the school and with officials in the LEA;
4   copies of recent school reports;
5   a copy of the psychologist's report and recommendations.

Finally, it is open to you to write a letter to one or more of your local newspapers setting out the problem you face and the difficulties you have experienced in trying to get something done about it. It is probable that if you persist in this way, some changes designed to meet the requirements of your exceptionally able child will be made.

3 The intelligence test

Estimating your child's ability

It is very difficult for parents to judge their own children's level of intellectual ability. And as readers will have discovered from the previous pages, obtaining a professional assessment of a youngster's IQ does incur some time, effort and, possibly, expense. If you are right in your assumption that your boy or girl possesses exceptional ability, you can gain some reassurance from using the parents' check-list (Table 2) and the ability test on p. 105. These will make it easier for you to approach the head or some other senior teacher at your child's school, and tell him or her that the work your child is being given is not sufficiently stimulating and advanced.

The check-list and the ability test are two different ways of judging the standard of your child's mental development. At the same time, they are complementary. The check-list enables a parent to take into account many factors which have affected the standard that a particular child has reached, whereas with an IQ test you know only whether the answers he gives are right or wrong. In the case of pre-school children particularly it is often difficult to persuade them to focus their attention on answering specific questions; here the check-list may give parents a better idea of their child's ability than they had previously been able to gain. The chief disadvantage of this test is its subjective nature. It is very easy to err by being too generous or too stringent, however careful and fair one tries to be in making a judgment. For instance, it is very difficult for a parent to say (unless he or she has had experience with many other children) whether, in comparison with other children of the *same* age, a little boy or girl can 'count up to ten' 'about the same' or 'much better'. On the other hand, using only an objective test has disadvantages as well. With the vocabulary test, for instance, it may be that for some reason or other a child has not had the opportunity to learn the meaning of the particular words used. It is for reasons of this sort that even using both methods you cannot expect to gain an accurate assessment of your child's ability – only an indication

Table 2 A parents' check-list of a child's level of mental development

Please put a tick in the appropriate column for your child's ability compared with other infants of the same age:

Pre-school children			
	not so well	*about the same*	*much better*
1 Did he walk?			
2 Did he talk in sentences?			
3 Build with stickle bricks (e.g. Lego)?			
4 Do very simple jigsaw puzzles?			
5 Recognise representations of people and things in picture books?			
6 Recognise numbers and letters?			
7 Count up to ten?			
8 Remember things, either actual events or cards or numbers in games?			
9 Begin to read?			
10 Start to write?			
5- to 11-year-olds			
11 Does he ask continuous and numerous questions?			
12 Does he have an exceptional memory?			
13 Recognise relationships between things and events?			
14 Show unusual ability to concentrate on doing some task or hobby?			

Table 2 *continued*

		not so well	about the same	much better
15	Like wrestling with puzzles or playing chess?			
16	Is he very interested in reading?			
17	Accepted by older children as an equal?			
18	Has he an abnormally wide range of different hobbies?			
19	Are his vocabulary and speech unusually mature for a child?			
20	Is he exceptionally advanced in school work?			
	Total			

If you have placed 5 ticks in the third column in either group of 10 questions, your boy or girl is probably bright or very bright and it is worth investigating the level of his ability further.

as to whether it is worthwhile seeking professional advice.

Before parents give the test, it is necessary to explain how it operates and what it can tell us. As has been illustrated in earlier chapters, some children learn more quickly than others. This learning results from the use of a number of different abilities, both physical and mental. For instance, children learn language from hearing it spoken and come to know that certain words mean certain things. Later they are able to recognise that the same things vary with different conditions – a road is not the same when it is wet as it is when it is dry, and in summer a stone wall feels warmer when it is in the sun than when it is in the shade. Later the child starts to relate the effects different things or processes have on each other and the changes which take place as a result. For instance, a child comes to realise that a wet road dries more quickly in those places where the sun shines on it directly than where it is in the shade.

During their babyhood infants begin to learn their mother tongue. As they grow older they increase their vocabulary and accumulate a knowledge of the things and processes going on around them. By the end of their pre-school days they have a practical knowledge of the effects many of these things and processes have on each other.

Although there are quite marked differences between babies – some are more advanced at learning to walk and others with talking – by the time they are two years old most infants have reached about the same stage in their development. A baby of a year old is usually only able to say a few words, but by the time he is two he is expected to have learnt to toddle around and to be able to say short, simple sentences. Most three-year-olds are fully mobile, can talk fluently and notice detail. By the time they are four they are able to fit simple shapes together, know the names of, and recognise, the main colours and begin to play games with other children. Children of this age usually cannot read or even recognise the letters of the alphabet or the symbols for digits, but four-year-olds are expected to be able to follow simple instructions like 'Go upstairs and bring down the book which is on the chair.' Psychologists have used the facts (1) that all children have to learn about their surroundings, and (2) that most mentally normal children of the same age have reached about the same stage in their learning, as two of the pillars upon which to construct intelligence tests.

How intelligence tests are devised

A third pillar upon which IQ tests have been built is the natural variation found amongst the individual items making up a group of the same things. Nature is full of examples of differences of this sort: take, for instance, a cluster of daffodils growing in a garden. The majority of the daffodils are of very nearly the same height, but a few are on stems which are markedly taller or shorter – and so just one or two of the flowers stand out from the group as being much taller or shorter than the rest. This pattern of natural variation is found, too, with man-made things. For instance, in a residential area of an ordinary town, most of the houses will be very nearly the same size, but there will also be a few which are larger, and some which are smaller. The bell-shaped pattern formed by the num-ber of daffodils of each height, and by the frequency with which houses of the same size occur, demonstrates the 'normal curve' of distribution. It depicts graphically the much larger number of individual items making up a large group that will be at or near the average level for the whole group, the much smaller number of items at levels distinctly different from the average, and the increasing rarity of items furthest away from the average for the group (see Figure 5). The normal distribution is an important factor in the construction of intelligence tests.

The experience of teachers and others has shown that most children with similar cultural backgrounds will have reached about the same stage of mental development at approximately the same age. In other words, most youngsters if tested would be found to be at the stage of mental development which is normal for children of their

Figure 5 :
The curve of normal distribution: the heights of a group of 101 daffodils

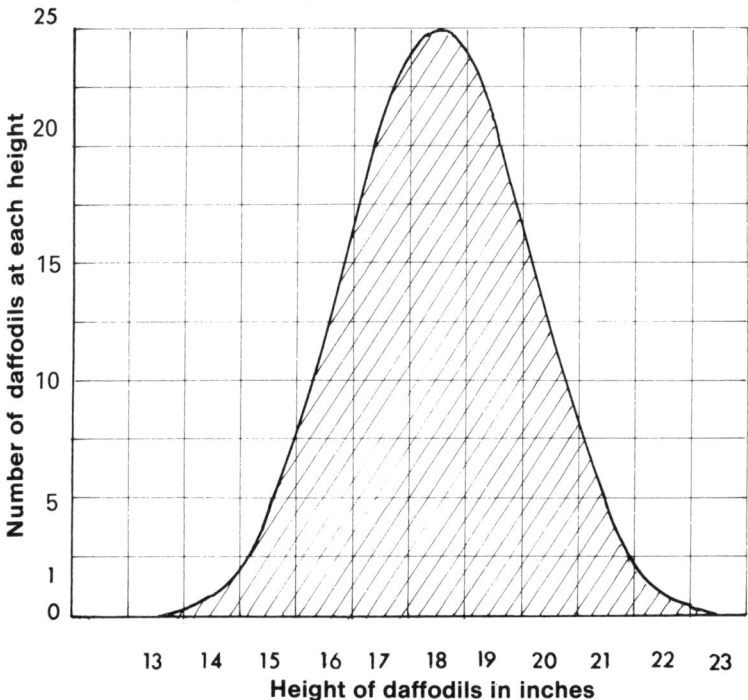

Note: Average height of daffodils is 18″.

age. Of the remainder, some would be found to be mentally more advanced, while others would be at a level below that expected for children of their age. Psychologists thus have two ways of expressing a child's age. The first one is 'chronological age', time by the clock and according to the calendar. The second is 'mental age', the measure of a child's mental development. For the great majority of children their chronological and mental ages must be about the same. This is so on account of the way the concept of mental ages has been reached. The stage of mental development attained by the majority of, say, five-year-olds (chronological age) has been taken as the standard for a mental age of five years. It follows that if Robert and Irma are two typical children with a chronological age of eight and ten, it is to be expected that their mental ages will also be approximately eight and ten.

But while the averages of chronological and mental ages for most children will coincide, it is quite likely that for any particular individual there will be a slight difference between his chronological and mental ages – sometimes the one will be a little higher, sometimes the other. However, taking the age group as a whole it is also to be expected that, as with the daffodils and the houses, there will be a large number of children whose mental ages are clearly just above or below the average level and a few cases where the discrepancy between their chronological and mental ages is large. These will be the very bright and gifted on the one hand and the mentally less able and severely retarded children on the other. Figure 6 again shows a normal distribution. The great majority of the individuals making up the total group of children are clustered around the average, and the number becomes smaller and smaller the further away the individual's level of ability is from the majority of the age group.

As has already been said, slight differences between chronological and mental ages occur frequently and are partly the result of day-to-day influences. To the extent that these discrepancies do indicate a genuine difference in ability either above or below that of average children, the variation is small enough for the education authorities to expect that the normal school curriculum is sufficiently flexible to cater for the discrepancies, without special

Figure 6 :

A normal curve showing the probable distribution of IQs in a large unselected group of children

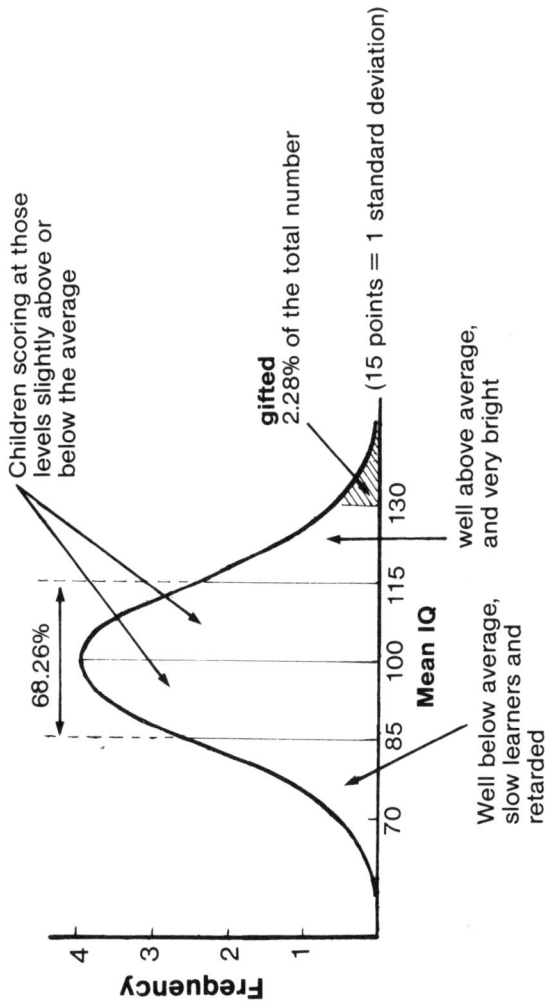

Children scoring at those levels slightly above or below the average

68.26%

Mean IQ

gifted
2.28% of the total number

(15 points = 1 standard deviation)

well above average, and very bright

Well below average, slow learners and retarded

Frequency

4
3
2
1

70   85   100   115   130

The number of children with IQs at each level is indicated by the height of the curve educational provisions being necessary. Nationally, the average IQ score gained by two thirds of the children of school age is between 85 and 115. It is generally accepted in educational circles that pupils in this band can be considered to be near enough to the average in their ability for the usual school curriculum to be adequate to meet their needs. Nearly all schools can cater for this range of ability by making use of extra books and materials for broadening the work undertaken by the above average pupils, while many of those in the lower average group will somehow manage to keep up with the essential work covered by the class. However, many of the children whose school performance falls below the expected average, and all of those classified as 'retarded', will be given additional teaching. But as we have already discovered, it is rare for appropriate additional learning facilities to be made available for the corresponding groups of able and gifted children.

How the IQ is calculated

An IQ is an intelligence quotient which traditionally has been calculated by dividing a child's mental age by his chronological age and multiplying by 100 in order to remove the decimal point. To give an example: if John aged ten years exactly had a mental age of eleven, his IQ would be $(11 \times 100) \div 10 = 110$. Similarly, if Jane aged nine years six months had a mental age of nine years three months, her IQ would be $(9.25 \times 100) \div 9.5 = 97$ to the nearest whole number. Both these children fall within what is considered by psychologists to be the normal range of ability, and the curriculum in their school classes ought to be adequate to meet their needs.

There has been criticism by some psychologists of the use of the term 'mental age' for the purpose of calculating a child's IQ. As a result, modern tests usually use 'deviation scores'*, which are calculated from the standard devi-

---

* 'Deviation scores' are scores which are calculated so that they indicate how far away individual scores are from the average for a whole set of marks. For instance, when 50 is the average mark obtained by a group of children, if one boy obtained a score of 45 and another of 55, the deviation score would be the same for both children although in the first case it would be negative and in the second positive.

ation* upon which the spread of the scores obtained in the test are based. The procedure is too complicated to explain here and in any case, the different method of calculating the IQ rarely makes more than one or two points difference. The method using mental age explained above is quite adequate for parents to be able to judge approximately the level of their child's mental ability.

As we have seen, the scoring on an IQ test is usually arranged so that the boy or girl of average mental ability will score an IQ of 100. Although this is the intention, it does not always happen – for several reasons. First, tests go out of date. Most children in England and Wales today would not be able to do a simple calculation referring to 'half crowns' or 'florins' because they probably would not have heard of these coins. If a child failed to give the correct answers to questions referring to outdated money, this would not indicate a lack of ability on the child's part but only the unsuitability of the test. Second, children with the same degree of intellectual ability are not spread evenly over the country, so the average IQ might be above 100 in one district and below it in another. Local averages which are above or below national norms rarely differ by more than a few points. Third, where children belong to the families of ethnic minorities, most of the usual tests are probably unsuitable. This is because these children have a different cultural background from those on whom the tests have been standardised† (mainly children from ordinary English or Welsh families, most of whom were pupils at local education authority primary and secondary schools). So the usual tests, particularly those used by teachers, cannot be relied upon to give a good indication of the mental capabilities of children who have a different family background or who have recently arrived from abroad. An example will illustrate why this should be so. The Moslem religion forbids the pictorial representation of the human form and of other living things. Most intelligence tests make use of pictures of people doing various things, or of animals or trees. A Moslem child may be in

*The term 'standard deviation' is explained on p. 57.

† Tests are standardised by giving the sets of questions to a large group, generally some thousands of children. The average score gained by children of the same age will then be equated to an IQ of 100.

such a state of mental conflict when asked to do something forbidden by his religion that his test score will probably be too low to give a reasonable indication of his ability.

The intelligence test given at the end of the chapter is for parents to use in order to gain some idea of whether their child is gifted or bright. It has been devised specifically for very able children and is not suitable for those of below average ability. The test is not a substitute for an assessment on the Wechsler Intelligence Scale for Children or the Stanford-Binet Intelligence Scale by a qualified psychologist. The use of these two tests is very strictly controlled, and only those professionally qualified are allowed to use them. But the test provided in this book will help parents decide whether to arrange for their child to be tested by an educational psychologist. If it shows the child to be not very bright, parents may decide against paying a substantial fee to an educational psychologist to find out whether he is gifted. On the other hand, should there be behavioural problems, signs of stress and so on, it would probably be a good thing to go to a psychologist on this account, irrespective of the probable level of the child's ability.

It is important to emphasise how essential it is that the instructions for using the test should be followed implicitly. Apart from that, there are two great dangers which can easily lead to the results becoming invalid. First, it is natural for parents to want to help their child and to want him or her to score well. Yet if they give way to this inclination in the slightest degree, it will only mean that there can be less confidence placed in the IQ result, which may be higher than the child's mental ability justifies. If a false picture of this sort is given it can have harmful results. An inflated IQ score can lead to parents expecting more from their son or daughter than he or she has the ability to achieve. It is extremely upsetting for a child who is genuinely doing the best he can with schoolwork to be unable to satisfy his parents. In an extreme case a youngster can suffer so much stress as a result of being unable to come up to the expectations of those he loves and desperately wants to please, that he can become mentally ill.

There are also risks in the opposite direction. Intelligence test designers assume that a child is motivated to do the test – that he or she is concentrating on the questions and doing his or her best to answer them correctly. When children are in school amid a general atmosphere of settling down to work among a group, it is reasonable to assume that nearly all of them, if not all, will be motivated to score as high as they can. At home a child is probably not used to having to settle down to work. It may be that a child does concentrate for long periods on some interest or other, but this is because he or she has chosen to do it. It is quite a different matter when a youngster is asked by a parent to sit down and give his full attention to a test in time which he has come to think of as his own. Also, the social and emotional relationship between parent and child is very different from that between teacher and pupil. Precisely because a child knows his or her parents so well and feels close to them, there may not be the same feeling of having to do something – in this instance the intelligence test – whether he or she wants to or not. There is, too, the possibility that the child may think of the test as something of no great importance, and consequently not as a task requiring maximum concentration. A gifted child may be so accustomed to being presented with easy tasks that he may not be prepared for the real challenge to his intellectual ability which will be presented by some of the test questions, and so not apply himself fully to answering them. If, on the other hand, the parent should over-stress the significance of the test and the need to concentrate on getting the right answers, the child might become over-anxious or resentful, with the result that fewer right answers are given than are really within his capabilities. For any of these reasons the IQ score which is calculated may be lower than the one which would most truly reflect the child's mental ability.

A clever child will almost certainly enjoy doing the test. Many of the questions and puzzles are intriguing and are designed to capture a child's attention. This leads to the last warning that must be given to parents. A bright youngster is quite likely to be interested in this book and, if it is lying around, to pick it up and start reading it. If he does so, he will almost certainly find the test and start having a go at some of the questions. Should this happen and later on you use the test to estimate your child's ability, it will invalidate the test results.

The dangers outlined above should not deter you from trying to assess your child's IQ. The warnings given are intended to help parents obtain the best estimate possible of their youngster's level of mental ability.

Choose very carefully the time when you test your child. If you ask him to stay in when he wants to go out to play football, his motivation is likely to be poor and his score an inadequate reflection of his intellectual ability. Similarly, if you ask your daughter to work through the test at a time when she wants to visit her friend, go swimming, or go for a cycle ride, again the motivation is likely to be poor and the score not do justice to her ability. Any youngster is likely to be annoyed and uncooperative if he is asked to do an IQ test at a time when he particularly wants to see a programme on TV. Nor should you expect to get a satisfactory result from the IQ test if you ask him to do it at the end of a long day when he is tired, nor if he is trying to work out answers to the questions against a background of teasing and chaffing from a brother or sister. If you have more than one child of school age, or just below, it is advisable to make arrangements for the other children to be fully occupied so that they do not disturb the boy or girl you want to test.

As has already been said, most bright and gifted children enjoy working through intelligence tests, which they see as a challenge. There are times when most of them will be happy to do the test, particularly when they have nothing much else to do. The most opportune moment will not be the same for all children, since a lot depends on the way the family spends its day. Probably early evening on a Saturday or some other time during the weekend would be a good time in most families.

Once you have decided on a suitable time, you need to think carefully about how you are going to approach your child about doing the test. It is usually best to tell him the truth, but in brief and simple terms. You want the youngster to realise that he must try hard, without allowing him to become anxious. The sort of thing you could say is that 'Mummy [or "Daddy" or "Both of us"] want(s) what is best for you so we [I] want to see if the work they are giving you in school is just right or too easy.' The child will probably respond in some way and a question and answer session may ensue. If, after this, he seems willing to work the test, you can then say something like: 'All you have to do is to work through some puzzle questions and see if you can find the right answers. Some will be too difficult for you so you can guess them or miss them out. Just do what you can. You'll find them interesting and you'll like doing them.' At this point the youngster may say he does not think he will be able to do the test. You can then reassure him: 'I'm sure you will be able to do some of it. The thing to do is to have a try and see what you can do.'

If your son or daughter should signify that he or she does not want to do the test, it is better to drop the subject and to raise it again at an opportune moment a couple of days or even a week later. It is probably better, too, to avoid using the word 'test'. When your child does eventually get down to trying to work out the answers, it is essential, as has already been said, that you give not the slightest hint as to what these might be.

How to use the test
The test questions are graded with the easier ones first. They gradually become harder so that at the end of a section they can be very hard indeed. As you will see, there are a number of different types of question. The first section consists of sets of pictures and is a vocabulary test. The second is another vocabulary test, but without illustrations. The third section is on absurdities.

When your child is working through the test you may find that he cannot do one of the easier questions but is able to answer one or two further on which are apparently more difficult. The same sort of thing may happen between the different sections. A child may be able to do very little with the second vocabulary test (the one without the illustrations), but be able to provide nearly all the right answers in the one which follows. The reason for these apparent anomalies is the natural variation between people. When you give the IQ test to your child, remember to make sure he is comfortable and able to concentrate. For children, particularly the younger ones, who cannot concentrate for long stretches of time, it is best to divide the test up into two or three sessions. But it is against the test rules to go over any of the questions asked in the first session a second time in a subsequent session.

How to mark the test
Answers to the questions will be found either in the text of the test itself or on the score sheet (p. 248). As we have said before, great care must be taken that the children do not have an opportunity to see the book when it is in the house. Obviously, if the child you are testing has had an opportunity to do some of the questions and then look up the answers of those he cannot do in the back, the results of the test will be invalidated.

When marking the test, you should award one point for every completely correct answer given. The rules do not allow you to give half a mark for answers which are partly right. The scores table on p. 249 gives total scores for gifted and bright children at certain ages.

From Table 3 you will be able to gain some idea of how intellectual ability is distributed in general. The table shows the proportions, on average, of all children (which, of course, includes the less able ones) that may be expected to be found to be gifted or very bright. However, the table cannot take account of variations between different geographical and residential areas.

Table 3   Ability categories according to IQ

IQ score above	Approximate level of ability	Proportion of age group expected to gain score
145	highly gifted	0.13% or 1.3 per thousand
140	highly gifted	0.4% or 4 per thousand
135	gifted	1.0%
130	gifted	2.25% or 25 per thousand
125	very bright	5.0%
115	good average	16%
100	average	50%

4 Should we have our child assessed?
Ability test for use by parents

General instructions

Make sure the child is feeling cooperative and that you will not be interrupted.

The test will take about 20–30 minutes. With a very young child it may be best to tackle each section on a different occasion.

There is no time limit except in sections D and F.

Do *not* tell the child if his or her answers are correct or not. When the child has responded say, 'Thank you', or 'Next one', or just smile and proceed to the next question. Where prompts are permitted, this is indicated in the text.

Score 1 point for each correct answer throughout.

Section A: Picture vocabulary

Instructions   Say, 'I am going to give you a word and show you four pictures. Please choose a picture to illustrate the word. Do you understand?' (Repeat if necessary.)

1. PRICKLY

2. INFLATE

a.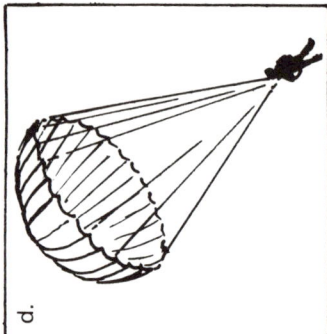

b.

c.

d.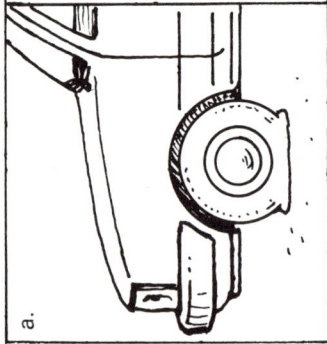

3. REPTILE

a.

b.

c.

d.

4. ARTISTIC

a.

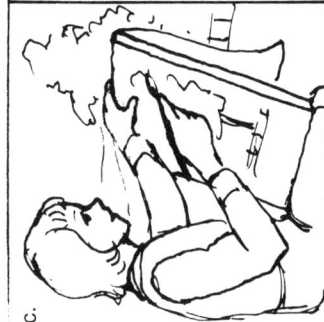

b.

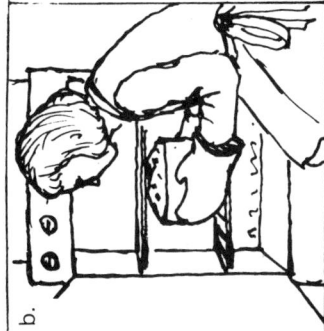

c.

d.

5. HAWK

a.

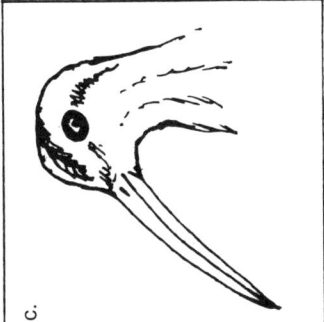

b.

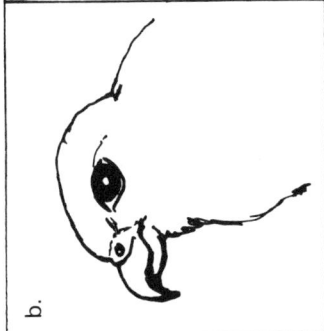

c.

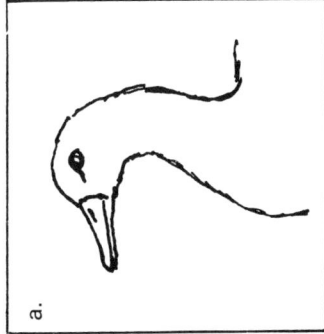

d.

6. SILHOUETTE

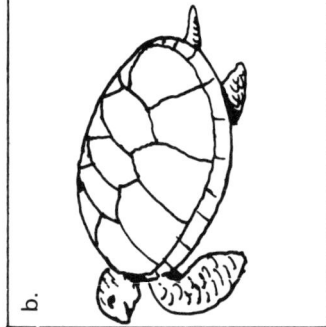

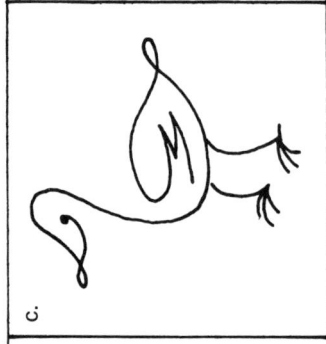

7. TRANSPARENT

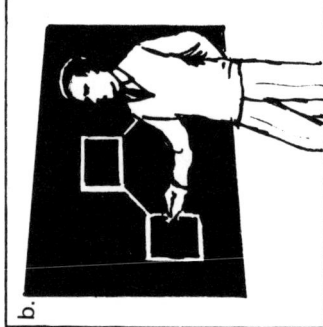

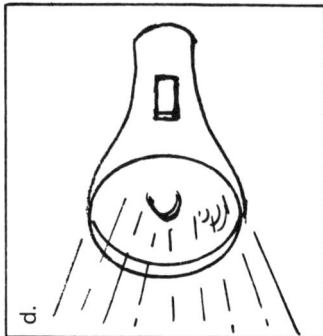

8. POLLINATION

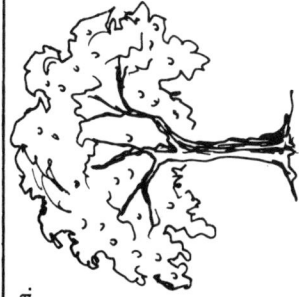

a.

b.

c.

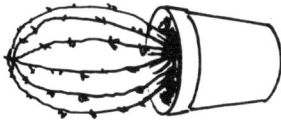

d.

9. AMPHIBIAN

a.

b.

c.

d.

10. CHAUFFEUR

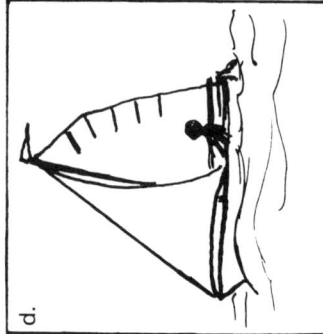

a.

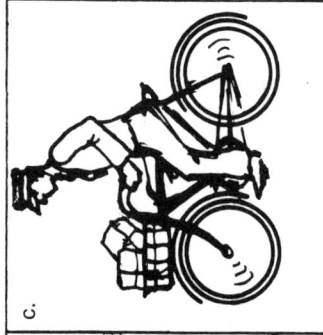

b.

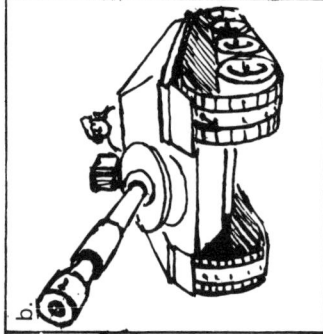

c.

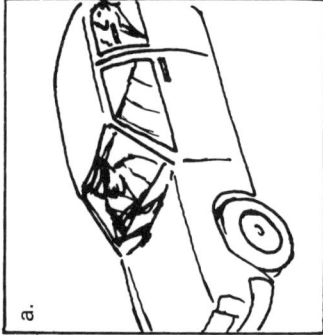

d.

11. PHARMACY

a. HARDWARE

b. BOOKSHOP

c. CHEMIST

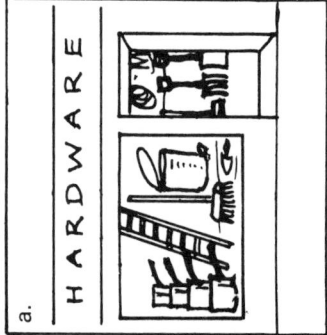

d. GROCER

12. ARTIFICIAL

a.

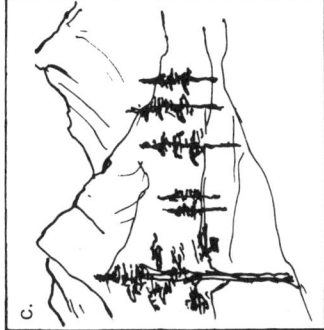

b.

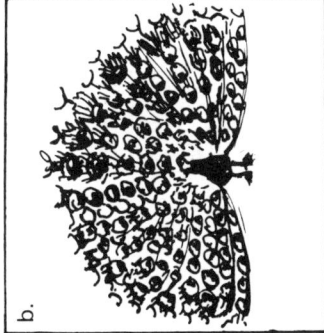

c.

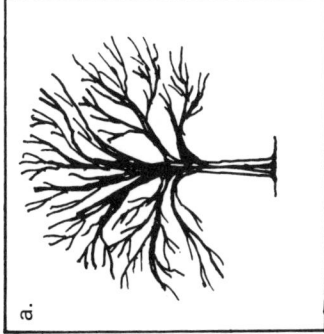

d.

13. FESTOON

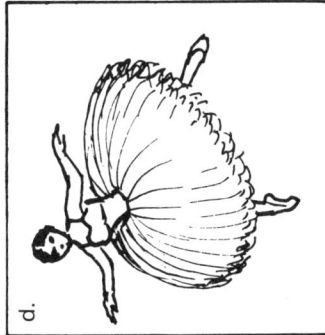

a.

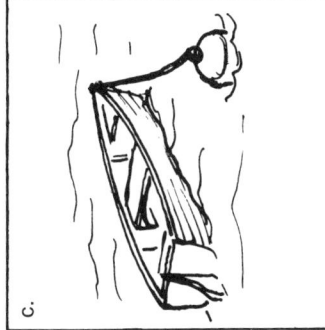

b.

c.

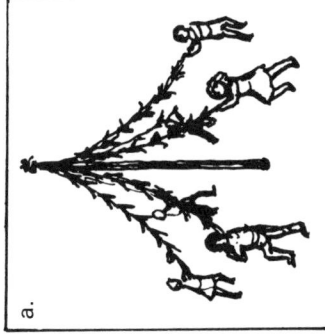

d.

14. OBELISK

a.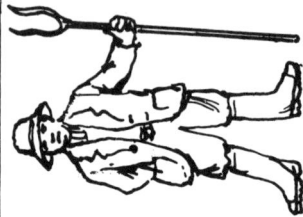
b.
c.
d.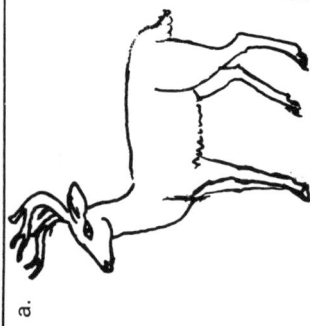

15. CREATION

a.
b.
c.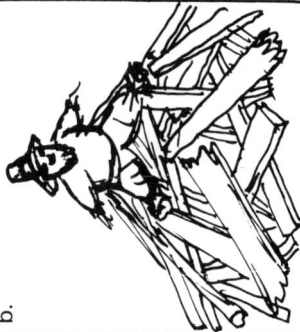
d.

16. INCISION

a.

b.

c.

d.

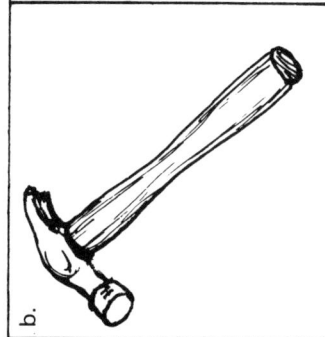

17. INSPIRATION

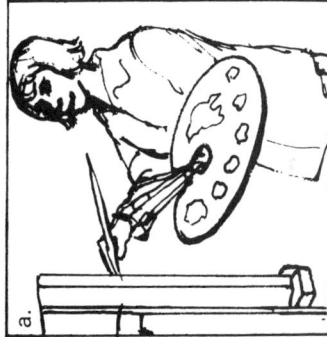

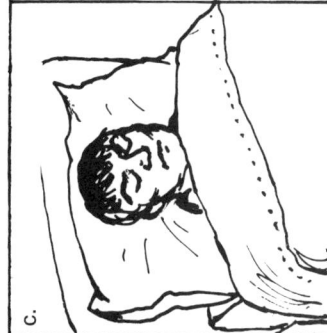

a.

b.

c.

d.

18. LEGAL

a.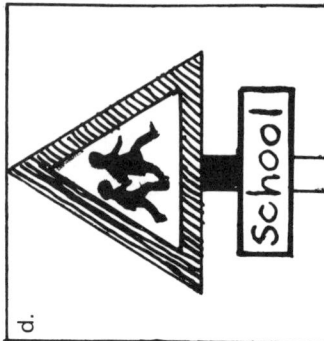

b.

c.

d.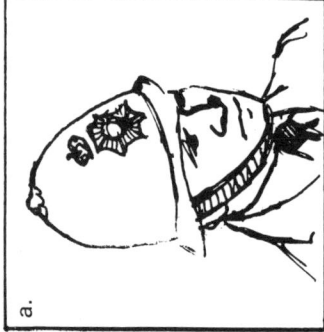

19. INGESTION

a.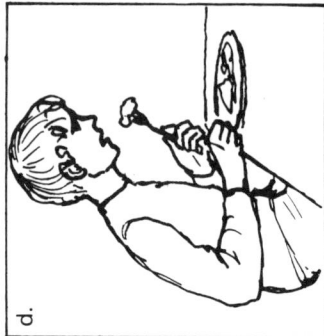

b.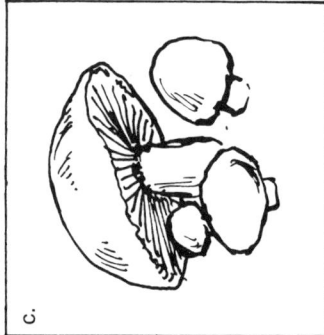

c.

d.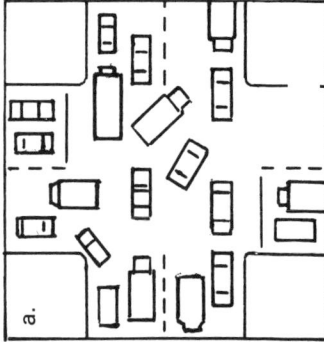

20. GREAT EXPECTATIONS

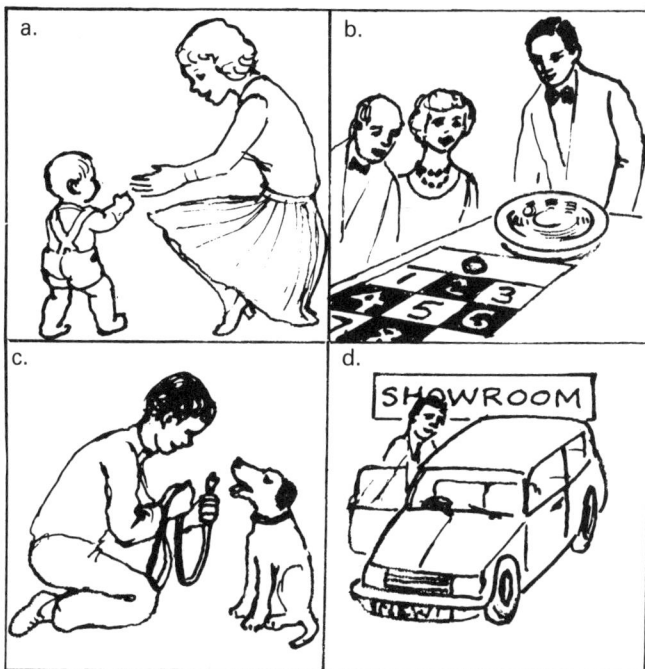

Section B: Vocabulary

Instructions Say, 'Now I am going to read you a word and I want you to tell me what the word means.' If the child clearly knows the word but has difficulty defining it adequately, say, 'Can you tell me more about the word?'

With pre-school children you may ask them to show you what a word means.

Where words have more than one meaning any one is sufficient for a mark.

When a child fails to score on three consecutive words proceed to the next section.

1	APPLE	fruit; computer
2	LETTER	symbol; epistle; written communication
3	QUIETLY	with little or no motion or noise; without disturbance
4	GENTLY	with mildness and sensitivity
5	RAPIDLY	very quickly

6	AGGRESSIVELY	unpleasantly; crossly; in a quarrelsome manner
7	GRADUALLY	proceeding by steps or degrees; progressively
8	VENUS	planet; goddess of love; a beautiful woman
9	AMBITIOUS	ardently desiring power, rank, office; aspiring; showy; pretentious
10	GRAVITY	force of attraction, especially of objects to earth; tendency of mass of matter towards centre of attraction; seriousness; sobriety of conduct
11	INTERMEDIATE	between two extremes; in central position; intervening; exam preceding finals
12	SUMMARISE	present briefly and concisely
13	STAMPEDE	sudden, frightened rush especially cattle/crowd; to put into a state of panic (Answer must include fear/panic/mad. If child says, 'Many animals rushing', ask 'Why?')
14	SINISTER	evil-looking; threatening; unlucky; on the left hand
15	PRECISE	exact; unequivocal; formal; punctilious
16	CONCISE	brief; shortened; condensed; comprehensive
17	IMPENDING	imminent; threatening; hanging over
18	TRANSITORY	continuing for a brief while only
19	VACILLATE	move to and fro; waver; fluctuate in opinion
20	PARSIMONY	excessive thrift; undue economy; stinginess

Section C: Absurdities

Instructions   Say, 'I am going to read you some sentences. If there is anything wrong or funny about them please tell me what it is.'

Read each statement twice if necessary.
When the child fails to score on two consecutive statements proceed to the next section.

1 Mother asked her child to take the trifle out of the fridge so it would not get too hot.

2 The telephone exchange operator told me that my line from the exchange was not working so he would be unable to talk to me.
(Child must indicate either that the line must be working or that the conversation could not take place.)

3 The man told the child to turn off the stop watch in order not to waste time.
(Child must explain that there is no connection between the stop watch and wasting time.)

4 To the question 'Which comes first, the chicken or the egg?' The child may reply with great certainty that it could only have been the egg as chicks hatch from eggs and grow to be chickens later.
(The child should explain that either answer could be correct, since the chicken produces the egg; in other words, it is impossible to say.)

5 In order to remedy the very high birth rate in a country, they have passed a law that only those over the age of sixty are permitted to have children.
(Child must explain that women over sixty can't have children and that the long-term effect would be to reduce the population dramatically.)

Section D: Rhymes

Instructions Say, 'I am going to read you a list of words fairly quickly and you have to try and give me the name of an animal that rhymes with the word I give you. For example, if I say 'fog' you could reply 'dog'. Don't worry if you can't think of one. Do you understand?' (Read again if necessary.)
Read the words to the child at fifteen-second intervals. As soon as he responds go on to the next word immediately.

If the child gives you a correct answer to an earlier word before you have finished the whole list, score a point.

If the child fails to think of a rhyme for four consecutive words, proceed to the next section.

The answers given below are only examples. Other animal rhymes are acceptable.

1	HABIT: rabbit	6	ALLOW: cow
2	COURSE: horse	7	REVEAL: seal
3	BIG: pig	8	DIPLOMAT: cat/rat/bat
4	STAFF: calf/giraffe	9	ROPE: antelope
5	TONY: pony	10	DECEIVER: beaver

Section E: Picture oddities

Instructions Say, 'I am going to show you a picture with silly mistakes in it. See how many you can find in one minute, starting now.' Time.

If the child gives value errors, e.g. pram is unattended, say, 'No, not that sort of mistake – just faults in the actual picture.'

Section F: Circles

Instructions Say, 'This time I am going to show you a large patterned circle with the centre missing and you have to choose the correct centre.'

Point to the first large circle and the six small centres as you give the instructions.

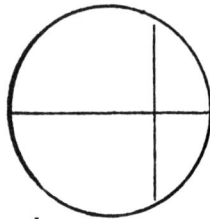

2.

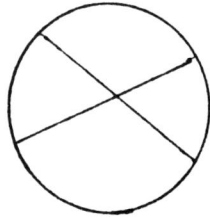

4.

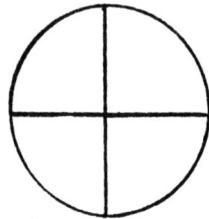

6.

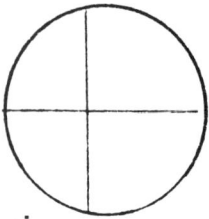

1.

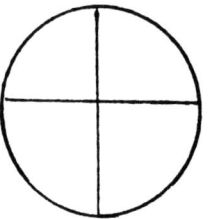

3.

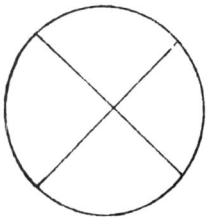

5.

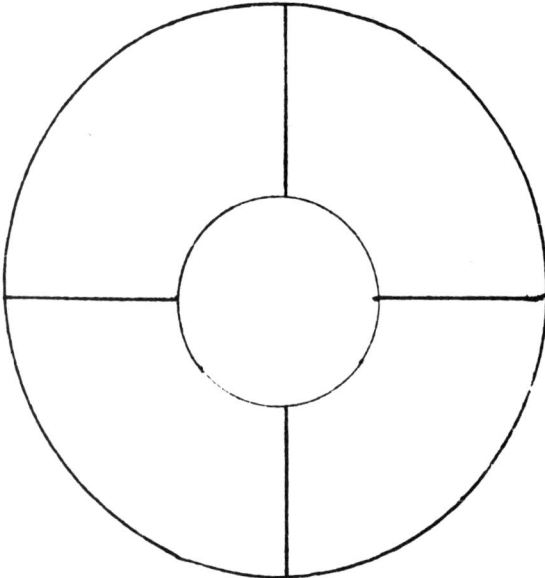

1

2

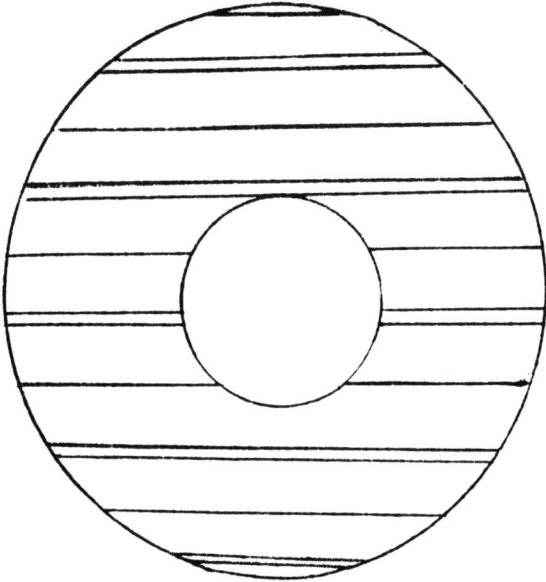

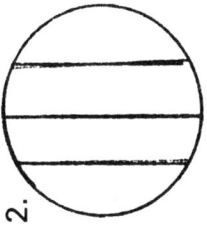

1.

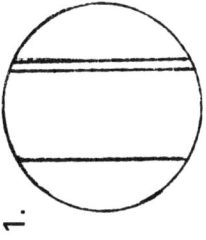

3.

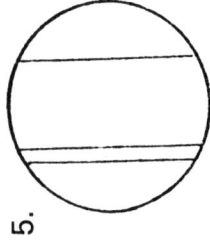

5.

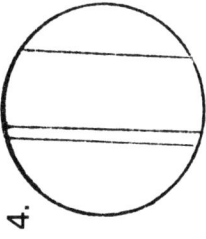

2.

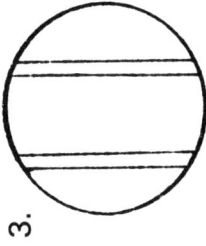

4.

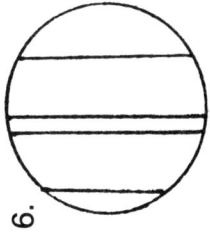

6.

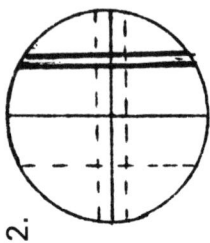

2.

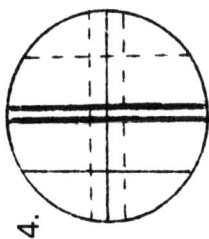

4.

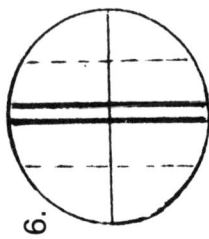

6.

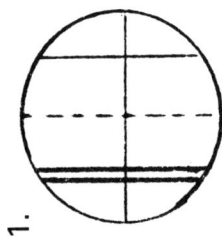

1.

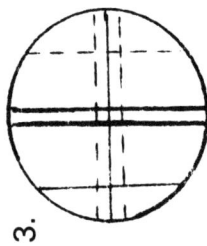

3.

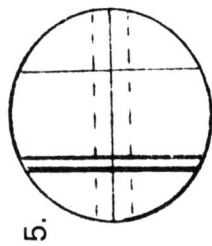

5.

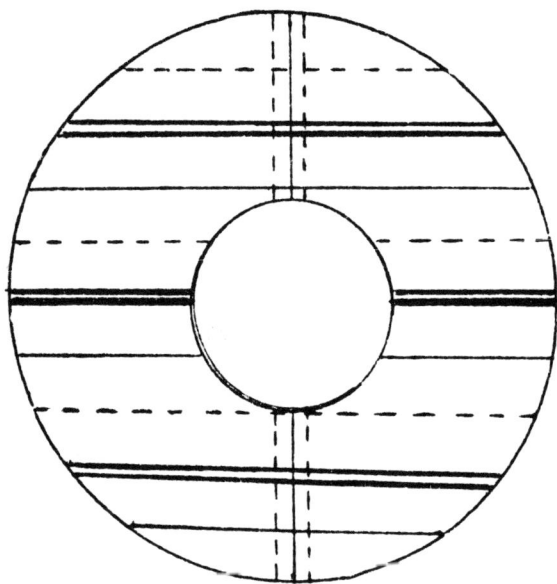

3

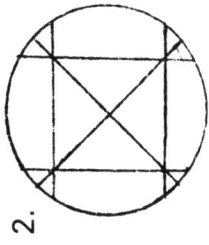

2.

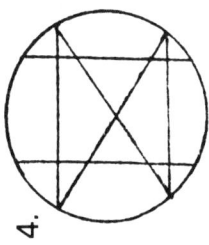

4.

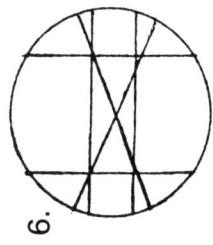

6.

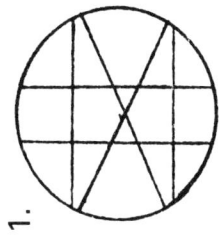

1.

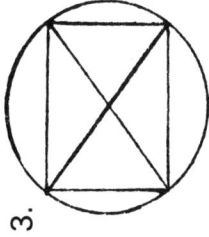

3.

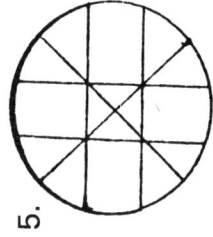

5.

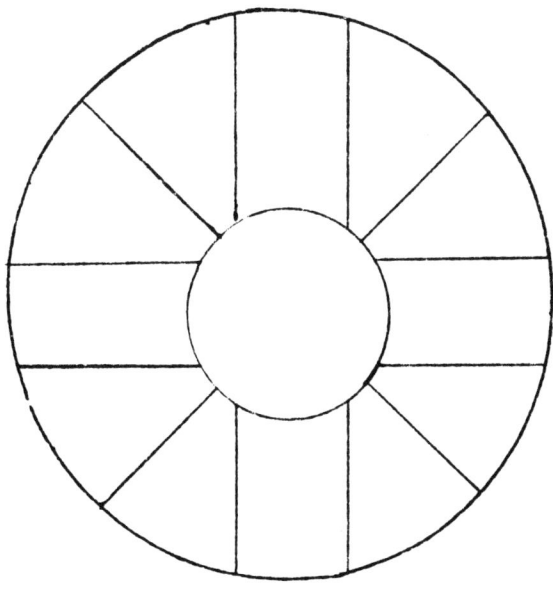

4

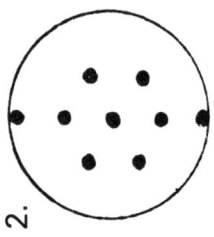

2.

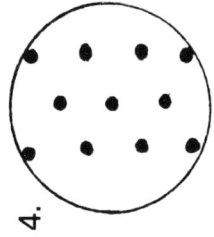

4.

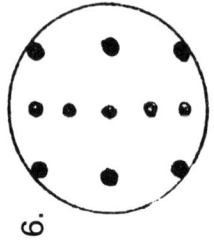

6.

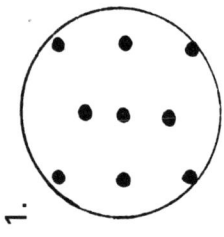

1.

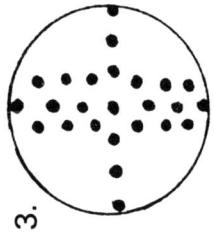

3.

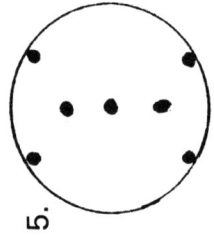

5.

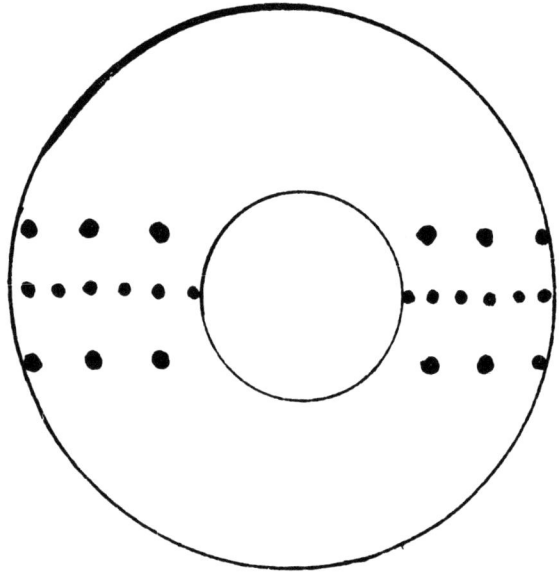

5

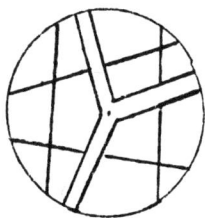
2.

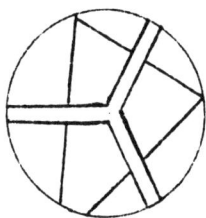
4.

6.

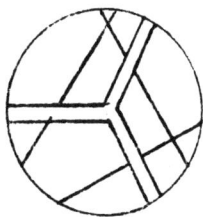
1.

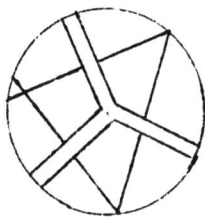
3.

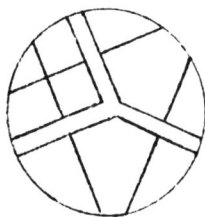
5.

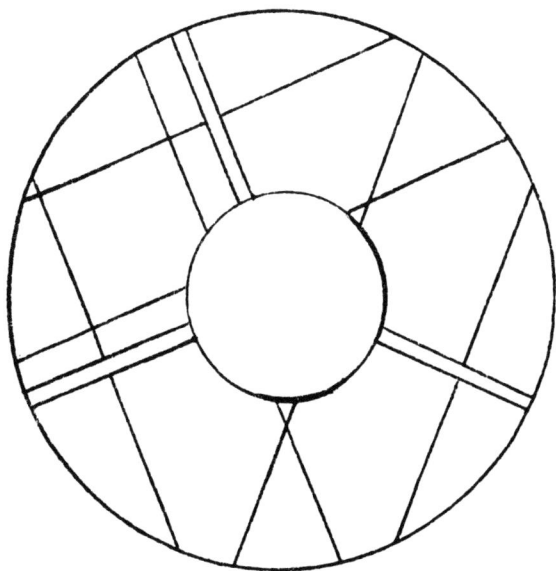
6

2.

4.

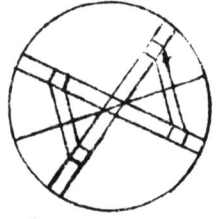

6.

1.

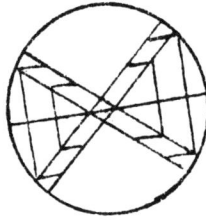

3.

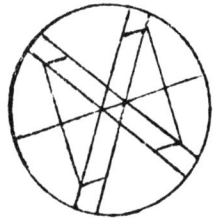

5.

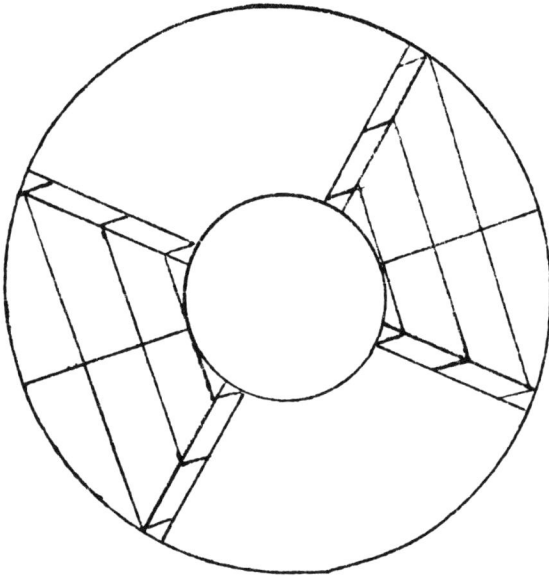

7

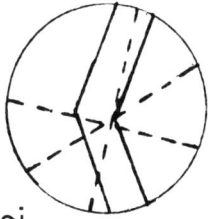

1.

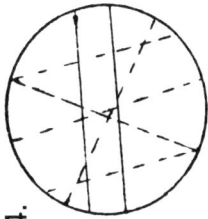

2.

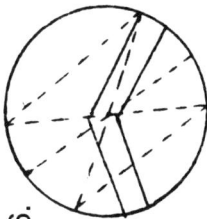

3.

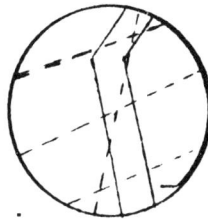

4.

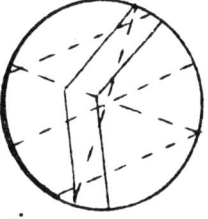

5.

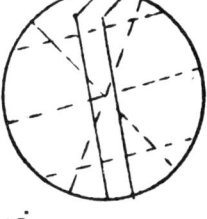

6.

8

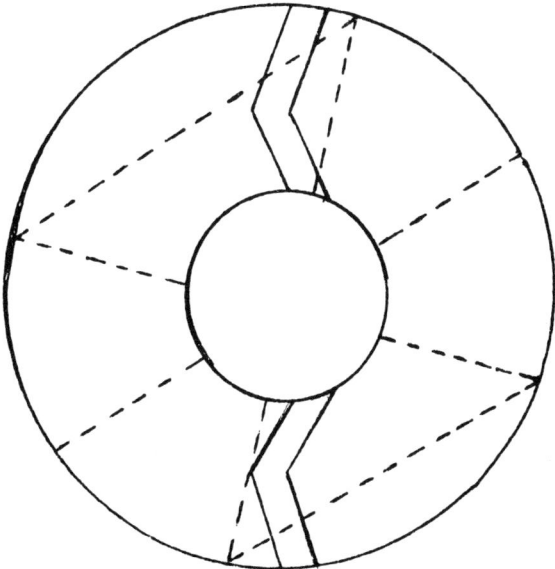

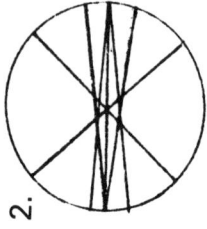

2.

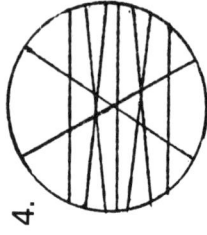

4.

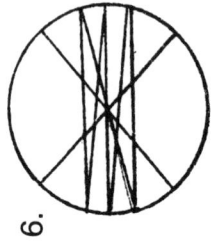

6.

1.

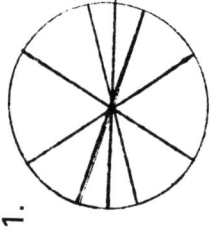

3.

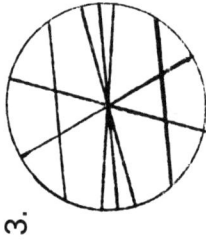

5.

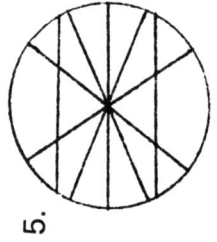

9

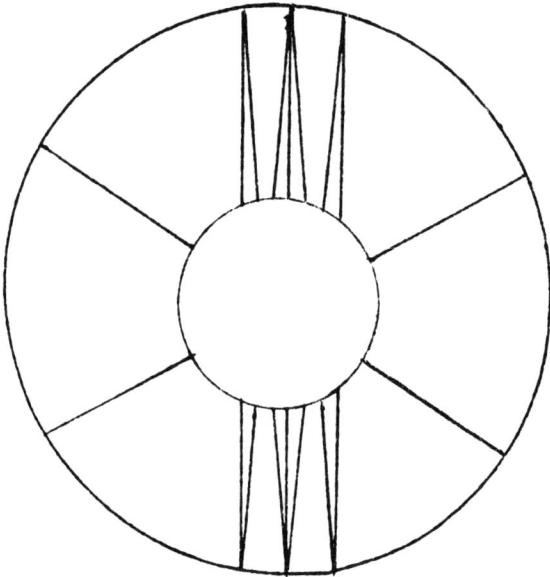

4   The Pre-School Years

The early learning that takes place in the pre-school years is of very great importance. At no other time in their lives is there such a rapid rate of development in human beings, both physically and mentally.

The newborn baby grows rapidly during the first few months, learning to sit up, then perhaps to crawl around and to bounce in a baby-bouncer. During the time when babies are still in their prams there is also a marked growth in their mental abilities. Very tiny babies soon learn to recognise their mother and to know the routine of feeding, washing and being settled down to sleep. A baby's mental awareness grows rapidly during the first months of life, and by the end of the first year most can say a few words.

The speed with which a child develops depends partly on his genetic endowment and partly on the stimulation received from the people and the things in his surroundings. Genetic endowment sets the pattern and the limits within which development will take place: for instance, it is entirely responsible for a child's general shape, his blood group and the colour of his eyes. Heredity also sets limits to the extent to which a child can develop. In some respects, such as how tall a child will be when he is an adult, the environment plays a very important part in addition to the genes which he has inherited. An adult's height will depend partly upon how well he was nurtured in childhood, that is how well he was fed, the suitability of his physical surroundings at home and the extent to which he had the opportunity and encouragement to take plenty of healthy exercise. To give an example from young people's physical growth. In the 1950s and subsequently, infant care in Britain made great advances. A large expansion in pre- and post-natal clinics allowed the health and diet of expectant mothers and infants to be carefully monitored.

Vitamin tablets and concentrated orange juice were distributed widely, and once the mother and her baby had returned home from the maternity unit, calls from the health visitor provided extra support and advice which helped to ensure the satisfactory progress of both. Those babies of the 1950s are now young adults, and it has been found that, on average, they are taller and healthier than their parents were at the same age. The difference between the generations is shown clearly by the shoe sizes in popular demand. Today many girls in their twenties take a size six. Formerly this was comparatively rare, and in the 1920s most girls took sizes four and five. It is probable that there will be further advances in the future and that the average height of the population will rise still further, with their feet becoming correspondingly larger. Yet there is obviously a limit to which height can be increased, (perhaps to seven or eight feet?) set by genetic endowment.

To take another example, how well will a particular child be able to swim in adulthood? Obviously, the genes which she has inherited will affect her physical and mental potential for becoming an outstanding swimmer, but the realisation of the potential will depend upon the environment in which she grows up. At least three sets of environmental influences will play their part. First, the adequacy of the physical surroundings she experiences for the development of her physique; second, the opportunities she has to learn and practise swimming (how far she lives from the swimming-baths, for instance, and the standard of instruction given there); third, the psychological factors, such as the extent to which she is encouraged to swim by her parents or by her school, and the degree to which she has been encouraged by early successes to strive for greater achievements.

These three aspects of a child's environment, the adequacy of the provision for his physical growth, the opportunities for learning available in his neighbourhood, and the psychological atmosphere and encouragement provided by his family and his home, are all-important for a child's eventual fulfilment of his intellectual potential, perhaps more so than they are for the realisation of a child's latent ability to become an exceptional swimmer. Certainly it is more difficult to recognise the effects of the environment on a child's intellectual development and scholastic progress than it is to see the effect upon an individual's achievement in some form of sport.

A young child's progress is affected from birth onwards (and even at the pre-natal stage) by the environment in which he is born. Being given the opportunity and encouragement to use his limbs and, as he becomes older to practise sitting up, crawling, bouncing and walking are all of great importance in a baby's development. Although there is probably an inherent disposition for a child to walk upright, the baby still has to learn this skill, which he masters by trying out and practising the use of arms and legs. The interaction between genetic endowment, nurture, the feeding and care of the child and his own efforts to become mobile, brings about the child's development. Even a very young baby is aware of the happenings around him. He watches a person moving about a room, and research has shown that by about three months he can recognise his mother's face and distinguish it from others.

It is easy to see that the three elements operating in a child's physical development – heredity, nurture and practice – are also active with regard to the growth of mental abilities. However, it is extremely difficult to prove that this is so, and heated arguments continue between psychologists on this topic – the geneticists on the one hand stressing the importance of heredity, and the environmentalists on the other emphasising the major effects of physical, psychological and social factors on mental development. But when the two arguments are examined, it is found that, in nearly all cases, the debate is not about whether it is *either* heredity *or* environment that governs a child's mental development, but only about the proportions in which they each do so. It is rare to find a psychologist who makes a strong case for heredity as the dominant influence who would deny that there are also environmental factors, and similarly, those psychologists who see environment as the major influence nearly always accept that genetic endowment has some part to play in children's development. This highly academic debate, often conducted in technical terms with arguments supported by mathematical formulae, has, nonetheless, an important relevance for parents. Over-simplified and sometimes erroneous versions of the theories put forward by others of the theories debated by the two groups of psychologists can have undesirable effects on everyday practice in educating children.

During the last twenty to thirty years the views of the environmentalists have had a dominating influence on the opinions of those in professions concerned with child development, including teachers in schools. This is partly because those concerned with children's welfare realise that they cannot alter their genetic composition but that they can improve aspects of their environment. This has led to emphasis on deficiencies in children's family backgrounds as the major cause of differences in IQ.

This popularly held view can equally be ascribed to the dominant social attitudes reflected by both public opinion and governments during recent years. One should not discount, either, the effects of the enormous expansion of the welfare and educational services which has taken place during the post-Second World War period. As a result, some (perhaps many) teachers and social workers believe that the children who are intellectually advanced are so because they have the advantage of belonging to middle-class families, whereas other children are backward because they belong to socially deprived families. Of course, sweeping assumptions of this sort completely ignore the fact that not all middle-class children are bright, and that gifted children are to be found in the families of unskilled manual workers, in fairground families, and so on.

Heredity and environment

It is important for mothers to recognise that both heredity and environment contribute to their babies' development. Although these two elements are interwoven in such a way that they cannot be completely separated, appreciation of the ways in which each contributes to a baby's development can help a mother play a more actively constructive part. The contributions made by these two factors in human growth will, for the sake of clarity, be considered separately.

There are two main ways in which a baby's genes affect his development.

First, there is a very large number of genes that determine that a child shall have those characteristics common to all mankind – the basic physical framework and the power to think. As a consequence of this genetic pattern, a human being passes through a number of inevitable stages: infancy, childhood, adolescence, maturity and old age.

During infancy the precise order of developmental changes can vary from baby to baby. One may produce one or two teeth earlier than most but be rather slower in sitting up and crawling, while another may be advanced in his ability to move about. Some babies are toilet-trained earlier than others, others start to feed themselves sooner or talk before others, but by the time they are three years old all normal children will have passed through these stages – although some, particularly boys, may still have toilet 'accidents'.

There is a tendency, too, for particular aspects of a baby's development to happen in fits and starts. For instance, when he is teething, progress in other ways may slow down or even seem to stop altogether. It is important for mothers to know that variations of this sort are quite natural, and if their babies are earlier doing one or more of these things it does not mean that they will necessarily develop into very bright children, although there is a likelihood that at least a few of them will do so. Equally, if a baby seems to be developing more slowly than those of friends and neighbours – seems to be behind in walking and talking, for instance – it does not necessarily mean that he will not grow into a normal toddler.

Although there are no clear-cut indications that a baby is likely to become a gifted child, there is an air of alertness about some babies which can be indicative. Some infants seem to take in everything that is going on around them while still in their prams. Vague and imprecise though it is, this apparent greater awareness is probably the only indicator that a baby may grow into a gifted child. The story that follows will be discounted, and rightly so, by psychologists and others professionally concerned with child development, yet it is nonetheless striking. Six hours after a baby girl's birth, the nurse proudly showed

her to her mother for the first time and said, 'Doesn't she
look intelligent?' She did not say, as might have been
expected, 'Isn't she sweet?' The baby grew into a gifted
child and later a gifted woman who became secretary of
one of the branches of Mensa, a club for people with
exceptionally high IQs.

The features which make a child a human being are, or
course, all inherited from his parents. These characteristics have an essential composition which makes the
human child uniquely different from any other mammal.
At the same time these characteristics are subject to
variation.

The particular variation of any given attribute that a
child inherits is also transmitted by the parents. Since an
infant receives half of his genes (many of which are
dormant in his parents) from his mother and half from his
father, it is a matter of chance which particular variation
of a feature possessed by the mother or father will be
inherited. (Incidentally, this process does explain why
there are easily recognisable physical resemblances between parents and child.) If both mother and father have
brown eyes there is a strong likelihood, but not certainty,
that their offspring will have eyes of the same colour. It
may be that one of the grandparents or perhaps an earlier
antecedent had blue eyes, which means that there is a
slight chance that the child of two brown-eyed parents will
have eyes of some other colour (blue, perhaps). It is to be
expected, too, that the child of two dark-haired parents
will also have dark hair. But hair colour, unlike eye
colour, is a characteristic which shows fine gradations,
and the range of shades that may be found among the
population of Britain forms a continuum from the very fair
to black.

The child of two dark-haired parents will probably have
hair which is distinctly dark compared with the average
hair colour to be found among the population, and yet the
child's hair may not be as dark as either parent's. A
further example of this phenomenon, and one which is
more frequently quoted, is that of an individual's mature
height. A man may be shorter or taller than either of his
parents, but, since his mature height may also be affected
by the manner in which he was nurtured during child-

hood, the extent to which his height is the result of inherited characteristics is not so clear-cut. This is illustrated in the example given above regarding the greater average height of today's young adults compared with their parents, which is attributable to the improved standards of child-care which have become general in Britain during the last twenty to thirty years.

It may be seen, then, that parents pass on to their children not only the characteristics inherent in being a human being, but also to some extent the particular kind of physical features that they themselves possess. Look at a family photograph: there is usually some facial resemblance in all the children to both mother and father, yet none of them is an exact replica of either parent or of each other.

Just as physical characteristics are inherited from parents and earlier forebears, so are the basic mental abilities that distinguish, under normal circumstances, a human being from other mammals. Mankind's genetic constitution provides that potentially all human young will have the power of meaningful speech, of imagination, reasoning and other mental abilities which are essential for thought processes to take place.

As with physical features, variation is found within the basic pattern of human mental abilities. And, again as with physical features, it seems reasonable to suggest that there may be a propensity for children to inherit the particular variation in mental characteristics possessed by their parents.

It is at this point that a considerable amount of controversy arises as to the extent to which genetic endowment determines a child's mental abilities. It is easily recognised that for a baby boy to become outstanding at football, three conditions are necessary. First, he must have inherited a suitable physical frame and constitution which will enable him to become a fast runner and an agile mover. Second, he will have to be taught how to play football expertly. Third, he will only become a first-class footballer if he spends a great deal of time playing football. The first of these conditions depends upon his parents; the source of the second will be his cultural, social, economic and family background; the third will depend upon how the boy makes use of his inherited potential and the opportunities provided by his environment. It is reasonable to suggest that the same conditions will hold with regard to the development and application of a child's mental abilities: his potential intellectual capabilities will be determined by his genetic endowment, and the fulfilment of his potential will depend upon his environment and the extent to which he will make use of his mental abilities and opportunities.

Although most people professionally concerned with child development do not deny that these three conditions are operative for both physical and mental growth, there is little agreement on their relative importance. The three strands – heredity, environment and the individual's personality and motivation – are so entangled that they cannot be separated with precision. For instance, two professional tennis players who have a strong, healthy and normal child and who provide him with every opportunity for developing into an expert tennis player cannot be sure that he will follow in their footsteps. The infant as he becomes older may lack the will to practise tennis sufficiently. Nonetheless there is a strong probability that the baby will become a good tennis player and a likelihood that he will at some time play professional tennis. Conversely, the baby brought up in a deprived inner city area who has inherited through, although not directly from, his parents a potential for high intellectual ability, may subsequently become successful, say, in the legal profession, through hard work and a determination to secure for himself a different lifestyle. I know of several such cases, where the children have inherited an ability to undertake difficult intellectual work. They have grown up in a home environment that has not favoured intellectual activity, yet their burning desire to obtain qualifications and acceptance in one of the older professions has led to success. But although some have achieved their goals in spite of poor childhood environment, it may be expected that there were many more potentially very able or gifted children who failed to overcome the handicap of a disadvantaged upbringing. There is no doubt that parents can increase their children's chance of becoming well adjusted and successful young men and women.

The development of intelligence

The growth that takes place both physically and mentally during a child's pre-school years is much more rapid and lasting in its effects than is the development that occurs during any comparable subsequent period. Since infants normally spend these years in the home, the parents, and most frequently the mother, are a major influence not only as regards the ways in which the infant progresses during his first five years, but also in setting the pattern for his future progress. It is easily seen how much an infant benefits from careful attention to his physical needs. It is less obvious that what happens in these early years has as much, and probably more, effect upon a child's mental development as upon his physical well-being.

Research* has shown that there are similarities in the patterns of children's physical and intellectual growth. Both kinds are cumulative, until a platform is reached in maturity, and a decline sets in in old age. As a child grows older he becomes taller, and although the rate of growth varies, at no time before old age, except as the result of an accident or perhaps illness, does he lose height. Similarly, the degree of intelligence possessed by an infant increases with age until a stable level is established when the individual becomes a young adult. The rate at which this growth takes place varies but, in all normal circumstances, once a given level of mental ability has been reached it does not usually decrease in maturity until senility sets in with old age – although there may be some loss during adult life if an individual's mind lacks stimulation.

A child may be expected to gain more than half of what will be his maximum height as an adult by the time he is four years old. Similarly, an infant has developed by that age more than 50 per cent of the intelligence he will possess at the age of seventeen and when he is a young adult. So, as far as height and intelligence are concerned, an individual will have attained before going to school well over half of the totals he will possess in maturity. These percentages are given by B. S. Bloom, an acknowl-

* *Stability and Change in Human Characteristics* by Benjamin S. Bloom, John Wiley & Sons Inc., 1964.

edged authority on the development of human characteristics.

What must interest parents and others concerned with
the upbringing of young children is the extent to which, if
they improve their children's environment, they can help
them not only while they are still small but also for the
future. Research indicates that children's physical and
intellectual development, and their prospects, are improved when, as infants, they experience a very favourable environment (as opposed to deprivation), and that
this holds true particularly in relation to the first three or
four years of life. As we have already seen, children's
height is a good indicator of improved physical development, when two generations from the same ethnic background are compared. As evidence of the beneficial effects
of better diet and conditions, Bloom quotes from a study of
the kibbutz settlements in Israel. There, given a near
optimal diet drawn up by nutritionists, the children have
been found to grow on average to as much as a head taller
than their parents, most of whom grew up in poor conditions in Central and Eastern Europe.

The importance of a child's experiences during the
pre-school years for the development of a well balanced
personality and of his potential abilities is widely recognised. A number of research studies have been undertaken to find out to what extent a child's IQ is affected by
the sort of environment in which he grows up. The results
show that the effects are greatest during the period from
birth to four years, and Bloom suggests that sharply
contrasting environments during this early period can
account for as much as ten IQ points' difference. Only
extreme circumstances are likely to cause as much difference as this in a child's mental abilities: for instance, if
children are reared in a psychologically deprived environment such as an orphanage where although their bodily
needs are satisfactorily met they have a minimum amount
of contact with adults, their average IQ level will probably
be about five points below what it would be if they were
growing up in a normal family. By contrast, in ideal
surroundings where a child enjoys affection, plenty of
opportunity to hear people talk and to learn to say words
and sentences himself, and plenty of educational toys to

play with, he is likely to score an IQ about five points above what is normal for his age group.

Five additional IQ points is a significant amount to have gained by the age of four. But this is only likely to be achieved if an infant enjoys a really stimulating environment. In practice this usually means that someone, usually one or both of the parents or grandparents, must spend a great deal of time talking to and playing with the baby and young child. There is the compensation here that research shows that the extra gain in IQ level is likely to be retained unless the child subsequently suffers severely adverse conditions. So it is fairly safe to predict that the boy or girl will grow up with a greater mental ability than otherwise would have been the case.

A systematic study of what it is in a child's environment that affects IQ has been made by R. M. Wolf.* He sets out three groups of influences. First, the sort of expectations held by parents as to what a child is going to achieve; second, the opportunities enjoyed for learning and using language; and third, the number and variety of experiences he has for general learning. Wolf's views on how a child's situation with regard to learning can assist the development of mental abilities will be looked at again in more detail in the next chapter, which deals with the effects that can result from different sorts of schooling.

Practical ways of developing a baby's IQ potential

Everything is new to the baby at birth. Within a few hours he learns to suck, and then soon gets to know the things in his immediate surroundings. It is not long before a baby can use all five senses – feeling, touch, smell, hearing and seeing – in order to find out about the world.

The very young child is immobile, so all learning must happen in whatever place he has been laid down. He is able to get to know the things in his cot and pram by touching them, and becomes familiar with the sounds and sights that he can hear and see. He comes to recognise, too, his mother when she comes over to the pram or cot, picks

* R. M. Wolf, 1964, 'The identification and measurement of environmental process variables related to intelligence', PhD dissertation in progress, Univ. of Chicago. See also B. S. Bloom, *Stability and Change in Human Characteristics*, 1964.

him up and feeds him. Even in his restricted environment, there is a great deal for the baby to learn about.

All the same, if the baby's immediate surroundings are not varied enough, he may not receive the stimulation required to promote the maximum growth of his mental faculties. However well cared for the child may be as regards feeding and being kept clean if, to give an extreme example, he is only picked up four times a day for the minimum amount of time necessary to carry out these essential functions, and the rest of the time is placed in a pram facing a brick wall until he is put in the cot for the night, his mental development will certainly not be encouraged. Even where there is not such a marked lack of stimulation as here, preoccupation with an infant's physical requirements together with a lack of appreciation of the fact that the mind needs feeding as well as the body, may result in a child's mental abilities not advancing as quickly as they could.

Even before he begins to walk or crawl, a baby learns from doing things – from looking at what can be seen, from pushing and pulling what can be reached, from listening and trying to talk. Parents should be careful to see that their baby has opportunities to learn in all these ways. If he is put out in the garden in his pram, then turn it so that he can see the trees and flowers moving gently in the breeze, and hear the birds sing and the sound of people at work. But most of all the baby needs the mother or father to go over to smile at him, to talk to and play with him. Human love and attention is vital to all children, whether tiny babies or teenagers.

Of course, there are great differences between babies. By the time they are two months old some can begin to play with toys which, if well chosen, can help their mental development. Cuddly soft animals and rattles are usually popular. A baby can squeeze a soft toy, and will smile and gurgle when his mother shakes a brightly coloured rattle just over the pram. Rattles on an elastic strap can be fixed across his pram or cot, and he will be thrilled when, by stretching out, he succeeds in touching it, making it move and eventually making it rattle. Bright mobiles, too, hung above the cot or where he can see them from the pram, hold a baby's attention and help him learn to focus his eyes.

Once he has learnt as much as possible from the first pram string rattle, it can be replaced with another one, more colourful and more exciting. First the mother plays with the baby, showing what can be done with the new toy, and he then tries to do it too until finally he can. The baby has made another important step forward.

Once he begins to move himself about by rolling or crawling along, a whole new world opens up. There are many colourful and exciting toys with which a mother can play with her baby, helping him to learn to roll them about, push, pull, pile them on top of each other and then knock them down again. Sometimes advertised in toy catalogues are a twin rattle made up of two smiling faces revolving in different directions, which helps a baby learn to manipulate, and a seven-piece pull-apart clown stack with a tinkling bell which rings as the clown rocks to and fro. A toy called 'Active Baby' consists of four parts, each a brightly coloured different shape which can be rattled and pressed so that the four pieces fit together. Another exciting toy for a baby of over a year is called 'Lock-a-Block': Six different chunky shapes can be posted through the right holes in a bigger block, and the door of the bigger block locked with a plastic key (available from Offspring, see address at back of book).

The toddler
Once a baby is able to walk, the opportunities for learning about his surroundings increase enormously. He can now move about himself and start to explore the house and garden. It is an exciting time for the young child, but also a dangerous one. Now that he is going from place to place, poking, pulling and pushing, accidents are particularly prone to happen even though precautions such as fitting gates across the bottom of the stairs are taken.

From the age of two years onwards many bright and gifted toddlers can begin to do jigsaw puzzles, of which there is a very large range available. The simplest are inset puzzles which consist of a wooden or plastic tray with cut-out shapes: they usually show pictures of animals, trees, fruit, and so on. These will probably soon be too easy for the very bright child who, when still only two, is quite often ready to go on to the more difficult picture jigsaw puzzles designed for children aged three and four. Two 'train' jigsaws that are available help children learn the letters of the alphabet and the symbols for numbers. One of the jigsaws has letters on the train compartments and the other has the numbers one to ten. Of course, the pieces only fit together in the correct alphabet order and number sequence.

At about the age of three – for some toddlers a little before and for others soon after their third birthdays – most very bright and gifted children are ready to start learning to read. To be able to do this a child must have learnt to distinguish between the different shapes of the letters and words represented on paper. This is one of the reasons why toys with different pieces which have to be fitted together are so useful, as they help children to learn about shapes, an essential prerequisite for learning to read.

There are two main ways by which children read, which for very bright and gifted children are complementary – not causing confusion as may happen with average and less able infants. The first is the 'look and say' method. Very able three-year-olds soon notice the letters and numbers on car number plates and the words printed all around them, and ask what they say. When being driven in a car, or walking about when their mother is doing the shopping, their sharp eyes notice such words as 'Car Park', 'Way Out' and 'Road Works' and they soon learn to read these for themselves. At home, the very bright and the gifted notice the words printed on the labels of various kinds of foods and they quickly learn to read some of these too.

There are also plenty of educational materials which parents can buy to help their child learn to read – for instance, 'picture-word cards'. They consist of two sets of cards, the first of which has pictures of well known animals and of familiar things and the second just their names, such as 'dog', 'tree', 'chair' and so on. A bright child rapidly learns to match each picture to the right word. Mother and child can have great fun playing with these cards, and then the little boy or girl soon learns to read the words in a book. The second and complementary way of learning to read is for the child to become very familiar with the letters of the alphabet, and then to start using them to make words. Here car number plates are very useful, and when out for a walk an exciting game can be to see who can read a car number plate first. Sets of letters made of card or wood, and plastic ones with magnets, can be bought, and there are numerous ways a child can play with them, perhaps picking out the letters to form a word spelt out by his mother or copying the word at the bottom of some of the picture-cards. Soon, with a little help, he will start reading his first book.

Pre-school children can learn to use numbers in much the same way as they can learn to read. Again car number plates are very useful. A bright child will recognise the digits quickly, and if his parents give him suitable educational toys he will be able to make a start with number work. The first essential here is the abacus, a counting frame with five rows of ten brightly coloured beads which can be moved along a thin rod. The beads can be used to teach a child addition, subtraction, multiplication and division. Sets of cards can be bought, too, which make the meaning of numbers clear by, say, printing a bold three, giving the word 'three' in letters, and then a picture of three of the same things, perhaps cars or circles. Once the basic concepts associated with number have been grasped, a 'counting and sums board' gives children an opportunity to experiment with numbers. Sixty small cards are provided on each of which is printed a single digit or one of the four signs for add, subtract, multiply and divide. A child can set himself countless sums on the board and then try to find the answers. Any pre-school child who has become thoroughly familiar with these three educational toys, who enjoys playing and experimenting with numbers and who has grasped the basic concepts of adding, subtracting, multiplying and dividing, will have an excellent foundation on which to base more advanced work in mathematics in the future.

Besides helping their children gain an early start with reading, writing and number work, there are other ways in which parents can help under-fives to increase their mental abilities. The two most important are by extending their powers of imagination and by encouraging them to think logically.

Imagination is the source of richness and colour in an

individual's mental life. It is even more difficult to define or measure than other mental characteristics because of its very nature, yet it is a quality of great importance. Apart from enriching an individual's experience of the world about him, it is essential for gaining a better understanding of himself, of other people and of the events of daily life.

There are at least three ways in which the imagination can be stimulated. The first is by make-believe or 'pretend' games. The children imagine they are in all sorts of different places – some of them are unreal like 'where the rainbow ends', others actual places like 'at Auntie Joan's' – and they pretend that they are different things, animals or people such as 'mothers and fathers'. These games, though possibly 'silly' to adults, have an important part to play in a child's development. A few words from the mother, an old (and preferably large) cardboard box and some old clothes for dressing up can keep several children playing happily for an hour or more pretending they are mother, father and baby with their own house and so on. This, in the language of sociologists, is 'role-playing'. The second way a child's imagination is fed is through stories – 'Once upon a time . . .', and the story follows. There is probably no substitute in terms of the comfort it brings for a child to be able to listen to his mother telling him a story as he settles down to sleep at night. Bright and gifted infants are no different from other children in their need to be told or read a story at bedtime. They do differ, though, from most others in that, being often naturally imaginative, the terrible giants, dragons and so on which are often found in children's stories can be more real to them and so more terrifying. It is probably wise, particularly at night time, to try and avoid frightening stories.

As we have said, the gifted and very bright are different in that they learn to read at a much earlier age than most children. Once they can do so, a new world is opened up and they can read simple stories and books for themselves; reading increases their general knowledge and at the same time encourages the growth of their imaginative powers. Parents may like to buy books for their child – this helps develop the habit of owning books and forms a beginning to the child's own library. In addition, parents will find many delightful books in the junior department of their public library. When choosing books it is an advantage to look for a variety – say, one with very few words and attractive and colourful pictures, another which is simple but humorous, and two more difficult books designed for children one or two years older than your child, one of which is fiction and the other likely to increase his general knowledge.

The third way of increasing children's imaginative power is by encouraging them in creative activities. Most children love to draw and paint and to make things, and the gifted and very bright do too. There are plenty of things in most homes which can be used for this purpose, and materials can be bought from toyshops, craft and hobby shops. The usual difference here between the very able and most children is that, in spite of not having had time to master even to an elementary level the techniques of drawing and painting, the very bright child will show from time to time an exceptional degree of perceptiveness in art work. In craft work the gifted will be interested in making models and other things that are considered normally too difficult for children of their age, and will concentrate on their task for unexpectedly long periods of time.

Another most important way of helping children gain an early start in our technological society is by encouraging them to think logically. Experiments with young children have shown that under the age of about six or seven most cannot see the simple logical relationships that are so obvious to adults, so obvious in fact that it is difficult for adults to appreciate that they can be difficult to recognise. For instance, if a number of small cubes are put close together on a table and then the same cubes are spread out on the table, most pre-school infants and those in their first year at school will think there are more cubes when they are spread about, even though they can see that no extra cubes have been added and none taken away. Another well known experiment is with water in glass beakers. Even though the young child sees that the same amount of water is poured into each of two glasses, if they have a different diameter he will say, when asked, that there is more water in the glass with the narrower diameter than in the one with the wider diameter. This is because the water in the narrower glass can be seen to come higher up.

Parents can buy educational toys which help young children grasp elementary logical concepts regarding area and volume: for example, plastic or wooden blocks of different thicknesses and geometric shapes. There are many sets of coloured cards which encourage a child to recognise logical sequences. Some cards have different numbers of dots on them, and the child learns to put them in the right order, and – which is much more difficult – he learns *why* the order is correct, that is, that one more dot is added in each case. Other cards show a series of pictures which, if put in a logical order, tell a story. For instance, there might be a series of four pictures, one where a man is getting out a ladder, another where he is climbing up it, a third where he is painting a high wall and a fourth where he is coming down the ladder. The cards are muddled up and the child is asked to look at them carefully and to put them in the right order so that they tell a story. Although parents may think this is an easy task, most pre-school children do not find it so, and it is probable that the game will have to be played several times before the child places the cards in the right order with confidence and can explain *why* this particular order is the correct one. Rather more advanced for a child, although again very easy in the eyes of parents, are the 'Thinking Skills' booklets, available from Pullen Publications, Knebworth, Hertfordshire. These are more difficult, and it will be only when a child has mastered the easier exercises in logical thinking and knows *why* a particular answer is the correct one as well as being able to memorise it, that he will be ready to start on them. The easiest ones are the 'A' booklets, of which the one with shapes, in which the child is asked to draw another shape to complete a pattern, is probably the easiest.

Play and work

It is natural for young children to want to learn, and they do so during the course of playing. The last section has considered ways of making children's learning more efficient by guiding their play into particular channels and assisting their mental development with the aid of educational toys. An essential element of all this has been that the various activities are just games and the children are just playing. When they are given educational toys, the learning aspect is incidental.

Playing means doing something because you want to. You do not have to play in some particular way when you have lost interest, or are tired of it. If you have not chosen a particular activity because it interests you, then it is not play but work. This does not mean that a child may not be quite willing and happy to do some work, but there is an element of compulsion in work which is not present in play. When a child plays with educational toys in the way described here, or when a parent using educational toys plays with a child, the result cannot but be beneficial, as the only difference between this and playing with any other toy is that the child is probably learning rather more.

The same activity, say the arranging of four pictures so that they tell a story, can be either play or work for the little boy or girl concerned. Which it is depends upon the child's subjective attitude to the activity. If he wants to do it and is only doing it because he likes doing it, then it is play. If he is engaged in this activity because he has been told to and so feels he has *got* to do it, or if he feels he must do it because he wants to please his mother (though it is very unlikely that pre-school children will have this attitude, as they are usually essentially egocentric), or because he has been promised a sweet or some other treat when he has done it, then it is work.

It is not necessarily wrong for a young child to do a very limited amount of work in this way. What is important is that parents should distinguish between what is play and what is work, since the element of compulsion may be stressful for the child. Children do, of course, vary a great deal, and ten minutes' or so work with the promise of an ice-cream at the end of it – and the promise *must* be kept at all costs – may be quite enjoyed by a child who considers the ice-cream well worth the effort. With another child an undue amount of stress may be caused, with harmful effects or counter-productive results, such as resentment of the particular type of learning involved. Parents, then, who put any sort of pressure on their children to learn must do so with the utmost caution.

Whether or not it is desirable for a parent to teach his child depends upon the attitude of the child to the activity concerned. Some fathers and their small sons can sit on a settee and have enormous fun playing with numbers, adding them up, taking them away, and so on. Here the fathers are undoubtedly teaching the children, and the children are learning, but this is just play and there is no stress. Similarly, a mother may play with her small daughter by reading a story-book with her, or the child may try to make words with cardboard letters while the mother suggests words for her to spell and tells her when she is right. Again the parent is obviously teaching the child, but there is no stress in the situation providing the activity stops as soon as the child wants it to.

As we have seen, almost all bright and gifted pre-school children are keen to learn, and so, for that matter, are most other infants. But it is the bright and gifted who are so incessant with their questions – the word 'Why?' seems to be constantly on their lips. There is no doubt that finding simple yet accurate answers to all these questions and expressing them in language which their small children will understand can be very exhausting for parents. There is no doubt, too, that parents are called upon to show a great deal of patience. Yet children learn this way probably more than by any other, so it is most important that parents do their best to satisfy their little ones' curiosity.

It cannot be wrong for parents to help their children find out about the world in which they find themselves when the initiative comes from the infants, even when there is an overlap with what the infant teachers will expect to teach them when they start school. What is certainly wrong is to put a brake on children's learning, and if parents hold back from telling them what they want to know, this is precisely what they are doing. Very bright and gifted infants are sufficiently forward when they are three or four and still at the pre-school stage for the sort of learning which most of the other infants of the same age are only ready for at the age of five when they start school.

Reading
Most of the problems connected with children's pre-school learning are concerned with learning to read. When discussing these matters with me, parents have shown a sense of guilt if their child could read before starting school. For instance, it is often the case that they are reluctant to admit that their child learned to read at home and, when they do admit it, they may add hastily, 'But we didn't teach him. He taught himself.' In one case a mother said, 'She wanted to learn to read but I stopped her', and looked up expecting approval, not knowing that what she had done was damaging to her child's mental development.

The reason why many parents feel guilty at helping their children learn to read is because it is sometimes with disbelief and even displeasure that infant teachers greet the information that a child who is just starting school can already read.

There are at least three reasons for this. First, in many instances the teacher's own training has not prepared her to appreciate how great can be the differences between children's mental abilities, even when they are only five years old. Second, great emphasis is given in teacher-training courses on how to teach a child to read. Attention is directed to the advantages of the various techniques, which are analysed in detail. Of course, there are difficulties in teaching many children to read. This is true of most, if not all, of those of average ability and of the less able – the two groups of children who form the greater part of the age group. Hence, many infant teachers do not *expect* infants to be able to learn to read easily. When pre-school children are found to have already acquired this important skill, the tendency is to assume that they have been forced to learn by selfish parents who wish to 'keep up with the Joneses' and be able to say that their child is cleverer than those of their neighbours. This, of course, is a completely wrong assumption where the parents of genuinely very bright or gifted children are concerned. The third reason for disapproval is probably the least excusable.

Most schools have a reading scheme – a sequence of books which new entrants are expected to work through. By the time the children have done so it is anticipated that they will have become fluent readers, and extra help will be given to those who have not achieved this target by the time they are due to transfer to the junior school. If a teacher is inexperienced or just inflexible, those infants who enter school already able to read present a problem: what is she to do with them? Such teachers find the classroom situation much easier when all the children start school knowing nothing. Of course, infant teachers with this outlook also tend to assume that all children learn at the same *rate* when they are in school. This in its turn leads to bright children having to mark time while the rest of the class catches up – a matter which will be discussed in the next chapter.

The only valid reason for not teaching a child to read before starting school is because the child himself does not yet want to learn. The convenience of a teacher, or of a school, is not a valid reason. The function of schools is to aid the educational development of all their children. It is detrimental to very bright and gifted children to be held back, and their parents must insist that appropriate provision is also made for them. The mothers and fathers of mentally handicapped infants have demanded that the special needs of their children are met. Having achieved recognition of the rightness of their demands, the extra teaching and facilities followed. It is now up to the parents of the exceptionally able to fight for recognition of their children's needs. And like the parents of the children at the other end of the scale, they must be prepared to face opposition and derision from teachers and neighbours, for it is the welfare of their children that is at stake.

Family relationships and neighbours

Difficulties may arise within families when one of the children is intellectually gifted or exceptionally talented in some other way, and other brothers or sisters are of normal ability. If there are, say, three children whose ages are spaced at two-yearly intervals and the middle child is gifted, then it is likely that the mental age of the second child is higher than that of the eldest of the three. Here is an illustration to show how this situation may arise.

There are, say, three brothers aged 6 years 8 months, 8 years 4 months and 10 years 5 months whose IQs are 105, 135 and 104 respectively. Their mental ages may be calculated from the simple equation *IQ* × *chronological age*/100 = mental age.* The results give the mental ages of the three boys as 7 years 0 months, 11 years 3 months and 10 years 10 months.

This situation can cause serious difficulties within the family. The mental development of the middle brother is more advanced than that of his elder brother but, as he was born two years after his elder brother, he is not treated as an equal with the older boy either by the parents or the elder child. To know he can do most things (excluding probably physical activities) as well as his brother, but for the most part not be allowed to because he is younger, is extremely frustrating for the gifted boy. Such a situation is likely to lead to arguments between the two boys and a feeling of being unfairly treated by the middle boy which, in extreme cases, can lead to the development of 'a chip on the shoulder' which may persist through later life. As for the youngest boy, he is almost in the position of an only child, for he is mentally about four years behind his two brothers.

What can parents do about a situation of this sort? First, a big step towards finding a solution has been taken once a mother and father recognise and accept that one – sometimes more than one – of their children is mentally very advanced for his age and is far cleverer than their other children and most others. That this is so should be treated as a fact of life. Nor should an attempt be made to keep the boy's exceptional level of ability hidden from him. He will in any case be aware that he can learn things much more quickly than his contemporaries and that he can solve problems easily which others find difficult, and so on. Not to admit to the boy that he is much cleverer than other children can only lead to confusion in his mind and may sow the seeds of distrust of his parents.

---

* See page 98 for fuller details regarding the relationship between chronological age, mental age and IQ.

As far as they are able, parents should tell their gifted child the truth about his ability – neither exaggerating nor understating it. It should be explained to a child who has been confirmed as gifted by an educational psychologist or by some other objective means that – while most children are about average – just as it is natural that some are much taller and others much shorter, so some are intellectually gifted and others educationally subnormal. Some people are afraid to tell their child that he is gifted in case it makes him conceited. It is unlikely that this would happen in the case of a *genuinely* gifted child. It is more often a question of the wishful thinking of parents that their child is gifted, when in fact, although above average, the boy or girl is not exceptionally able in any way.

Being gifted brings with it difficulties as well as advantages, which a child who knows his or her true level of ability will be in a better position to deal with. He or she should be prepared for a certain amount of hostility from other children, who are naturally antagonistic to someone who seems to know more and can apparently do most things better than they can. There will be adults, too, relatives and friends of the family, who compare the gifted child with their own or other children they know and conclude that he or she is 'odd' or 'pretentious'.

Wise parents will explain to their child the reasons for concealing the high level of intellectual ability he possesses in certain circumstances. But they will also explain the dangers of always concealing it, or of allowing it to become a habit. For example, a gifted girl (IQ 145) was sent by her parents to a local Sunday School where she joined the infants' class. She did not misbehave, but at the end of the year she was not moved up to the next class with the other girls. When her mother asked her why this was so, she replied, 'Because my work was not good enough.' At that time the child attended an independent school where she was in a class of children a year older, among whom she was in the top third for attainment in classwork. What had happened in the Sunday School was that she had concealed her ability so cleverly that the teacher (who was a trained primary school teacher) thought her to be on the

slow side. In fact, some gifted children counteract the
boredom they are experiencing by amusing themselves
with seeing how well they can convince a teacher (and
sometimes other adults) that they are stupid. The danger
is that the gifted become such experts at concealing their
ability when in ordinary schools that the teachers fail to
recognise them. Then when the appropriate time comes
they are not entered for examinations and so on. One must
also bear in mind that even highly gifted children will
not always find their work easy, and they will have to
use their abilities to the full. One of the advantages of
being gifted which might be mentioned to the child
is that, because he is able to learn more quickly, he
need spend less time on the basic subjects and so
will have more for finding out about other interesting
things.

A second way in which parents can avoid tensions
within the family when one child is gifted and the others
are normal or bright-average, is to take account of the
differences between their offspring in the way they treat
them. This does not mean that the gifted, or for that
matter, that the normal or less able children, should be
favoured. What it does mean is that when there are
marked differences between children, the same measures
are unlikely to be equally appropriate for all of them. Most
parents want to be fair to each of their children and
interpret this as 'treating them all the same'. But there is
no fairness in treating those who are very different from
one another as if they were the same. This point will be
considered more fully in the next chapter, where choice of
schools is discussed.

Most mothers will have friendly contact with other
mothers living in the same road or district. As they are
likely to have many common interests, quite often
friendships which have started in the ante- or post-natal
clinic continue through the years that follow. But whether
they are well established contacts of this sort or slight
acquaintances from a casual meeting, the topic of conversation between mothers of young children is likely to
be about the latest development to occur with their child.
The parent whose child is showing signs of giftedness
needs to be cautious on these occasions, particularly if her

child is well in advance of the others. If a three-year-old is starting to read or a four-year-old is becoming interested in numbers, it is altogether preferable to talk about the other things he or she does which are more usual for pre-school children.

Local services
From birth to a child's fifth birthday, his welfare is the responsibility of the Department of Health and Social Security. Until a baby is six weeks old regular visits are made by a health visitor to ensure that mother and baby are making good progress. After that, visits are made from time to time and as thought necessary. Developmental tests are given to the child to check that there is no malfunctioning and that he is not retarded. Providing his responses come up to the minimum required level, the authority is satisfied. Officially no account is taken when a baby's or toddler's development is found to be exceptionally advanced, but occasionally a health visitor will tell the mother that this is the case and make a few positive suggestions. It is, of course, open to the parent to contact the local office of the DHSS and ask for the health visitor to call, whereupon she can ask for advice as to how to meet the needs of her child who is presenting problems as he appears to be very forward for his age.

Playgroups and nursery classes
Information regarding playgroups may be obtained from the local DHSS office and about nursery schools for children who are a little older, from the LEA office.

There is a great deal of variation as to the facilities available in different localities. The DHSS and the local authority are not legally obliged to set up playgroups or nursery schools for the under-fives. However, the local council has the right to do so if it wants to, and the DHSS may give a grant towards the running costs. Some playgroups are initiated by churches, by other voluntary bodies or simply by groups of mothers who have felt the need for some such facility; other groups are set up by private individuals. Once established these groups, too, are often eligible for financial assistance from public funds.

In recent years it has increasingly become recognised that young children learn a great deal from the activities they enjoy in a well run playgroup, and that they benefit from mixing with each other. There is no doubt that, in general, very bright and potentially gifted children gain from the stimulation they receive in such groups, even more than most of the other children.

There are four different types of group which cater for the under-fives: mother and toddler groups, those organised by childminders in private houses, playgroups held in church halls and similar locations, and nursery school classes. There is a clear distinction between playgroups and nursery classes in that the former are the responsibility of the DHSS and the latter of the Education Authorities. In other respects there is a considerable amount of overlap between these four categories, particularly with regard to the things the children do. There is a great deal of variation between one group and another within each of the categories. In one playgroup the infants may enjoy a variety of stimulating activities and ample learning opportunities, while another lacks originality and choice in the ways the children spend their time.

There are also distinct differences between the four types of group. Those for mothers and toddlers are usually supported most by mothers with babies under the age of two, although a considerable number of children above this age attend as well. The main distinction between the mother and toddler and the other groups is that the mothers *stay* with their children. Playgroups organised by childminders in private houses are allowed to accept children from their second birthday, but the regulations do not allow the larger playgroups which are held in halls to take children under the age of two and a half. The mother and toddler groups are usually held only once or twice a week. The playgroups may be held every weekday but probably cater for different sets of children. The same children usually attend only two or three mornings or afternoons a week. Quite often playgroups do not provide for children over the age of four. On the other hand, nursery classes do not take children until they are three and often not until they are four. In practice, a bright or gifted child will probably learn very little in some nursery classes. Although those in charge may claim that they meet the children's individual needs, the nursery-teachers are often afraid they may 'poach' on the work infant teachers do if they allow a child to do more than recognise letters and be able to write his name. How much work the children do depends almost entirely on the nursery teacher in charge. In some Local Authority nursery classes outside London, there is a reading scheme in operation for those who are ready, and the children also write and do number work. Private nursery classes usually have the children only in the mornings for five days a week in term time. Nursery school classes which are attached to primary schools often keep the children all day and parents are not asked for any payment. In nearly all other cases the parents have to pay for their children to attend these pre-school groups. The charge is usually between 50p and £1 per session.

The sort of benefits a potentially gifted infant may be expected to gain from a well run playgroup may be seen from the following example. A playgroup supervisor started the group and continues to run it in her own home. She takes infants from the age of two and keeps them till they are three, when they are ready to move on to the nearby nursery school. At any one time there are ten or twelve little ones attending for a three-hour morning session twice a week. The supervisor, now married with a toddler of her own, is a trained nursery nurse and formerly worked for two years in a large inner-city nursery. Her background and experience, together with her pleasant personality, combine to make this playgroup probably one of the best organised, happiest and most stimulating of its kind. Although there is a maximum of twelve infants attending at any one time, there are three adults to play with them and see to their needs, one in each of three rooms. The first of these is called the 'dry room', where the two-year-olds play with stickle-bricks and Lego, push pegs into pegboards, learn to use scissors, cut out coloured pictures, thread and sew and make collages. The next room is the 'wet room': here the children play with sand and water trays, and do finger- and bubble-painting as well as painting using an easel. The third room is known as the 'quiet room', and this is where the children can sit down quietly and look through picture books and do simple jigsaw and other puzzles. At different times during the morning the whole group of twelve two-year-olds and three adults come together to listen to a story, to have a sing-song and for a ten-minute session of music and movement. Halfway through the morning there is a drink of orange for all the children. These very varied activities stimulate the children's interest and learning. In addition, the two-year-olds learn to mix with other small children, become accustomed to being with other adults besides their mothers, and begin to get used to having to share things with others like themselves.

In most towns and villages there is usually a playgroup to be found – and if there is not, it is open to any mother to start one. Apart from benefiting the children, it is also pleasant and helpful to parents to meet others with young children living in the same vicinity. If you do not already know of a playgroup in your area you may see one advertised at the doctor's surgery or can ask the receptionist where there is one. Another place at which to inquire is at your local church or post office. Alternatively, since all playgroups must be registered with the Department of Health and Social Security, you can ring up or call in at your local DHSS office for their names, addresses and telephone numbers.

Organisations and suppliers of educational toys
The Pre-School Playgroups Association claims more than twelve thousand members throughout Britain (the address of its headquarters is given at the back of this book). Membership is open to any group or individual interested in working with, or rearing, young children. The association arranges meetings and conferences where, after the serious business has been dealt with, members have an opportunity to meet each other and make new friends. The organisation publishes two magazines. The first, *Contact*, is produced ten times a year and has news about playgroup activities, well informed articles on child development and useful advertisements. The second,

Under 5, is quarterly and costs only 15p. This is a lively magazine that helps parents share their views and offers them ideas that they can use in their own homes.

Early Learning Centres have now been set up in eighteen towns, including Oxford, Bristol, Reading and Southampton, and more will be opening soon. These are not just shops, as each centre has a play area where children can try out many of the things on sale, and trained staff are available to give advice should parents require it. In the holidays, too, there are various play activities at these centres, including music-making and story-telling sessions. Parents who join an Early Learning Centre receive an information sheet called *Early Learning News*, which contains descriptions of educational toys which the centre has selected for each of four age groups – babies, toddlers, pre-school and school-age infants. The prices of the various toys are given in a catalogue and they may be ordered by post, using the order form which the firm provides. The headquarters address of this firm is: Early Learning Centre, 1 Hawksworth, Swindon SN2 1TT.

Another organisation, Purnell Publishers Limited, have produced the 'Three Four Five Nursery Course' and the 'Three Four Five Ready to Read Course' which, they say, 'has been specially designed to help you develop in your child the basic skills leading to reading, writing and counting through natural play activities.' If you decide to enrol your child and pay the required fee, you will be sent twelve monthly packs. There are three main parts to the course – 'Developing Speech', 'Pre-Reading Activities' and 'Number Sense'. If your child is advanced for his age, the best time to start with the course would probably be when he is two and a half to three years old. Explanatory notes on how to use the packs are included.

Another scheme which aims to help parents choose and buy educational toys is 'Offspring – Learning Through Play'. A fully illustrated catalogue, giving the ages for which each of the educational toys is suitable, will be sent upon request. Some of the items such as rattles are designed for babies from birth up to a year old, and there are quite a number of toys for those aged three to eighteen months. There are also many games, puzzles and construction sets for toddlers and older pre-school children. The names, addresses and telephone numbers of these firms will be found at the back of this book.

5   Which School?

All children in the United Kingdom must have a regular
and formal education from the age of five to sixteen years,
and their parents are under a legal obligation to ensure
that they do so. Just as most parents have no choice as to
the age at which their children will start school, in practice they have very little real choice as to which one they
will attend. Yet, as we have seen, there are great differences between individual infants, and the very bright and
gifted on their fifth birthday may have a mental age of six
or six and a half (IQ 120 or 130). The difference between
the mental ages of these advanced children and the rest of
their age group is likely to increase as they grow older, so
that at the age of ten a boy with an IQ of 120 has a mental
age of twelve, and one with an IQ of 130, of thirteen.

Types of school
The choices facing parents as far as schools are concerned
are of two kinds. The first is a general choice between the
different types of school available; the second is the choice
that particular circumstances impose on the individual
family. The available schools divide into two main types.
There are the schools paid for out of rates and taxes, which
are administered by local education authorities and which
children attend as of right, without any fees being paid by
their parents. These schools are known as 'maintained'
schools, as they are maintained out of public funds (rates
and taxes). They are also known as 'state' schools. Taken
together, these free schools form the 'maintained sector' of
the educational system.

The fee-paying schools, where fees must be paid in order
that a child may attend, are the second main type. Taken
together, these schools form the 'independent sector' of the
educational system. The individual schools are free to
administer and organise their schools in whatever way

they see fit, providing they act within the law. They must comply with the requirements of the various Education Acts as regards the education provided, which must be efficient and full-time. These establishments must, and of course do, carry out the health and safety regulations laid down by national and local authorities. There are considerable variations between them with regard to their curricula and the manner in which they are organised and administered.

State schools
There are several kinds of schools in the maintained sector. The great majority, known as 'county schools', are wholly financed, controlled and administered by the LEAs. In addition there are schools which were founded, usually in the last century, by voluntary organisations, mainly the churches. Subsequently the founding bodies did not have the financial means to modernise and expand their schools, so arrangements were made whereby they should be financed and mainly administered by LEAs. A degree of independence has been retained by these schools. They are known as the 'voluntary-aided', 'voluntary-controlled' and 'special-agreement' schools. They vary as to how many of their own governors they are entitled to appoint, and accordingly they have a greater or lesser control over the day-to-day conduct of their schools. Usually it is in matters of religious instruction that these schools differ most from the county schools.

Under the state system there are primary and secondary schools, and children transfer from one to the other at the age of eleven. The primary schools consist of schools that cater for both infants and juniors in separate departments, and those which are infant or junior schools only.

Most secondary schools are comprehensive. Some of them cater only for pupils up to the age of sixteen when, if they wish to continue their education, they may transfer to a sixth-form college. Other comprehensive schools have sixth forms and are able to take their pupils up to university entrance level. In a few local education authority areas there are still selective grammar schools to which entrance can only be gained by passing a selection examination. These, too, have sixth forms.

A few LEAs have first, middle and upper schools catering for children aged five to nine, nine to thirteen and thirteen to eighteen. Where this arrangement is in operation, the children usually change schools twice, but recently some first and middle schools have been combined, which means that pupils transfer only once at the age of thirteen.

Independent schools

The schools in the independent sector may be classified into five broad groups: preparatory, public, private, specialist and miscellaneous. Most of the schools are single-sex, but there are also coeducational ones for both juniors and seniors.

Preparatory schools These cater in particular for children between the ages of eight and thirteen. Many also have pre-prep departments to which children are accepted at four to four and a half years. During these early years the main attention is on teaching the children the essential skills of reading, writing and number work. They do many other things as well, of course, such as history, geography, nature study, arts and crafts, music, swimming and other sports. There is usually a businesslike approach during lesson time and an emphasis on producing work of a good standard.

At the age of eight in most prep. schools, the children start new subjects. The prospectus for Kingshott, a boys' preparatory school in Hertfordshire, says:

> The youngest boys, in the overall care of a Form Master, will start basic French, Latin and elementary Science at this stage. After this the number of Science periods in each week's time-table increases with specialisation beginning in Chemistry, Physics and Biology. Art, Music, and Speech and Drama are important parts of every boy's study. Painting, drawing, mosaic work, collage and papier mâché take place in the art room.

The boys are prepared to take the common entrance examination in order to gain admittance to a public school at the age of thirteen. In some cases they leave to go on to a new school at the age of eleven.

Public schools Winchester, Eton, Harrow, Haberdashers' Aske's and Rugby are probably some of the best known 'public' schools, but there are many others as well. Some of these have only boarders, others only day pupils, and still others take both.

There have been marked changes in recent years, but most of the public schools still demand and achieve a very high standard of work from their pupils. Academic studies are of a particularly high level in the more usual subjects and in a wide range of optional subjects. There are also exceptional opportunities in music, art and sport, and again the levels of performance expected and obtained are extremely high. Research by Sharon Robinson reported in the *Sunday Times* magazine in 1981 shows a 'league table' of the schools which, in proportion to the number of their post-GCE O level pupils, gained the largest percentages of Oxbridge university places: the first sixteen were all independent schools.

The well known public schools are very selective, and admission can only be gained by passing the entrance examination. This usually consists of a group IQ test* or similar test of intellectual ability, two or three written papers in English, mathematics and perhaps general knowledge, and for those who have been successful in this part of the selection procedure, an interview with the headmaster. For those who enter the scholarship examination there will probably be a two-day selection procedure, and in the case of boarding schools, candidates will stay in the school for one or two nights.

As will be realised, it is not easy to gain admittance to one of the country's leading public schools. In order to do so a child must be intellectually very able and have achieved a high standard in his academic work, and the

* The use of the three well-known IQ tests which are administered individually, the Stanford-Binet, WISC and the newer 'British Ability Scales', is restricted. They may only be used by a qualified psychologist. In addition, there are also 'group IQ tests' which may be given by teachers. These are paper and pen tests and may be administered to a number of children at one sitting. Like the individually administered tests, the group IQ tests are objectively scored and the questions are designed to test, as far as possible, reasoning ability independently of the extent of a child's stock of knowledge.

parents must either be able to pay fees ranging from £3,000 to £6,000 a year or be able to obtain financial aid under the government's Assisted Places Scheme (see p. 214) or from some other source.

The normal age of entry into most public schools is thirteen, but some admit new pupils at eleven, others have a fresh intake at both eleven and thirteen. In most public schools highly gifted children whose academic work has reached the required standard will be accepted under-age, that is, at ten or twelve.

Private schools These schools are very varied but it is probably true to say that on average their academic standards are not as high as in the public schools. Many are small, and the atmosphere is often less formal than in the large establishments, but in spite of more limited resources a number of them do obtain very good results in academic and other fields. Some of the schools have a less conventional philosophy and endeavour to create by it an atmosphere in which young people will be encouraged to develop their own interests. Parents may find among the variety of private schools one which is exactly right for a child who is 'different' from others.

Specialist schools These are schools which cater specifically for children talented in music, ballet and drama. They are described in a later section (p. 181).

Miscellaneous schools The EEC has set up a school in England to provide a multinational education. There are also schools set up by the nationals of other countries, such as diplomats and businessmen who are resident in this country, and by different ethnic and minority groups. A few independent schools have been established for maladjusted, emotionally disturbed and slow-learning children.

The choices for parents
What should be done with a very bright five-year-old who already knows all that he will be taught during the first two years in an ordinary infant school? For most parents there is no satisfactory answer to this question as things stand at the moment. Partial solutions are offered below.

Before considering the choices facing parents, a point made in the last chapter must be reiterated. Parents should not hold back from encouraging their children to learn. Some parents feel they ought not to help their children in case, during the following school year or whenever, it will make them even more bored. This may indeed happen, but it is the school situation which must be made to suit the child, not the other way round.

There are psychological reasons why the provision of educational toys and going to a playgroup are likely to be beneficial. If a child is at some time going to lack learning opportunities and a challenging and stimulating environment, it is preferable that it should occur when he is older – that is, when he is five rather than at the pre-school stage. The older children become, the less vulnerable they are to the damage which may be done to their personalities and mental abilities by being bored through an absence of learning opportunities. As has already been shown (see p. 137), more than a half of a child's mental and physical development takes place *before* entering school. Of the remainder of what will be in maturity the full level of intellectual ability, the greatest proportion will be achieved during the earliest school years.

The alternatives open to parents are to look for a suitable infant school or independent school, or to educate their child at home (see Chapter 6). The advantages of these different options will be considered in turn. For most parents, however, there is little real choice, and they are faced with no alternative to sending their child to the local infant school.

The first thing that parents should do, if possible well before their child reaches school age, is to collect together as much information as they can about as many schools as possible, both state and independent. They can do this by asking all their friends, neighbours and relatives about what happens in the schools their children attend. Although useful, the views expressed must be treated with caution, since other parents can only give their own subjective view of a school – a view which, quite often, is based upon a single incident, good or bad, which has impressed itself upon their minds. Second, what has proved to be a suitable school for someone else's child may not be so for your bright or gifted infant.

An example will make clear how this may happen. The mother of a highly gifted child asked a friend, who was a teacher, about an independent school in which formerly she had been teaching. The woman replied saying it was a terrible school as all the children thought about was doing their work and passing exams! The mother thought that this sounded the right sort of school for her very bright daughter, sent for the prospectus, went along to see the school, and decided to send her child there. The girl was very happy, worked and achieved well, won the music prize, took part in all the other activities which were going on, and got on well with the other girls.

Infant schools

Under the 1981 Education Act parents now have a legal right to choose the maintained school they wish their child to attend. The changes in the law are discussed more fully in the next chapter.

The curriculum followed in most infants schools is very uniform. There is often an assumption that when children start school they have not been away from their homes before, or mixed with other children. So the infant teacher spends the first few weeks getting the children used to the new surroundings, to each other and to herself. They spend their time playing with sand and water and with educational toys, doing painting and taking part in classroom games. At some time during the day a story will probably be read to them. When a start is made with learning to read, it is generally assumed that none of them have done any reading, writing or number work before. By the time they are due to move on to the junior school when they are seven, it is expected that all of them (as far as possible) will be able to read, write and do number work. Care is usually taken by the teachers to prevent any sense of competition developing amongst the children.

There are, of course, differences between infant schools, arising from differences in the personalities of the heads and from differences in the ways in which the schools are administered (see p. 160). Some heads will allow a child to take his or her own reading book to school instead of making him or her work through the normal reading scheme. In a few cases a head may consent to a gifted child moving into an older group of infants – say, a five-year-old may move in with the sixes – but this does not happen very often. When asked by a mother whether her daughter could be transferred into an older age group, one head said very firmly that children could not be put into classes according to their academic aptitude. She went on to say that it was her job and that of her staff to see that the clever children suffered academically as little as possible, and that if the parent was dissatisfied the best thing she could do would be to send her daughter to a private school.

Independent schools
You may feel you would like to investigate the possibilities of sending your child to an independent school. Many of the parents who do so have only modest means and have to cut down their expenditure on other things in order to pay the fees. They may, for instance, decide to move into a less expensive house, or manage with an old car, or forego expensive foreign holidays in order to afford it. The fees vary considerably from school to school: probably at the present time (1983) they are mainly between £200 and £400 per term for five- and six-year-olds, but it is usual for the fees to increase as the child becomes older. Although at first sight these may seem such large amounts that most parents feel they could not afford them, after giving thought to the problem many families find that they can do so with some rearrangement of their finances. There are, after all, a quarter of a million children in independent schools!

If parents are to make sacrifices in order to pay school fees – and there are very few with children at independent schools who do not have to do so – they will want to feel confident that their child will benefit sufficiently to make the effort worthwhile.

The first important advantage that parents who decide to send their child to an independent school have is greater choice. They will be able to select a school which they consider will most nearly meet the needs of their child. If he is obviously very bright, they will probably choose a school which has a reputation for high standards in academic work in spite of the fact, say, that the sporting facilities may not be as good as elsewhere. Their views as to which class or group their child should be in and the sort of work he should be given will almost certainly carry more weight than they would at the local infant school. An independent school will be more likely to make greater efforts to meet the wishes of parents than a state school since, of course, it is the parents who pay the fees!

A good prep. or private school will have advantages for a very bright or gifted child who has already learnt to read, write and do number work at home and in playgroups and nursery school. First, such a school usually has an entrance test which ensures that all the children accepted are above average intelligence. The probability will be, then, that there will be a larger proportion of bright children in the school – an obvious advantage for your bright child as he will be much more likely to meet other children of his own age with approximately the same level of ability. On the one hand competition, and on the other common interests, encourage a bright child to be alert, and assist in the further development of his or her mental abilities.

Where a gifted child is still at least a year ahead in his general mental development and knowledge among a selected group of infants of well above average intellectual ability, an independent school will almost certainly favour moving him up into the next class. To do so will bring him into a group of children who are nearer to him in mental age and with whom, therefore, he is likely to have more in common. On very rare occasions it may be beneficial to put a child in a class two years ahead.

A child with high intellectual potential who enjoys a stimulating home environment and who has benefited from well run and imaginative sessions at playgroup and nursery school, is likely to be very much ahead of his contemporaries in self-awareness, in creative and other mental abilities, in manipulative control of pencil and pen, paint-brush and scissors, and in reading, writing and number work. Where a child has a very favourable genetic endowment for intellectual work and has experienced excellent learning opportunities during his first years, he will probably have covered at least the first two years of the work/play curriculum of the typical infant school before he starts attending.

There is the question of whether a prep. or private school will provide the most suitable curriculum and learning environment for, say, a five-year-old boy or girl who is two years in advance of the average child of his or her age in schoolwork. There are great differences between schools in the independent sector, and while most prep. schools may encourage their pupils to do work of a high academic standard, some may consider this to be less important, perhaps, than encouraging a cooperative spirit among the children. There is a tendency for prep. schools to be more traditional in their approach, which usually means that for at least part of the school day the children settle down to work. In general there is less of the 'learning through play' which is found in many, or most, of the maintained infant schools, and progress with reading, creative writing, number work, general knowledge and art work will usually be at a much faster pace.

Acceleration This is the semi-technical term for putting a child up in school into an older age group. There are two reasons why a child may be advanced with his schoolwork: first, the high level of his natural intellectual ability, and second, the fact that he has been provided with more opportunities for learning during his pre-school years than most children. In this case he will have acquired a stock of knowledge and a level of understanding which is ahead of most children in his age group. This will give him a very good start when he begins school, and his self-confidence will be increased as he finds that he is able to do the schoolwork more easily than the other children.

But there are dangers as well as advantages in accelerating a child, which is why schools are loath to put any boy or girl more than one year ahead. First, the parents should assure themselves that their child *is* very bright or gifted and so naturally a fast learner, and that his forwardness in schoolwork is not mainly the product of having been provided with a much more stimulating learning environment during his pre-school years than the majority of other five-year-olds. Where this is the case, acceleration will lead to unjustifiably high teacher- and parent-expectations, which the child will be unable to satisfy two or three years later when he will be overtaken by other naturally faster-learning children. When this happens, stress results from trying to keep up to a level of work he or she cannot manage, and disappointment and frustration are felt all round by the child, the parents and the teachers.

Does this mean that where children are only good-average to bright it is not worth spending effort, time and money in providing an enriched learning environment during the pre-school period, following it up with the financial effort required to pay for a boy or girl to attend a private school?

The answers to both questions are a definite 'No!' The enriched learning environment in the pre-school period will have lasting benefits, providing it does not lead to the kind of unduly high expectations described above. As explained in the last chapter (see p. 138), the child will probably have gained two or three points in IQ level, which will be retained through life. Finding that the work is not as difficult as he had expected will boost his self-confidence and encourage him to tackle new and more difficult learning in the future. Also, an experienced and competent teacher will be pleased to find that your small son or daughter has already made a good start with reading, writing and number work, for these skills form the basis of future progress in schoolwork. It is, after all, the main function of teachers and of schools to promote children's educational development, and this includes learning the basic skills. The teacher's approval of your child's early learning will probably find expression in her dealings with him in school, and her favourable attitude will give him a sense of achievement and well-being which will augur well for future progress.

Is it worth the financial effort for a boy or girl to attend a private school if his or her level of intellectual ability is not more than good-average to bright? The answer is again yes, as parents are able to choose the school which is most likely to suit what they see as their son's or daughter's personality and aptitudes. Then, too, they as parents will have a much stronger say in the way their child is handled at school, and it is more likely that he will acquire a sound foundation on which to build his future progress, even if the high fees at secondary stage should prove beyond their means.

Although a private or prep. school is *more likely* to be of greater benefit to a gifted child than the local educational authority's primary school, there is no certainty that this will be so in any particular case. This point cannot be stressed too strongly. The reason for this is that not all private schools are efficient and well run, and some are less so than the typical primary school. If you should find that your nearby LEA primary school can cater adequately for your child, sending him there will, of course, have the added advantage that you will not have to pay fees.

There are two other considerations to be discussed in connection with the suitability of a private school. These are accessibility and travelling distances, and the social background of the children.

Travelling For most parents an independent school is unlikely to be situated as conveniently as the local primary school. Some parents send their children to private day schools which are as much as ten miles away from where they live, though this very rarely means that the parents must make a twenty-mile round trip every morning and afternoon. Many independent schools run their own school bus which collects children if not from their homes at least from conveniently placed pick-up points. In rural areas most families have cars – and the mothers coming from one direction will arrange between themselves a rota for their mutual convenience, which usually results in each mother collecting and delivering about five children twice a week. These journeys can be very enjoyable: listening to the chatter of five or six small children who seem to forget the presence of a mother-driver can be both informative and entertaining. They also help to establish friendships between the parents.

Social background The children who attend independent schools today come from all types of families. Fifty years ago it was largely the children of the rich and of those whose work took them overseas in the diplomatic corps or in the armed services, and the sons and daughters of the clergy for whom many schools had special endowments, who went to the fee-paying schools. Today, children from families of this sort are still to be found in independent schools, but in addition there are boys and girls whose parents come from all walks of life. The head of a well recognised prep. school told me that he had among his boys the son of one of the stall-holders in the local market. It is not uncommon for mothers to take a job in order to earn the money with which to pay the fees.

Maintained primary and junior independent schools compared

Compared with local authority primary schools, most prep. schools and many of the other private schools have retained a traditional approach to academic work. In most independent schools there is a more serious attitude towards work, and the subject divisions – history, geography, etc. – remain. Latin and French are commonly taught, although Latin is usually only taken by the abler children. Almost without exception the level of academic work is higher than that of children of a comparable age in the primary schools. It is rare for there to be any feeling that a child should be held back in his academic work in case he is not sufficiently emotionally or socially mature, as is often the case in local education authority schools. There is usually less reluctance, too, to accelerate a child into a higher class if his work warrants it, or to hold him back to repeat a year if it is felt that insufficient progress has been made. The formal approach of organisation into forms, and the commonly found work ethos, result in good classroom discipline. There are usually plenty of opportunities for such activities as sport, music and the arts and crafts.

Private schools which do not claim to be prep. schools do not gear their curriculum and organisational structure to the public school system. Usually their curriculum, organisation and general approach to education is nearer to that found in LEA primary schools. One fairly clear-cut distinction between preparatory schools on the one hand and other private junior and LEA primary schools on the other, is that the preparatory schools employ subject specialists who move from form to form teaching their own subject, whereas in most of the other private schools and in all state primaries there is a class teacher who teaches her class all, or nearly all – if there are exceptions it is usually for music and games – of the subjects in the curriculum. The other private junior schools are less flexible than prep. schools with regard to keeping children grouped strictly according to their chronological age and not according to their natural ability or the level they have reached in their schoolwork. However, the private junior schools are more flexible about these matters than LEA primary schools. After all, they do have to please the parents.

A local education authority is legally obliged to provide a school place for every child between the ages of five and sixteen years resident within its administrative area. The normal age of transfer from primary to secondary school is eleven – all those children whose eleventh birthday falls on or after September in one year up to 31 August in the next being taken as a year group – and they will both enter and move up the secondary school as a unit. This is in spite of the fact that a child whose birthday is on 30 August will be a year younger, give or take a few days, than one born in early September.

As we have seen, the level of a child's ability is not usually taken into consideration in state schools when placing him or her in a school year; the argument offered is that although a child may be intellectually forward, he or she may not be equally advanced in social or emotional development, and it would therefore not be in the child's interest to move forward into an older age group. If this argument does not convince the parent as to the rightness of keeping a very bright boy or girl in a class where all or most of the work is at too elementary a level for the child to be making academic progress, the head will probably explain that every child is treated as an individual and accordingly is given work to do which is at a suitable level. If the parent is still unsatisfied that his or her child is making satisfactory progress, the head may explain that he cannot let one child move up to the next class, because if he did so many of his other parents would want their children to go up as well. The justification of these points will now be considered.

Why primary schools do not group children by ability

The argument put forward by primary school teachers that an intellectually gifted child is not as advanced in emotional and social development is nearly always true. However, the largest and best known research study* on gifted children found that although they were not as far ahead emotionally and socially as intellectually, the academically gifted were more mature in these respects than the majority of their age group.

It is not perhaps surprising that a child who is advanced in this mental development and consequently also in the sort of things in which he is interested, should from time to time become exasperated at being forced to spend his time only in the company of those much younger than himself in every way except chronologically. When a gifted child finally bursts into an angry protest at this situation, he is said by the teachers to be socially immature; if, on the other hand, the child chooses to go into a corner and read a book or to withdraw into himself and daydream – perhaps of the things he will do once he gets away from school – he may be described as socially immature.

Mental traits are notoriously difficult to measure, and it is on these grounds that the validity of intelligence tests has been challenged, yet although there are no tests readily available to the ordinary teacher regarding levels of emotional and social maturity – with few exceptions these are only available to qualified psychologists – parents of bright children are frequently told that their child cannot be moved up to the next class because he is not sufficiently emotionally and socially mature!

The second common reason given by primary school heads for not putting a child up into a higher class is that there is no need, as all the children have their work set individually by the class teacher and so each is catered for adequately. There is no doubt that this is a most desirable aim, supported by virtually all teachers. In reality it is extremely difficult to achieve, and it is my experience that

* See vol. I, Ch. 18, 'Trait Ratings', p. 542 and preceding pages of *Mental and Physical Traits of a Thousand Gifted Children*, L. M. Terman, Stanford University Press, 1925, repr. 1968.

usually, as far as bright and gifted children are concerned, it amounts to little more than lip-service, since the schools do not have the facilities to put it into practice. It is true that a great deal of the work in primary school classrooms is done by children working in small groups at a table, and that the work is a little more or less advanced from one table to another. While this may well accommodate the needs of most children, who fall into the broad category of being just below and just above the average, it rarely meets the needs of the very bright and gifted on the one hand, or the less able on the other – but the latter do, of course, usually receive extra teaching, so their requirements are met. One head told me when I visited his school that all his bright children were well catered for, since the range of books available included some for twelve-year-olds! This, in a school where the normal leaving age was eleven-plus, illustrates how many primary school teachers fail to appreciate how very far ahead the gifted are.

The second reason why it is rare for sufficiently advanced work to be provided for very able children in the ordinary primary school classroom is that, whereas there is a very large range of special books and materials directed towards the needs of the less able, the suppliers of educational equipment provide little in the way of special teaching aids for those of high ability. It seems that the four Schools' Council work-packs produced by Globe Educational and the one on North Sea Oil by Able Children are the only materials in the UK which have been produced specifically to enrich the curriculum of bright and gifted children. There are, however, other intellectually stimulating publications which can be obtained such as 'Thinking Skills' and 'Amusements in Mathematics' booklets (also from Able Children) and games like chess and 'Scrabble'. Primary school teachers need aids of the sort that can be used by the very able pupils for independent learning, particularly in the older junior classes, as the teachers are usually required to cover the whole curriculum and cannot be specialists in every subject.

Then comes the third reason for not putting a child up which primary schools often give – that other parents will demand that their children move forward as well. There is a great desire in schools both to be fair and to be seen to be fair. No one can argue with a child's date of birth, and if the school adheres to the rule that placement in classes is determined by birthdays, then it cannot be accused of favouring one child and not another. What is open to argument, of course, is whether categorising children according to their exact age is a sensible thing to do in the first place.

Why is it that the independent sector finds it can move children up and down between year groups, in spite of being far more directly responsible to parents than are the LEA primary school heads?

One might almost say that a primary head is not directly responsible to any individual parent. A school must carry out its legal duty under the various Education Acts, and although the practicalities of how this shall be done in any particular school are theoretically the responsibility of the school's governors, they are largely under the jurisdiction of the Education Committee – one of the committees of local councillors elected in local elections. Those councillors who are on the council's Education Committee are responsible for the appointment of the chief executive and administrative officers (including the Chief Education Officer, or whatever other title may be given to this job) of the authority's education department. These officials in their turn recommend the appointment of the other senior members of the education department, including the heads of the schools. The national government passes the laws, and it is the function of the Department of Education and Science to draw up the regulations for their implementation and to see that local education authorities carry out their legal duties. There is a legal requirement that children should be educated according to their 'age, ability and aptitude' (the 1944 Education Act), but schools claim that they do this anyway. It is not easy for parents to prove that in the case of their own child the school is not doing so. Far from there being any official requirement that children should be grouped in school according to their mental age, the recommendations of leading educationalists and of the schools' inspectorate have tended rather in the opposite direction – that pupils should be grouped according to their chronological age.

This brief look at the hierarchy within the state system shows that it should be much easier for heads of state schools than for those of independent schools to group their pupils by ability. Parents do not have any direct power in a state school. Any parents who are dissatisfied with the education their children are receiving can send them to another state school, although in practice they rarely do so. A primary school head may be unpopular and there may be an unpleasant atmosphere in the school, but he is secure in his job providing he does not break the law. The case of Tyndale School, London, in 1975 demonstrated this. The head was eventually suspended and later dismissed, but only after about two thirds of the children had been withdrawn from the school and protests had been made by at least one member of the teaching staff and governors.

In the independent sector, grades rather than birthdates are the main criteria for placing children into groups or classes.

In the state sector, the tripartite system under which children sat a selection examination at eleven-plus for grammar school places has been repudiated by most modern educational theorists. With the introduction of comprehensive schools at secondary stage, there is only limited pressure on state primary schools to bring their pupils up to the standard considered to be the 'average' for their age group. 'Streaming', the predominant system for grouping children by ability, has been discontinued almost everywhere. Recent years have also seen the disappearance of other methods of registering children's academic performance, such as numerical marks for individual pieces of work, term and examination marks and grades. This is also the case in the lower forms of some secondary schools. Many primary schools do have objectively scored tests for the teachers', and particularly the head's, use, but it is rare for either the parents or their children to be told the results. It is now very difficult to tell in primary schools whether intellectually able children are functioning satisfactorily, since it is rare for educational statistics to show in any detail the level of performance of the brighter children. The dominant view in state schools is that there should be no academic selection between children in the primary schools, and usually not before the third year in secondary schools. The only exceptions to this rule of non-selection are sport and music.

Almost exactly opposite is the approach of the independent schools. Almost all preparatory schools have an entrance examination or test at the age of seven which children must pass before they can gain entry. Many of these schools also have a 'pre-prep.' department which takes children from the age of four and half. Although there is usually no entry test at this stage, parents will be unlikely to enter children they consider to be on the slow side. There are, though, other private schools which will take such children, usually those which do not gear themselves specifically to preparing children for entry to the public schools.

Once a child is in a prep. school he is taught most subjects by subject specialists, and he is set regular homework which is carefully corrected and marked. There are also marks for classwork and tests. These various sets of marks are added up for each subject, and are used to calculate class positions, usually monthly and termly; at the end of the school year there are formal examinations and in some schools there is another set of examinations halfway through the year. From all these sets of marks, teachers, parents and the children themselves can see how each boy or girl is progressing relative to the rest of the class. Using these marks as evidence to back up the opinions of the school staff, a head is in a position to give a child's parents a clear picture of his progress and so, as usually happens, justify leaving him in the same group to move up the school in the normal way. Alternatively, should the head believe it to be in an exceptionally bright child's interest to move into a higher class, he will be moved up. Conversely, another child who has perhaps been away from school on account of illness and whose marks are well below the class average, may be kept down to repeat a year. The reasons for putting a pupil up or keeping him down can be explained clearly to parents.

As we have seen, the main choice open to parents is between the independent fee-paying system and the free state-maintained schools.

Within the independent sector a parent can choose geographical location and type of school – a prep. school, or a private school not orientated towards the public school system.

Another consideration is whether a child shall be sent to a day or boarding school. Although most parents will not want their children to go away from home when they are very young, it is common for boys to enter many of the better known prep. schools as boarders at the age of eight. The main advantage claimed for children boarding from this age is that they are work-orientated from early on. Second, it is easier for regular habits as regards homework and bedtimes to be established and maintained in a community where regulations relating to things of this sort are accepted by everyone. Third, no time is wasted travelling to and from school. Bright and gifted children will benefit from boarding probably rather more than most other children, as they will be more able to benefit from the atmosphere of work, regular routines for homework and bedtimes, and the saving of travelling time.

However, parents may consider other factors of greater importance than academic progress and may doubt the advantages of a boy or girl becoming accustomed to the strictures of an established daily pattern of life. First, the child's personality may be such that if he is sent away from home at the age of eight he will be so upset, that any possible benefit is more than lost by his distress at leaving his mother and his home. Second, the mother in particular may decide that she wishes to keep her children near her, so that she gets to know and understand them better as they grow up. Even if it is decided that the children will go away to school at the age of eleven or thirteen, a mother will have had a few more years in their company before they do so. Again, from the gifted child's point of view, whether or not he will benefit from attending a day school rather than a boarding school will depend primarily on his personality.

Scholarships
The fees for independent education are high. Fees for those attending boys' junior schools are most commonly about £450 to £500 per term, but may be as little as £200 or as high as £800.

Many independent schools give scholarships for children showing exceptional academic ability. These are usually awarded as a result of a child's performance in the school's entrance test and/or as a result of an interview with the head. From the school's point of view, a system of scholarships serves to promote an atmosphere in which high standards of work are accepted by staff, parents and pupils as an important and desirable objective. A school usually sees its scholars as the pace-makers for the rest. Being a scholar is prestigious for the child and usually earns certain small privileges such as sitting in a special position during school assembly. Providing the boy's natural ability warrants the position, it is also likely to have a beneficial effect upon his current and future attitude to academic work.

What most scholarships do not do these days is to make a significant reduction in the fees that must be paid to keep a child at an independent school. Out of a termly fee of £500 an average scholarship would probably be worth about £50. No doubt parents find such a reduction helpful, but it is not enough to remove the financial burden that results from keeping a boy or girl at an independent school. Exceptionally, a scholarship may account for as much as a third of the normal fee payable. Many schools also give bursaries, whereby a needy parent is given financial assistance from either the school's own fund or from trust funds. Except in very rare cases, this will probably cover only a part of the total fees.

There are other ways in which parents can obtain financial help with school fees. Children whose fathers are serving overseas in the diplomatic corps or armed services are eligible for grants or allowances. Several multi-national companies and organisations operate similar schemes. Then there are some professional associations that have foundations that will give help with school fees for the dependants of members of their profession. Local education authorities are allowed to take up places at independent schools without obtaining permission from central government, but at the present time (1983) it is rare for them to be willing to do so except where financial help is necessary to enable a bright child to continue at an independent school after the death of a parent. A few authorities have raised money on the rates to pay for scholarships at independent schools, and it is worth finding out whether yours is one of them. Lastly, there are some grant-giving trusts which assist the children of the clergy, those from broken homes or in other very difficult circumstances, and orphans. Full information regarding the availability of scholarships and grants may be obtained from the Independent Schools Information Service. The address is given at the back of this book.

Specialist schools for the talented

The term 'talented children' is usually taken to mean boys and girls who have outstanding ability in music and dancing. Sometimes it is used more broadly to cover acting, drawing and painting. Commentators in the mass media use the phrase 'talented performer' even more broadly, to include anyone who displays exceptional ability in the circus arts, gymnastics, ice-skating, chess and any other form of sport or stage performance.

It is generally accepted that early childhood training is desirable if not essential for the development of outstanding violinists, ballet-dancers, acrobats and gymnasts, yet in this country there are only a handful of schools providing full-time education plus expert tuition in one or other of these arts. In nearly all cases the very early training is undertaken by the parent or some other member of the family. Then when it is apparent that the child has an aptitude for the particular art form, part-time attendance is arranged at a suitable school, to carry on his or her training and the development of his or her talent.

The opportunities are greatest for those children who possess musical talent. In most parts of this country it is seldom difficult to find a private music teacher reasonably near to a child's home. Once a child has started formal lessons it is usually fairly easy to see whether he or she has any particular aptitude. The teacher's judgment of his or her rate of progress and the child's liking for playing (and practising) music and listening to it will be the chief indicators here. There will also be some opportunity for learning music in either a primary or independent junior school, whichever the child attends.

There are four special music schools in England which

aim at developing and training professional musicians. These are the Yehudi Menuhin School in Surrey, the Purcell School, North London, Wells Cathedral School in Somerset and Chetham's School, Manchester. All four are coeducational and accept boarders – at the age of eight or above in the case of the Yehudi Menuhin School and from seven in the other three schools. Admission is on the basis of a successful audition, and although the child must have some knowledge of music, what the schools are looking for is musicality – an inherent understanding of and feeling for music – rather than an initial well polished technique. In any one year the total number of new admissions to these four schools is very small.

Other opportunities open to musically talented children are the Saturday classes held by various bodies. The best known and most prestigious of these are the sessions held at the Royal College and Guildhall Schools of Music in London, but entry cannot be gained below the age of ten. Entry is again by audition and is highly competitive. In many cases the fees for those accepted are paid by their local education authority. There are, in addition, Saturday and evening music schools organised by LEAs in many areas. It is usual for admission to these to be by audition. Usually parents are asked to pay something towards the cost, but less than the full economic charge.

Choir schools select boys with exceptional voices and aural acuity. The children have to be also physically fit and of above average intelligence, since choristers have arduous training sessions and church services to attend, all of which have to be fitted in with normal schoolwork. Admission to a school as a chorister is on the basis of an audition and other tests. Scholarships or financial assistance from the LEA are usually available where necessary, to enable parents to meet the fees for the few boys selected. The Wells Cathedral School, Chetham's School (associated with Manchester Cathedral), St Paul's Cathedral Choir School and St John's College School, Cambridge, admit boys as choristers. Entry is usually at the age of eight although the audition will have been held earlier, and they remain in the school until they are thirteen or fourteen or until their voices break. After that, arrangements can usually be made for them to continue in the school in the case of the Wells and Chetham's, but those in the two prep. schools, St Paul's and St John's, have to transfer to other schools.

The height of ambition for a talented dancer in this country is to gain admission to the Royal Ballet Company, and the most straightforward way of doing so is through the Royal Ballet School. There are only part-time courses available for children under the age of eleven. The classes are held in London and take place on Saturdays and during the early evening after school. Admission is solely by audition and children must be aged between eight and eleven on 31 August of the year in which, if accepted, they will join the classes. Although it is expected that applicants will have had some training in dancing, it is a feeling for dance from within the child herself that is likely to carry most weight with the adjudicators. Those who are accepted and attend these junior associate classes, as they are called, must pass a further audition at the age of eleven if they are to enter the Royal Ballet's full-time Lower School at White Lodge, Richmond, Surrey.

In order to obtain admission to the junior associate classes a child has usually attended a local private dancing school for one or more years. There is great competition between these schools with regard to obtaining places for their pupils. Few, if any, local education authorities provide classes in which is given the formal training necessary to enable even a naturally talented child to secure a place in one of the Royal Ballet classes. In this respect dancing and drama are treated differently from music by the education authorities. Primary schools do have 'music and movement' sessions, and very often a Christmas play or pantomime as a part of their normal curriculum, but the experience and training obtained in these activities would, almost without exception, be inadequate to enable a child to pass a Royal Ballet School audition.

Elmhurst Ballet School gives children from the age of nine professional training in ballet and drama as well as providing a general education. The school has both day and boarding places, and although most of the pupils are girls, boys are also accepted. Children are only admitted to the school on the basis of a dancing audition.

The Italia Conti Stage School is one of the best known and most respected of its kind, and many famous stage names were former pupils at the school. Vocational classes are held in London on Saturdays for children from the age of five. The types of stage work studied are acting, singing, ballet, tap and modern dancing. Admission is on the basis of an interview. Although this is not a formal audition, an applicant should be prepared to demonstrate the type of stage work he or she can do and likes doing. The Italia Conti Stage School, junior section, admits children from the age of ten to a full-time day school which gives professional stage training and a general education. Admission, once again, is by audition; the candidate must be prepared for the speech audition with three pieces of contrasting styles, and the dancing and singing audition must include, as far as possible, different types of dancing and singing. If accepted by the school, an application for assistance with the fees may be made to the local education authority if the child is over eleven. There is a licensed theatrical agency attached to the school, and pupils may obtain engagements from time to time. Preliminary training is advisable before a child attempts to gain admission to even the Italia Conti Saturday classes, and is essential before auditioning for the full-time junior section. There are a number of other stage schools in the London area which hold Saturday morning classes where elementary training can be obtained, and similar schools will be found in the major towns.

The broader meaning of the term 'talented children', as we have said, covers in addition drawing and painting and related subjects, chess and other types of performance – the circus arts, gymnastics, ice-skating and different forms of sport.

It is generally accepted that exceptional ability in drawing and painting – apart from the freshness found in very young children's work – is not usually revealed until adolescence. I for one would dispute this. I viewed an exhibition of children's art in Montreal in which accomplished young artists' drawings and paintings from early childhood (about the age of three onwards), middle and later childhood and adolescence were shown alongside artistic work by children of average ability. There was no question as to the superiority of the work of those who were subsequently recognised as talented artists. However, there does not appear to be any school in this country designed to give professional training to children who are potentially talented artists. Many, no doubt, may be born into families where one or both parents are professional artists who, when they are playing with their children, quite naturally show them how to draw or paint. The child who is encouraged in this way receives not only tuition but also practice in drawing, painting and other forms of art work.

As for chess, many gifted children of four and five enjoy learning and playing the game with members of their family. As the youngsters grow older they can often join a chess club in school and subsequently enter competitions drawing contestants from a wider area. Books showing the moves used in recognised games are available from local libraries, and it is possible for a gifted child to become highly proficient. There are, however, no special schools for chess in this country as there are in the USSR. So it is, too, with the other activities in which a child can be highly talented. Initially the teaching and training are undertaken by the parents, whether in the home or elsewhere, for instance the swimming baths or the ice rink; then as the child grows older and more proficient, he joins a club and, as he becomes more expert, he or she starts to win competitions. The one case where probably all the teaching and training is undertaken by the parents and other members of the family, is the circus arts.

Special schools, mainly part-time, have been established in the USSR for all these activities. In this country it is not only the level of a child's talent which determines whether she may become a professional artist, musician or stage performer, but also how much her parents are willing and able to help her. Parents have to be prepared to spend a considerable amount of time taking a child to and from classes, and to pay the cost of these during the early years. Once a child is ten, if she passes an audition into one of the recognised schools, a grant can be obtained, where necessary, to assist with the payment of fees, from the age of eleven. For the full-time music schools, grants may be payable from the time a child is admitted to the school.

6   Parents' Rights

Parents are legally obliged to educate their children up to the age of sixteen. What are their rights?

As we have seen, under the law parents are free to choose both how and where their child is educated, providing the child receives 'efficient full-time education suitable to his age, ability, and aptitude'.* Later in the same Act,† it is laid down that the minister and local education authorities 'shall have regard to the general principle that, so far as is compatible with the provision of efficient instruction and training and the avoidance of unreasonable public expenditure, pupils are to be educated in accordance with the wishes of their parents.' As regards *how* children are educated, parents have the choice as to whether this shall be in a school or elsewhere, for the same section of the Act continues '. . . either by regular attendance at school or otherwise.'

Parents have the right to choose whether their child shall attend an independent or publicly maintained school, and to select a particular school within these sectors. (Of course, this is not the same as saying that parents have the right to have their child admitted to the school of their choice.) There has always been freedom, in the independent sector, to select a school in any area parents may please. And under the 1980 Education Act, they have now a legal right of choice in the maintained sector as well. This means they can select a primary or secondary school for their child which is not in the area in which they live: nor need the school chosen be administered by the same local education authority. Of course, as before, this is not to say the children will automatically be admitted to these schools. The position with regard to the

* Education Act 1944, Section 36.
† Ibid., Section 76.

various options will now be considered in turn and in more detail.

Nearly all parents send their children to school: it is the accepted thing to do. The publicity given to the cases of Ruth Lawrence and the Harrison family by the media in recent years will have resulted in many more families becoming aware that it is quite legal for them to educate their children at home or at some other place of their choosing other than a recognised school, as long as, between the ages of five and sixteen, they are provided with a suitable full-time education. Without specifying what this shall be, the 1944 Education Act merely lays the duty upon the local education authority to see that parents carry out their legal obligations. In their turn, the LEAs (as far as I know) do not specify what they consider to be 'suitable full-time education', presumably because this is not easy to define and because they anticipate that all children apart from truants will attend school.

In exceptional circumstances LEAs arrange for a child to be educated at home by a peripatetic teacher. Usually this is a short-term arrangement where a child is physically unfit to attend school but is not in hospital. More rarely a peripatetic teacher is provided to give home-based education to a youngster who is maladjusted mentally. This was done in the case of Derek (see p. 22) after a succession of traumatic experiences at comprehensive secondary school; after two attempts to settle him in special schools had failed, Derek was provided with a home-tutor by the LEA. In another case, in a different LEA area, the Advisor for Special Education accepted that a boy was intellectually so highly gifted that the Authority had no suitable school place for him and the parents were provided with some assistance to help them educate the child at home, without the boy having first to suffer a series of disturbing experiences.

It is rare for parents who feel that their child does not fit into school life, whether because he is highly gifted or for some other psychological reason, to find that it is an easy matter to arrange for the child to be educated at home. For this reason 'Education Otherwise', a self-help organisation, was set up by a small group of parents in 1977 in order to offer support, advice and information to families practising or contemplating home-based education as an alternative to schooling. In one of its booklets, *School is Not Compulsory*, the organisation sets out guidelines regarding a curriculum that might be expected to satisfy a local education authority that a boy or girl was receiving an adequate education at home. It suggests that most parents would be willing for their children to work towards the following broad aims:

> Language skills: reading, writing and an ability for articulate and sensitive communication with others;
> Mathematical skills: an understanding of basic concepts, terms and notation;
> An understanding of the history and science of the world, including the development, properties and uses of the earth's resources – wood, water, uranium, etc.;
> Experience of artistic, musical and physical activities;
> The level of development in these areas will increase with the child's natural maturity.

No reference is made to the length of time a child should be expected to work when being educated at home. However, the book draws attention to an official specification in a particular case that the home education schemes provided by the LEA should be *a maximum* of five sessions per week, each session lasting for one and a half hours for children under eight and two hours for those of eight and over. It is also pointed out by Education Otherwise that LEAs usually determine their own criteria, which parents in their areas are expected to follow. Although there is variation between what the different authorities ask for, parents proposing to educate their children themselves may expect that they will want to be satisfied on the following points:

1 there will be regular, varied and flexible opportunities for learning and that for the younger age group this will include reading, writing and numbers;
2 there will be adequate opportunities for outdoor physical activities;
3 the children will have adequate companionship.

When learning on a one-to-one basis at home, progress is likely to be much more rapid than when a child is in a class of about thirty children. This is particularly the case where a gifted child is concerned. Ruth Lawrence, the girl about whom there was so much publicity, was educated at home by her parents and gained entrance to Oxford to take a degree in mathematics at the age of twelve. The faster the rate at which academic work is completed, the more time there is, presumably, for physical recreation and other social activities.

Which state school?
The 1980 Education Act strengthens Section 76 of the 1944 Act, which states that wherever it is possible to comply with parental wishes as regards their children's schooling, without undue public expenditure and misuse of resources, the LEAs should seek to do so. The new Act lays down that LEAs and the governors of the voluntary-aided (mainly church) schools must publish their rules regarding admission and the number of places available in the age groups in which children are normally admitted. It must also be made clear to parents that they may express a preference for a particular school, and what the appeals procedure is if their child is not given a place.

Under Section 6, Parental Preference, of the 1980 Education Act, the LEAs and governors of the voluntary schools must allow children to go to the school which their parents choose, unless there are valid reasons for not doing so. These are:

1 if it would 'prejudice the provision of efficient education or the efficient use of resources';
2 if it would be incompatible with the arrangements for admission made between the LEA and the governors of a voluntary-aided school, and
3 if, for a selective school, a child is unable to pass the tests for ability and aptitude.

Since what is, or is not, considered to be 'efficient education or the efficient use of resources' is not defined, schools are left to interpret these terms as they see fit. The new legislation does not mean that a child will be automatically admitted to the school a parent has chosen, but that the authorities should have justifiable reasons for refusing a parent's request.

These reasons can be of two types, between which there is a certain amount of overlap. Either your child does not come within those categories of entrants to which the admissions policy adopted by the authorities gives priority, and applications for a school place from eligible parents have left no spare places; or your child is not considered suitable for enrolment in the school you have chosen. The parents whose children are likely to be given priority for a particular school are those for whom it is the nearest school, or who already have one child attending. Although the 1980 Act provides for parents to be able to choose a school maintained by a different LEA, where a child lives on the other side of a county boundary there may not be a place available if the authority administering the school gives preference to children living within its own area, that is, the one over which it has jurisdiction. The voluntary schools, established by bodies other than the local education authority and most often by the churches, are now maintained by the LEA, and the salaries of the staff and other costs are paid by the County Treasurer. There are three categories of voluntary school, all of which have governors appointed by the body which originally set them up. The 'controlled' schools only have a fifth of their governors appointed by their founders, but the 'aided' and 'special-agreement' schools have a majority of their governors selected in this way. These last two types of voluntary school have separate powers and duties in relation to admissions, which are decided by their own governors. The admissions policy is likely to vary from that of the ordinary LEA schools (county schools) in that the church schools will probably give priority to children whose families belong to their church. They may also have certain other priority groups to which they give preference, such as one-parent families. However, no schools are allowed under the Act to discriminate between children on the basis of 'their colour or race'.

The second type of reason for a child being refused admittance to the school chosen by the parent relates to the boy or girl being considered to be unsuitable in some way. An example of this is in those LEA areas where there are still maintained selective secondary schools, that is, grammar schools. Where a child has not obtained sufficiently high scores in the entrance tests, he will not be given a place. It is probable that apart from a child's test scores, particularly if they are borderline, other factors are taken into account. All schools, primary and secondary, keep pupil records, and most authorities require primary heads to complete a secondary transfer form for all their leavers. Apart from grading a child's attainment on reading, writing, number work and possibly other subjects covered in the curriculum, there will probably be comments regarding the child's chief interests and his or her behaviour record in school. If at any time the youngster has been seen by the LEA's educational psychologist or educational welfare officer, their reports will probably accompany the primary head's report to the LEA's office or, when it is known to which secondary school the child will transfer, be sent direct to the head of that school.

Selective secondary schools, and comprehensive schools which enjoy a high reputation in their areas, are likely to have a demand for places in excess of those available. The heads of these schools, then, are in a position to select the children to whom they will offer places. They will do this in accordance with the published admissions policies of their respective schools, but to the extent that these leave them discretionary powers, they are likely to take into account the reports they receive from the children's primary heads. Parents have no right to see these reports, but there is nothing to stop a head from showing them, if he so wishes.

Apart from a child's record of schoolwork and behaviour, a gifted boy or girl may be refused admission to a school on account of his or her age. The local education authorities are not obliged to provide a child with a school place until after his fifth birthday. In many schools, it is left to the head's discretion whether or not he accepts a four-year-old. The chief criteria are likely to be how full his school is, the number of other four-year-olds in the area whose parents will also want him to accept their children, and the views of his teaching staff on the admittance of children under the age of five. Whether a child is mentally and physically advanced compared with most children aged four and is ready to attend school is not usually thought to be an important point for consideration. A four-year-old is unlikely to be offered a place if the answer to any of the three criteria is unfavourable.

A similar set of considerations is likely to be operative in the case of a very bright or gifted child transferring to a secondary school at the age of ten instead of eleven. Again relevant criteria are likely to be the number of pupil places available, how many other parents may also request early entry to secondary education, and the attitude of the teaching staff. There is the added obstacle that many primary school heads do not want an able child to leave their school a year before the normal age of transfer. On a number of occasions a gifted child has been moved up into an older age group during the earlier part of his or her primary schooling, only to have to repeat the fourth year in the juniors so as to be eleven when transferring to the secondary school.

It has become so much the recognised practice for children to transfer at the age of eleven plus, that many parents believe that it is illegal to do so earlier. This is not the case. It has become customary and it is convenient for the schools and the LEAs, but in the case of a gifted child it may be in his or her best interest to transfer early. It is, of course, administratively tidy for all children to move from primary to secondary schools at the age of eleven.

For a number of reasons the advantages and disadvantages of early transfer have not been presented to parents in an unbiased fashion. So frequently have the possible benefits of a child staying within a year group been reiterated and the detrimental effects received no mention, that many teachers in the maintained sector, heads among them, have come to have a genuine belief that it can only be right for all children to move upwards through the school system in groups determined by whether their birthdays fall between 1 September of one year and 31 August of the next!

As we have seen, in independent schools pupils are frequently moved up or down from one year to another according to the standard of their schoolwork and the level of their intellectual ability. There is no legal reason why the same practice should not be followed in the state sector. The law as laid down by the Education Acts applies equally in this respect to fee-paying and LEA free schools. Nor are there any apparent reasons why promoting children out of their age group should be any more detrimental to their emotional and social development in maintained schools than in independent ones. As far as I know, no research on the effects of moving children up and down in the fee-paying schools has been done. It is comparatively easy to find cases where the practice has been beneficial and others which have, in the long term, been shown to be detrimental – usually where a child was moved up two years. It has nearly always been the failures that have received the maximum amount of publicity. It seems, then, that the decision as to whether or not to press for a boy or girl to be accelerated must depend on the child's personality and the particular circumstances of the case.

Another reason for not accelerating a child often given by teachers in maintained schools is that, 'he won't be able to go on to the university anyway until he is eighteen so he'll have to lose a year somewhere. He might as well stay where he is.' It is certainly not the case that the universities do not accept entrants under the age of eighteen. Universities each make their own regulations, on the subject of the age at which they accept boys and girls as undergraduates as well as on other matters. It is not unusual for Oxford University to offer undergraduate places to youngsters of fifteen and sixteen if they have passed the qualifying examinations and interview; we have already mentioned Ruth Lawrence, who, in special circumstances at the age of ten, was accepted for admission two years later. Cambridge University, also, considers applications on their merits, and is prepared for a brilliant student to enter the university under the normal age of eighteen. London University accepts applications from fifteen- and sixteen-year-olds, but an applicant must have had his seventeenth birthday by the first day of the autumn term in which he becomes an undergraduate. The registrars of other universities will provide parents with information on this and other regulations upon request. Institutions of higher education which do not have their own royal charters but are empowered to award degrees, must comply with the regulations laid down by the Council of National Academic Awards (CNAA). This body stipulates that students should *normally* be aged eighteen years by 31 December of the year in which they start a degree or other course at a polytechnic or a similar institution. However, the key word here is 'normally', and where a boy or girl is exceptionally bright and has gained the requisite entrance qualifications, usually two or three GCE A levels, the admissions tutor has discretionary powers to accept the youngster. As regards colleges of further education, early admission to courses can generally be obtained providing the head of the school at which the individual is in attendance gives written permission. The normal age of entry to these colleges is sixteen, so younger entrants should still be at school.

Parents' rights of appeal

Under the 1980 Education Act, parents have legal rights of appeal with regard to their choice of a school for their child. These do not apply to the institutions of higher education which have just been discussed, nor to nursery schools.

As we have seen, when a child starts school at the age of five and at the time of secondary transfer, LEAs must allow parents to express their preference as to the school they wish their child to attend. At other times during the course of either primary or secondary schooling, a parent may feel that for one reason or another it would be to their child's advantage to move to a different school. If, when parents have selected a primary, middle or secondary school for their child, they are subsequently told by the LEA that the boy or girl cannot be admitted to the school in question, they have a legal right of appeal against the decision. The LEA may offer the parents a place in some other school and it will be for them to decide whether to accept it, to hold out for another alternative or to press their case through the appeals procedure.

If as a parent you should wish to appeal against an LEA ruling it is probably wise to do so in the following way. First collect all the information you can about your LEA's general educational policy, their admissions policy regarding their primary or secondary schools – whichever you are interested in – the names of the chairman and of members of the Education Committee, and the appeals procedures. All this information should be readily available at the education offices and should be given to you on request. Second, it is advisable to prepare very carefully your case for your child going to the particular school you have chosen. It is most unlikely that you would win an appeal case by stating that your child was exceptionally intellectually able and that you considered the school you had chosen had a better academic record than the alternative schools available, even though you believed this to be true. The gist of the authority's reply to a suggestion of this sort would probably be that all their schools were efficient and that their teaching staff took steps to make adequate educational provision for pupils of all levels of ability. In making a claim that your child is not, or will not be, receiving an appropriate education in the school offered you are, at least by implication, suggesting that your LEA is not fulfilling its duty under Secton 8 (1) (b) of the 1944 Act requiring all local education authorities to afford 'for all pupils opportunities for education offering such variety of instruction and training as may be desirable in view of their different ages, abilities and aptitudes . . .'.

If you wish to obtain a place in a school where you consider the curriculum and teaching will be more advantageous to your child, it is better to base your appeal on one or more of the following reasons. The school you choose is more suitable because:

1 it is the nearest or the most convenient as regards transport;
2 you prefer a single-sex or coeducational school, as the case may be;
3 you have some family association with the school or you have cousins, other relatives or close friends attending the school;
4 you have religious reasons for choosing the school.

Once you have decided to make a formal appeal for a reconsideration of your request, you should write to the Clerk to the Appeal Committee at the education offices, giving formal notice that you intend to appeal for a place at the school you name, giving your child's name and date of birth and setting out your reasons for making the appeal. Once the LEA has received your notification, the education office will let you know the procedures if they have not already done so.

Parents who require further information about the new provisions concerning parental choice of schools in the maintained sector and the related appeals system are referred to the 1980 Act itself and to the Advisory Centre for Education handbook, *Schools Choice Appeals*. However, no reference to the needs of gifted or very able children will be found.

Under the 1980 Act, Section 7, parents have a right to appeal to a local ombudsman, at the Commissions for Local Administration. The decision of an appeal committee is binding, but if a parent considers that the *composition* of the appeal committee is improper – for instance, no person should be on it who was responsible for taking the original decision against which the appeal is being made – this would be a matter to refer to the local ombudsman. Parents also have a legal right to complain to the Secretary of State for Education in England or Wales if they consider that an LEA is acting or proposing to act 'unreasonably' or is failing to discharge its duties.

Educating your child at home

As has already been said, you as parents have a legal right to educate your child at home if you satisfy your education authority that the education you are providing is efficient. At this point the question that will worry most parents of gifted and talented children is whether or not the all-round effects, including the long-term results, will benefit their son or daughter to a greater extent than if they stayed at school.

There is no simple answer to this question. Whether it will be to a child's advantage to be educated out of school will depend on the particular situation in which a gifted or very bright child is placed. In the hope of helping families reach a correct decision for the bright or gifted child in question, the most that can be done here is to set out some of the issues:

1   the effects of the social expectation that all children go to school;
2   faster academic progress;
3   the kind of learning materials and teaching that will be provided;
4   arrangements for regular work and discipline;
5   friendships and social relationships with other children.

It has been an accepted practice in our society that unless they are ill all children should, and with very few exceptions do, go to school. There are truants who, though sent to school by their parents, do not attend, and a few are kept away from school illegally to work with or for their parents, perhaps selling something, helping on the land, in fairgrounds and so on. In the first case it is the children who break the law, in the second it is the parents.

Education Otherwise, the organisation of families practising or contemplating home-based education (see p. 187), was set up in 1977, and in January 1983 claimed a membership of a thousand families or individuals; but, although they are becoming less so, children who are kept out of school for their own benefit are rare. The almost universally held view is that children should go to school and that parents who do not send them there are depriving them of the benefits of education and of the enjoyment of social and sporting activities with other youngsters of their own age. It follows, then, that people who keep their children away from school may be treated with a certain amount of hostility by neighbours and considered as rather peculiar. Some parents are so convinced that they are doing the right thing for their children in keeping them out of school – and in the case of a few gifted and talented youngsters it may be that they are – that they are prepared to put up with the criticism and unpopularity. As for the children, the attitude adopted towards them by the adult community may be one of sympathy, a feeling that the youngsters are being deprived by 'cranky' parents of their rights to schooling. Other children in the neighbourhood, or those belonging to relatives of the family, will probably view any child not attending school as 'lucky'. Certainly a gifted child kept out of school is unlikely to be any the less popular among his contemporaries than he would be if attending school in the usual way.

Usually a child will learn much more quickly when taught on a one-to-one basis at home than when in a class of, say, thirty children. When on his own he can work at his own pace and this, in the case of bright and gifted children, is likely to be very fast compared with most children of the same age. There are two reasons why an intellectually clever child will learn more rapidly in the home situation. The first is that he will not have to do 'more of the same' kind of work, as he probably would if he were still at a primary school; nor will he have to mark time while the slower members of the class struggle to understand the content of a lesson, as he probably would have to do if he were in a secondary school. The second reason is that there are all sorts of disturbances and interruptions in school. In secondary schools the first five minutes of a class can easily be taken up by the teacher making his way from another classroom; then the register may have to be taken and several more minutes often go by while the class is settling down, getting out the appropriate books and so on; time may be lost at the end of the class, too, when work is put away and books tidied up in good time for when the bell goes. In primary schools children have much more freedom to walk about the classroom and even about the school, and some minutes are needed for a class of thirty children to be moved into the hall or some other place in order to watch a TV programme, and yet more while they settle down again; and the whole process is repeated when they move back to their classroom.

Primary school teachers often claim that they meet the individual learning needs of their pupils by using work-cards of different levels of difficulty. Although this is so, the most advanced of these cards are unlikely to be sufficiently stimulating and challenging to hold the interest of a gifted ten-year-old. There seems little doubt that, as far as academic learning is concerned, a gifted child will probably make more satisfactory progress at home.

Who will teach the boy or girl and what books and other learning aids will be available? There are in fact plenty of ways in which a child can learn out of school. First, books: there are numerous schoolbooks available for all stages of learning, including the many topics of the complete primary and secondary school curricula. For four- and five-year-olds there are numerous general knowledge books, and workbooks for English and number work with blanks left for the child to complete sentences or fill in missing numbers. Similarly, there are more advanced books suitable for the use of eight- and nine-year-olds, and yet others for those at secondary stage. The best place to see these books is at one of the exhibitions held by educational publishers (the Publishers Association will tell you where and when on the phone). The World Education Service and the National Extension College offer home education and correspondence courses, respectively.

Most junior libraries have holiday sessions for children, in story-reading and other activities as well. Many library notice-boards give information about all sorts of clubs – from the more serious such as literary circles, French and German clubs and computer clubs, to those that are purely recreational or sporting. Not all of these will be found in any one area – except perhaps in the largest cities – but most parents will probably find two or three clubs which will interest their boy or girl. Most of these organisations are conducted by adults for other interested adults, and if children usually do not belong it is not because they are specifically excluded. Most children do not have sufficient knowledge or interest in the particular subject and are not mature enough in their general outlook, but in the case of many gifted teenagers, none of this applies. If one or both parents should also happen to have the same interest – for instance, in photography or in flying electronically controlled model aeroplanes – then father and son, say, could both join the club and take part in its activities together. There are museums and other places of interest where there is a great deal to be learnt, many of which supply worksheets with questions about the various exhibits, and children are encouraged to find the answers by going round the various items on display.

Much is to be learnt, too, from the BBC and ITN schools' programmes. Course booklets which accompany the programmes can be obtained from the BBC and ITN. The public libraries have a very wide range of books on their shelves and will obtain others for you on request.

Should your son or daughter need extra help with any particular subject, a small classified advertisement in the local newspaper for one or two hours' tutoring a week will almost certainly bring a response from such people as retired teachers who would be willing to give him or her some coaching for a reasonable fee. When the time comes for your youngster to take GCE O or A level examinations, you can enter him or her. There are really very few problems involved with obtaining the facilities to educate your child yourself.

How do you ensure that your child studies regularly, and how do you maintain discipline in the home? You will probably find it easier if realistic – not too long – regular hours for schoolwork are agreed upon by you and your child. Once made, the arrangements should be adhered to strictly, and only in really exceptional circumstances should the agreed hours of work be interrupted; everyday distractions should not be allowed to interfere with the schedule. Working at home requires self-discipline, and for most people this does not come easily. If a daily routine is agreed between all members of the family – the children as well as the adults – and it becomes habitual, less time and energy will be wasted on arguments as to who is going to do what at any particular time.

A definite period, say nine to eleven o'clock in the morning, might be set aside for 'book' work, and another period – not necessarily daily but possibly twice-weekly – for 'outside' work, when visits can be made to the library and shops to change or buy books. Many libraries now have loan services for such things as records, music cassettes and scores, cassettes of children's stories, adult fiction, and literature, plays by Shakespeare, Bernard Shaw and so on; there may be slide packs on different subjects, and 'subject folders' – collections of booklets, slides, tapes, etc. on specific topics. Some libraries may have video tapes on loan, and may either have or know of a computing centre open to the public. For instance, Stevenage has a computer centre which, although accommodated in a secondary school, is available for the use of any Stevenage resident, and puts on courses on computing.

A period of, say, two hours in the afternoon might be given over to some physical activity such as swimming, football, riding a bike, or whatever else the child happens to like doing. Then there should be 'free' time when, within reason, he does exactly what he likes. Late afternoon or early evening would probably be the best time for this, when other children are back from school.

A full day's visit to a place of interest such as the zoo, a historic building, the House of Commons if you live in or near London, the live theatre, a concert or a major sporting event might be made monthly. The sort of programme you devise depends, of course, on the age of the child, the sort of things he likes doing, the area in which you live and the facilities available.

Now for the question of discipline. Usually, but of course not always, discipline is easier to exert in a school situation. This is because most children do comply with school regulations and behave as they are expected to do. Normally, too, a gifted child will do as he is told as regards going into one classroom or another, getting out a particular book, carrying out a particular chemical experiment, and so on. There is a degree of formality (although possibly not very much) between teacher and pupil, and it usually comes more naturally for any child to behave in a similar way to the rest of a group of children. In the majority of schools, although the children are rowdy at times, they behave for most of the time in a law-abiding and disciplined manner. At home, the members of a family know each other very well and these days only exceptionally is there any formality between them. In many cases, whether gifted or not, a child will not do what a parent tells him to do without some argument. This is less likely to occur where a regular programme of work, physical recreation and free time has been agreed and so is another reason for adopting a definite plan of activities.

What sort of friendships with other children will a gifted boy or girl be able to make if he or she is not attending school? Perhaps surprisingly, in some cases it is easier for a gifted child to make friends when not attending school. As we have established, with an intellectually gifted child

whose mental age is both greater than his own chronological age and greater than the mental ages of the majority of the children in his class, it is more than likely that
there will be no one there who has reached his level of
intellectual maturity or has similar interests. Where this
is the situation, friendships tend to be one-sided. Often a
gifted child has no friends in school in the true sense, but
he puts on an act so as to appear on good terms with the
other children and so as not to be the odd man out.
Intellectually advanced youngsters often find that they
have more in common with older people, and they are able
to make real friends more readily in the less structured
situation of the neighbourhood than in school.

The division of children into age groups and then again
into classes makes it difficult in school for anyone to
become really friendly with a pupil in another year group,
or, for that matter, in another class. This is partly due to
the fact that pupils belonging to a particular teaching
group will usually move about a school as a set, and partly
– perhaps more importantly – because there is a tendency
for pupils in an older year group to consider themselves
'above' the lower forms. So although a boy in the fourth
year might, if he really came to know him, find he had a lot
in common with a gifted second-former, it is unlikely that
the initial psychological barrier, reinforced by the lack of
opportunity for fourth- and second-formers to meet in
school, would be overcome sufficiently for a friendship to
become established. On the other hand, it will happen
quite frequently in some schools that there are several
very bright or gifted children in one class. Where this
occurs, it is almost certainly easier for friendships of a
lasting nature to grow up between them and to continue
into adult life.

When should a child not go to school?
This is the key question. We have seen that it is legal and
possible for a boy or girl to be educated efficiently at home.
In the case of *your* child, will he or she derive more benefit
from attending school or from being educated at home?
There is no easy answer to this question, and the parents
of each child must consider for themselves in the light of
all the circumstances what is likely to be the best course to

adopt. Here all that can be done is to draw attention to some of the factors to take into account.

On balance, it will be better for your child to attend school than not to do so, but if he does not do so it does not mean that his future will automatically be prejudiced – in some cases prospects may be improved. One of the most important things to take into account is your child's personality. If he is a lively, outgoing boy who finds it easy to get on with people, he will probably be better off attending school even if you do not expect him to learn much with regard to academic subjects. It may well be that he will enjoy and benefit from the sporting facilities, and he will become accustomed to mixing with people, both children and adults. He will gain a knowledge of people, which is useful in itself. Also, he will have done the accepted thing, and so, when the time comes for him to fill in application forms for higher education or jobs, he will not be faced with the embarrassment of having to answer questions about what schools he attended. One couple that I know did send their boy to an LEA school for just these reasons, with the agreement of the headmaster. The school admitted that they were unable to teach him any-thing more academically, so it was agreed that the boy should go to school for the benefit of mixing with the other boys and for the sport, but that the parents would look after his academic work at home. They were both universi-ty lecturers.

The case is less clear-cut if a gifted child is quiet and shy. He may merely sit unhappily at the back of a class and come to feel that there is something wrong with him. Other children, and teachers, do not expect him to know and do the things that come so easily to him, and he realises that he is different from other people. In spite of being able to do so many things with ease, the one thing he cannot do is to 'get on the same wavelength' with the other people he is with. He knows that the other children, and quite likely some of the teachers, too, do not like him, and he may develop a sense of guilt about his intellectual abilities. All this can lead a child to cover up his or her intellectual ability. Sometimes it can lead to extremely naughty or, when older, delinquent, behaviour, as the gifted youngster tries to win the approval of others of his or her own age. In cases of this sort, it is probable that a child will develop more satisfactorily out of, rather than in, school.

Then there are those very bright or gifted children who are terrified of going to school because they are teased or bullied by the other children – this may happen, of course, to any child whether exceptionally clever or not – without the school staff being able to maintain discipline adequately. Sometimes the mental agony of going to school is so great that it gives rise to physical symptoms – tummy aches, sickness, loss of appetite, headaches, and so on. In all instances of this sort, parents would be well advised to see their doctor and to ask for the boy or girl to be seen by a psychologist (through medical channels rather than the educational psychologist attached to the LEA) and possibly by a psychiatrist. But in the end, when the experts have used their expertise to advise you on what they believe is the best solution to the problem, it will be for *you* to decide whether or not to take their advice; for no one, in normal circumstances, will know more about a child than his or her mother or father.

7   Adolescence: The Choices and Opportunities

While in their primary schools all but a very few boys and girls are children in the true sense of the word, but many of them, soon after they start at a secondary school at the age of eleven, begin to enter the period of adolescence. Physical as well as mental changes take place as the child gradually develops over three or four years into a young woman or man.

The period of adolescence is a difficult one in most families. The relationships which have been established between parents and child alter, and parents have to change their attitudes to their offspring and recognise that they are individuals in their own right. The boys and girls for their part have to come to terms with the fact that the world about them is far from ideal, and that their parents, their teachers, the school and other institutions with which they are involved all have their weaknesses as well as their strengths. Most importantly, the youngsters have to come to appreciate that besides having their rights, and many of the things that they need or want freely given to them, they have responsibilities too and must play a constructive part in their families, in their schools and in the clubs of which they are members. Teenagers have to learn to give as well as take from the community to which they belong.

The adolescent gradually has to recognise that he must take over the responsibility for his own future. Whereas, as a child, he did as he was told (possibly with a certain amount of grumbling) just because he was told to do so by his parents or teachers, as a young adolescent he questions the point of doing this or that. This leads logically, over a period of time, to a boy or girl asking him or herself what are the things he or she wants to do as an adult – which brings the youngster back to considering the options he or she should choose while still in school.

For the gifted child it is probable that adolescence will be an even more intense period than it is for youngsters in general. The vivid imaginations possessed by so many of the gifted are likely to make the fears and uncertainties which are normal in adolescence even greater than usual. For instance, in spite of indisputable evidence of exceptional academic ability, an adolescent may become racked with anxiety as to whether he will pass his GCE O level examinations. Intellectually gifted youngsters will, of course, go through the same developmental stages during the course of adolescence as others, but they may do so rather earlier than most. This is not likely to make the problems associated with adolescence any the less.

Differences develop between the sexes during these years. As well as the physical aspects of adolescence, distinct changes take place also in the interests which boys and girls have – old ones are given up and new ones emerge. It is during adolescence, too, that most boys and girls become particularly interested in and affected by others in their own age group. They become very conscious of their appearance, and are most anxious to look and do the same as others of their own sex in their own friendship group. While following, often slavishly, the behaviour patterns of youngsters in their own set, they become increasingly interested in those of about the same age but of the opposite sex.

The gifted youngster becomes, like other boys, self-conscious; he has doubts about his own academic capabilities, yet he may spend considerable time away from it so as to be 'one of the boys', and may perhaps spend even more time trying to attract one of the girls. The conflicts that he finds within himself often make him erratic and irritable, so that his family may find him difficult to live with. Girls behave in a similar manner. Boys naturally become a, if not the, major interest to young women. In one respect the distinction between gifted girls and most of the others of their own sex does appear to be greater than the difference between gifted and most other boys. Many of the intellectually outstanding girls have a liking for mathematics, the sciences and other technical subjects, whereas many girls either have no interest in, or dislike these subjects.

Even though it will not immediately create harmony

within the family circle, it will probably help the situation if parents realise that their son's or daughter's behaviour, however unreasonable and inconsiderate it may be, is typical of adolescence, and that in all likelihood it will be nothing more than a passing phase. If parents are able to understand some of the reasons for their offspring's behaviour, they may be able to find other ways of dealing with it other than by the head-on collisions which frequently occur in so many families with teenage children.

Which school subjects?
At LEA secondary schools normally all children, except perhaps a few of the less able, study the same curriculum for the first two years. In some schools one optional subject is introduced at the beginning of the third year, when the children are thirteen or fourteen. The new subject might be a second foreign language or an additional science, and the children who choose it are usually allowed to give up one of the practical subjects.

As we have seen, there is great variation between schools in the independent sector. Many of the fee-paying schools admit new pupils at either eleven or thirteen, whichever fits in better with the children's earlier schooling. Where youngsters enter a school at eleven there is usually a common curriculum for the whole year group, but one or two subjects like Latin and Greek may be either optional or studied only by the cleverer children. Pupils who enter a public school at thirteen must do English and mathematics, and usually there are a number of other subjects that are also compulsory. The choice is usually to do with which new subjects they will start rather than which are to be given up. In some public schools pupils are able to study four foreign languages, such as French, German, Spanish and Russian; alternatively, instead of two new foreign languages they may do statistics and additional maths.

Few intellectually gifted pupils would not take the opportunity of learning an extra language or another science subject at this stage, but in most schools the facilities will not be available for them to do so. It is open to parents to make private arrangements, perhaps with a correspondence college, for their youngster to undertake additional study, should he wish to do so.

The main subject choices which face parents and their sons and daughters come at the beginning of the following year, when they are mostly fourteen. In the English educational system this is when specialisation begins, and the choice is usually between a mathematics- and science-based curriculum and one made up primarily of the arts subjects such as English, foreign languages and history. The momentousness of the choice is often worrying to parents and to youngsters themselves, as the more advanced work they will do afterwards follows naturally from the choices made at this stage. And the alternatives chosen will also affect the higher education courses taken later on, which in turn will largely determine the type of career the youngsters will follow when their education is complete.

GCE O levels

The situation outlined above is the one which will face most parents with teenage children in LEA comprehensive schools. The school staff will probably emphasise the difficulty of the O level GCE work, and stress that it will be necessary for the boy or girl to work hard in order to obtain good grades. However, if the youngster is very bright or gifted, this will not be the case. A moderately intellectually gifted boy (say, IQ 130+) can usually manage one O level at fourteen and three or four more at fifteen while working, for him, at a reasonable and steady pace. If he has to wait until sixteen, the normal age at which to take O levels, the gifted pupil very often becomes thoroughly bored with the work. At the same time he experiences the normal adolescent's desire to be 'in' with the crowd, as well as a growing interest in members of the opposite sex.

In these circumstances it is not surprising if the gifted youngster pays scant attention to his academic studies and produces work of only average level, or even below. At school he is constantly badgered by the teachers to make more effort with his work and warned that he will not pass his O levels unless he does so. At home his parents reiterate what has been said at school. The boy struggles with himself to do the work in which he has no interest yet which seems to him, all the same, to be pretty easy – although those in the class who have expressed an interest in gaining O levels seem to be having to work hard enough. The gifted boy then begins to think that perhaps he has missed something after all and that it is much harder than he had thought. He may start looking for a different answer to a question from the obvious one – and be marked down in the examination for not having given the standard answer. He may then become thoroughly frustrated with schoolwork and turn his attention to other things – amusements with the 'gang' and courting the attention of an attractive girl!

How can a vicious circle of this sort be avoided? It is essential that a gifted teenager be given enough challenging work to do to maintain his interest. There will then be a healthy balance between the three main facets of his mental development – progress with academic schoolwork, participation in group or team activities with youths of his own age, and an interest in girls. And integral to the changes that are taking place in him will probably be a growing appreciation of moral and ethical standards.

Most teachers, particularly those in LEA schools, will almost certainly insist that you must not put too much pressure on your youngster. They are certainly right in saying that you should not make unreasonable demands, but the sort of boy or girl that teachers have in mind when they give this sort of advice is rarely the very bright or gifted. Their advice is appropriate for the majority of children – but not for your particular child *if* he is intellectually exceptionally able. Parents should be more concerned that their boy or girl is given sufficiently demanding work to do rather than that he or she may be being given too much.

Unfortunately parents often feel guilty when they go against the advice given to them by the teachers – the 'professionals'. It is certainly a great responsibility for parents to take upon themselves, and it is probably advisable for them to arrange for an educational psychologist to test their child privately. If the results support their belief that their child is exceptionally able, this will both give them confidence in insisting that he should have more taxing work to do, and provide the evidence to take to the school in support of their demand.

An 'enriched' curriculum

By the time a child has reached the middle of his secondary school years, it is unwise to move him up into an older age group as this will disrupt the friendships and other relationships that have grown up over the several years that the youngsters have been grouped together in the same form. It is also unwise to do so at this stage for academic reasons, for even if your child has a very high IQ, it is undesirable that he should miss out a whole section of the examination syllabus. In almost all cases, the most preferable measure will be to 'enrich' your child's curriculum. This semi-technical term simply means that he should spend less time on the basic school subjects – as he can work more quickly than the others he can cover the same work in a shorter period – while using the time he saves to study one, or very exceptionally two, additional subjects.

A few schools, generally ones in the independent sector, will provide exceptionally able boys and girls with an enriched curriculum without being asked. In defence of the maintained schools, it must be said that it is not easy for them to provide additional subjects for a very few pupils; it would add organisational difficulties to an already complex situation and, as we have seen, no additional funding is usually available to cater for bright or gifted pupils. If new subject matter *is* provided, your youngster will certainly benefit from the extra stimulation and knowledge.

For a boy or girl halfway through the secondary school, there are three ways in which parents can help: by drawing the attention of the school to the availability of the National Extension College correspondence courses; by seeking the head's permission for the youngster to attend a part-time day or evening course at the local college of further education; and by finding a tutor in some subject in which the child is interested – archaeology, electrical engineering, an unusual foreign language or a new branch of science, for instance – and paying for lessons out of school hours. It is a good idea, and where a youngster has not reached the minimum school leaving age usually necessary, for parents to obtain the head's consent to the arrangement, and to get him to agree to sign the form for the youngster to take an O level in the extra subject. He will probably agree to both these requests providing he is confident that the extra work will not interfere with the child's O level work in school.

In a good public school, pupils can usually start taking one or more O levels, usually mathematics and English, in the summer that they are fourteen. In the top stream the *average* IQ level is probably around at least 130 to 140. The *Sunday Times* magazine of 22 November 1981 reports the head of Winchester College as saying that in the scholarship house, the boys' IQs range from 140 upwards, while it is unusual for a boy to enter the school at all with an IQ of less than 120.

The leading independent schools are academically orientated, and it is not unusual for their ablest pupils to take eleven or twelve O levels, sometimes before they are sixteen. The same can happen in an LEA comprehensive school, but usually there are organisational and staffing difficulties which prevent a boy or girl taking more than eight subjects, and more often the number is five or six or less. Of course, whatever is said here does not apply to every school and every pupil within it, but there is little doubt that in general the opportunities for academic success are greater in the well recognised independent schools than in most of the LEA comprehensive schools.

Adolescent friendships

Turning to the second aspect of adolescent development, the desire of boys and girls in their teens to be members of a group with others of their own age and sex, all schools, with rare exceptions, cater well in this respect. The team games – football, rugby, cricket, hockey, netball – all provide opportunities for boys and girls to cooperate and act as a group in competition with other teams. In swimming, tennis, gymnastics and riding too there are similar occasions when the feeling boys and girls experience of needing to be one of a group can be satisfied. Parents should not consider that their children are wasting their time when they are taking part in such activities. Both boys and girls will do their academic work better if they feel themselves to be accepted and have a sense of belonging to a group.

To the youngsters themselves, an important indicator that they are 'one of the crowd' is their dress. However irritated parents may be with what they consider to be the unsuitable clothes their teenage sons and daughters insist upon wearing, they should try to appreciate how the issue is seen by the youngsters themselves. Their clothes are to them the badge of group membership. They do not view them from a utilitarian point of view, but as a symbol of their young manhood or womanhood, of their independence from the older generation – their parents included – and of their membership of their own generation. Parents who are tolerant of their children's clothes will find that toleration can lead to better all-round relationships between themselves and their children. From this acceptance of the youngster's rights to be an independent person, a mutual respect can develop, and a deep and satisfying friendship between the generations can result.

An area of possible conflict between teenagers and their parents is the friends they make, particularly those they meet in the neighbourhood after school. Parents are, of course, right to try and prevent their boy or girl from forming an unsuitable friendship but this is something which has to be done with caution, lest the youngster feels that his parents are unjustifiably interfering with his right to choose his own friends. Probably it is best for parents to try and tackle this sort of situation in an indirect way if at all possible. Rather than try to keep their child away from other youngsters after school, it is usually better to encourage him or her to take part in the local football or tennis clubs and any other healthy activity that goes on in the neighbourhood. This applies to gifted and talented teenagers just as much as it does to other boys and girls.

The third aspect of adolescent development referred to above is the emergence of an interest in the opposite sex. Probably the most universal anxiety of parents of boys and girls of about this age concerns their friends among the opposite sex. This is indeed a worrying matter, but again toleration, combined with a discreet watchfulness, will prove to be the best approach. To start with, most youngsters become interested in members of the opposite sex in a general way, but in some cases this can lead fairly rapidly to a friendship developing with a particular boy or girl, quite often someone who is a year or two older. It is natural that, once they have acknowledged that their child has become sexually mature, caring parents should want him or her to choose a girl or boy whom they, with their greater experience of the world, consider to be 'suitable'. If parents attempt to press their views on their child as to which member of the opposite sex he or she should associate with, it will almost certainly lead to arguments. It may, in extreme cases, even result in the boy or girl – when he or she is sixteen – leaving home. The Children and Young Persons Act of 1969, and the further Act in 1975, are rather vague. However, youngsters of sixteen are entitled to claim benefit from the DHSS in their own right. If a boy or girl wishes to leave home and co-habit with someone of the opposite sex, it seems they are usually free to do so. Although the parents may apply to the courts for an order for the youngster to return home, it is very unlikely that this will be granted unless there is reason to believe that the he or she is at risk from criminal activity. So if a youngster forms what the parents feel is an undesirable attachment to someone, it is usually better for them not to make a frontal attack and to forbid their son or daughter from continuing to see the person in question. Most young people like to make their own decisions. They feel they are grown up and perfectly capable of doing so. To them the issue is simple and clear-cut: he or she finds someone attractive, is liked in return, so that is all that matters. In such a situation a wise parent, who knows for some reason or other that the match is grossly unsuitable, will let the situation play itself out as far as possible, only interceding as a last resort.

Teenagers tend to be noisy and boisterous. They usually like to listen to pop music with the volume turned up, which often disturbs all the adults in the house. If they are given an abrupt order to turn the sound down, this will probably lead to an argument and a youngster's angry departure from the house. These characteristics are common to intellectually gifted as well as to other adolescents, but there is a greater likelihood of being able to discuss the situation with those who are highly intelligent.

The adults must accept the youngsters' right to their opinions and tastes in dress and music but, this having been agreed, it is usually possible with highly intelligent boys and girls to talk through the situation 'man-to-man' or 'woman-to-woman' and to come to some amicable agreement as to behaviour in the house, when, where and how late the youngster shall go out in the evening and so on. As to your children's choice of friends, whether of the same or of the opposite sex, caring parents will be wise to welcome them all, irrespective of their views on their suitability. Although having several visiting teenagers in the house can be extremely taxing on the patience of parents, this way they can at least know who their children's friends are. When a friend of the opposite sex is brought to the house, the parents – although they must keep in the background or the young people will go somewhere else – will be in a position to meet their child's friend and to exert at least some control over the situation. Where unsuitable friendships have been formed, after a time adolescents quite often come to see this for themselves. In spite of his or her feelings being involved and the fact that sexually aroused emotions are notorious for being unresponsive to reason, the gifted teenager will probably be able to see more easily than most when his or her interests and outlook are incompatible with those of a boy- or girl-friend.

The Assisted Places Scheme
During the earlier part of this chapter the opportunities available for gifted boys and girls to undertake challenging intellectual work in LEA comprehensive schools and in independent secondary schools were outlined. Although the general indications are that a very bright or gifted boy or girl is more likely to be offered a wider choice of subjects and greater stimulation with their academic work in a public school than in many maintained secondary schools, the first point to emphasise here is that this does *not* hold for *all* public or *all* LEA comprehensive schools. It may not be the case with particular comprehen-

sive schools known to you, nor is it with some or the minor public schools.

We have already discussed the greater flexibility of independent schools. In addition, many have excellent specialist facilities for a very broad spectrum of activities, so broad that only a few of them can be indicated here. There are, for instance, science blocks equipped with all that is required for the most modern technological work; music blocks with individual sound-proofed practice rooms; laboratories and workshops for electrical and mechanical engineering; art rooms with sophisticated arrangements for using daylight or artificial light, for all types of art work – painting, etching, ceramics, fashion design; craft rooms for metalwork, woodwork, stone-carving, pottery, jewellery, glass-blowing, and so on. The sports facilities in many of these schools include their own indoor heated swimming baths, indoor and outdoor tennis courts, extensive playing fields, a sports pavilion and a gymnasium. Most schools do not, of course, have all these facilities, but some of the best known establishments do have almost all of them.

In all the larger public schools the school's own chapel provides a place of repose to which the individual can withdraw when he feels the need to, as well as being a place of worship and an adjunct to the ethical and religious education given by the school. In some schools there is provision for pupils other than Christians to practise their religion. Probably most schools will expect all pupils to participate in some type of worship at least once a week. With non-Christians the precise arrangements are very much a matter for individual arrangements between the head and parents.

Although all schools, whether LEA maintained or independent, try to meet the individual needs of their pupils, many of the public schools take special measures to meet this end. In some, small groups of five or six pupils have a weekly meeting lasting an hour or more with a tutor who discusses with each of them the progress they have made and any difficulties they are experiencing with their schoolwork, what books they are reading and so on. In some schools, besides a small group meeting of this sort, the tutor sees each pupil individually each week to discuss his work. This happens particularly at the upper end of the school.

Under the government's Assisted Places Scheme, an opportunity of attending one of these schools has been extended to children whose parents cannot meet the full cost of the fees. The wide range of opportunities available makes it fairly safe to say that in at least one of the large number of schools taking part in the Assisted Places Scheme there will be the teaching and the equipment available to develop any aptitude or interest a boy or girl may possess. The scheme was introduced by the government in 1980 and came into operation in September 1981. Under it five to six thousand assisted places a year are available at selected approved independent schools for the academically able children of less well off parents. A government grant is also available to children who have passed the music audition but whose parents cannot afford the fees at Chetham's School, Wells Cathedral School, the Purcell School and the Yehudi Menuhin School, and similarly to children who have passed the audition for the Royal Ballet School. To be eligible for assistance, children must be 'ordinarily resident' in the United Kingdom, but where British parents are working overseas on contract or with the European Economic Community a child is not normally excluded.

All children, whether they are attending an LEA maintained school, an independent school or one run by the services overseas, are eligible to apply for a place under the scheme; but it is laid down that at least 60 per cent of the assisted pupils must have come directly from one of the LEA or armed services' schools. The usual age at which pupils awarded an assisted place will enter an independent senior school will be either eleven or thirteen. Where a child is particularly gifted, he or she can be admitted at an earlier age. There are also a certain number of places available for youngsters to go directly into the sixth form.

The way in which the scheme operates is for the parents who want their child to be considered to approach the head of the school they have chosen. For England and Wales there is a list of over two hundred schools that have been selected by the government as being of a good academic standard. The list is available from the Department of

Education and Science, and from the Independent Schools' Information Service, the addresses of which are given at the back of this book. The academically able children to be admitted under the scheme will be selected by the schools to which the parents have applied. The first stage in the selection procedure will normally be a written test set by the school. The children who pass this will probably then be interviewed by the head, who will select those felt to be most likely to benefit from admission to his school and most in need of what the school has to offer.

The amount of financial aid offered by the Government under the Assisted Places Scheme depends on the level of the parents' joint income. For the 1982–3 tax year, where the parents' income was not more than £5,617 the parental contribution was only £15 for tuition fees, the amount increasing proportionately for larger incomes until at £13,000 a year the parental contribution was £1,749. These amounts are adjusted to keep pace with inflation. The government scheme does not provide for help with boarding fees, but a number of the participating independent schools will provide assistance with these from their own funds. Some LEAs are also willing to help families with limited means to meet the boarding costs. The Independent Schools' Information Service will give parents further advice on how they can obtain help with the boarding fees. However, in the case of the four music schools and the Royal Ballet School there are different arrangements, and a government grant can be obtained to cover the boarding fees as well as tuition fees where necessary.

A question which must arise in the minds of many parents whose child attends an LEA maintained primary school is that, if they take advantage of the offer of an assisted place under this scheme, will they be doing the right thing for their boy or girl in sending him or her to a different type of school?

Although it is not possible to answer this question for any individual family, who must consider the pros and cons in the light of their own personal situation, it is possible nevertheless to give some general advice and information. The families with worries over this issue will be those whose children are currently attending their local LEA primary school, as those pupils attending a prep. or private junior school are already in the independent sector. As for the four specialist music schools and the Royal Ballet School, competition is so great and the child's talent has to be so exceptional for him or her to be offered a place, that it is very rare indeed for a family to decide in the end to reject it.

It is not accidental that the word 'family' instead of 'parents' has been used in opening this discussion about whether or not to apply for a place at an independent school under the Assisted Places Scheme. The first point that must be stressed is the importance of discussing the question with the boy or girl concerned. It is the youngster whose life is going to be affected – probably dramatically – though the short- and long-term effects will be different. To start with, the child may experience initial difficulties with adapting to a new type of school environment. If he decides he does not wish to stay at the independent school, he is free to return to his former comprehensive school, but if he succeeds in overcoming any initial problems of adjustment, there is probably greater benefit in the long term. As we have said, there is an increased likelihood that the individual's intellectual potential will be more fully realised, and that his career prospects will be improved. The young gifted adult will then have an enhanced opportunity of acquiring a job which is both more intellectually satisfying and more rewarding financially.

If a boy or girl who is attending a primary or the lower part of a comprehensive school is asked whether he or she would like to try for a place in a selective independent school, the reply in nearly all cases will be 'No!' There are two main reasons for this. First, almost everyone has a natural fear of the unknown. However unsatisfactory a child's current school, unless he is suffering from school phobia – the state of refusing to attend school, requiring the professional advice of an educational psychologist or psychiatrist – he will have more or less come to terms with the situation. In another case a child may apparently be progressing satisfactorily in the state school, but while his work may be good to average for the group in which he has been placed, for a gifted child this will still, almost certainly, represent underachievement.

The second reason for a gifted child's negative response to the idea of going to an independent school will probably be lack of self-confidence and an underestimation of the level of his or her own ability. It is difficult to know why high IQ youngsters often tend to underrate their intellectual abilities, but it may be that, compared with most people, adults as well as children, they have a greater awareness of the complexities of life, and so they think of themselves as knowing very little. It is often quite difficult to convince a gifted child that he or she can, and does, do things on average considerably better than other people. It is not unusual for the gifted to demand of themselves far more than is asked of them by others, either at school or at home. Quite often they are perfectionists and they do not like to fail. A mixture of reasons of this sort, engendering a general feeling that they would not be good enough, often gives rise to a fear of taking tests and a belief that they would not be able to cope in an independent school. Of course, if a child is very bright or gifted, these feelings of inadequacy are quite imaginary, and faced with the real situation they score highly on the test and usually adapt easily and quickly to an environment in which, as a rule, there is a greater appreciation of intellectualism than they experienced in their former school.

What then is the parent to do, for it has been suggested here that when the child has been consulted about a possible transfer to an independent school he will almost certainly reply in the negative?

Start by giving the whole question your most careful consideration. Collect together as much information as you can. The first step is to obtain the list of schools participating in the scheme, and to write to three or four (not just one) which for one reason or another you feel might be suitable for your child. When selecting schools to approach, consider whether each is near enough to where you live for your youngster to travel backwards and forwards daily or whether he or she would have to be a boarder. When you first consider the various schools, there will probably appear to be all sorts of insurmountable difficulties. Do not be put off; it is amazing how often, when the real situation is faced, a solution to what seemed previously an intractable problem can be found. If you live in or near one of the big cities there will also most certainly be one or more schools near enough for your child to travel to and fro daily. And even though you may be opposed to the idea of your son or daughter going away to a boarding school, it is worth your while to write to at least one so that you may compare them with independent day schools.

When you have received from the schools their prospectuses and have considered the education and other facilities they offer, it is a good idea to write and ask if you can look round the school, as you are considering applying for your child to be admitted under the Assisted Places Scheme. In reply you will almost certainly receive an invitation to visit, and will usually be offered alternative dates so that you can attend at your convenience.

While you are considering these various matters – in fact from the time you decide to send for the list of schools – it is nearly always desirable to involve your child in the discussions. If he should react by saying he does not want to go to 'one of those schools', you can reassure him that there is no question of him going to another school if he does not want to but . . . there is no harm in finding out about them, is there? A grudging agreement will probably be given to this suggestion. When the list arrives, the youngster can join in the 'fun' of going through it and help choose which schools to write to. Most bright boys and girls will become increasingly interested in the whole issue, and will probably make some very sensible comments as to why one school might be better than another. By the time they have studied the prospectuses and been along to see three or four independent schools, most parents will generally have come to some conclusion as to whether or not it would be a good idea to go ahead with an application under the Assisted Places Scheme. If their verdict is that going to an independent school would probably be in their son's or daughter's long-term interests, then they need to consider their next steps.

First, you must try and convince your child that he or she should at least take the entrance test at one of the schools. If the youngster passes, he does not have to accept the place if at that stage he should decide against it. On the other hand, if he does not apply to take the entrance test but later decides his career prospects would have been better if advantage had been taken of the scheme, by that time the opportunity of doing so may have been lost – although there remains the possibility of entering one of the independent schools at sixth-form level.

If you believe it to be in your child's interest to attend an independent school, then fill in the application forms of two, possibly three, schools. If in the end you or your child should decide against accepting a place, the offer can be turned down. It is very unlikely that this will cause much inconvenience at the school; the probability is that the vacancy will merely be transferred to the next child on the results list who would otherwise have been refused a place.

Opportunities for independent learning

A family may decide that they do not want a boy or girl to change over to the independent sector, but feel all the same that his time at school is not being used to the best advantage. There are other ways to help him gain as many qualifications as possible. Usually the first step is to make an appointment to see the appropriate senior member of staff at the school and to put these points to him. If the school cannot make any extra provision – and it is probable that the staffing and facilities will not permit it to – the head or his deputy may agree to give written permission for the youngster to undertake further studies outside school, via a correspondence course, attendance at a college of further education, or private tutoring. It is quite possible for a well motivated bright or gifted youngster to study for O and A level GCE subjects in these ways. The names and addresses of nearby colleges of further education can be obtained from your local authority's education offices, and the addresses of well recognised correspondence colleges are given at the back of this book.

School and public examinations

In our technological society, examinations are the means by which individuals are chosen for jobs. The marks awarded rank the examinees according to how well they have displayed the ability they possess in whatever subject or skill they are being examined. There are two points here: first, examination marks can only reflect what an individual *does* do, which is not necessarily the same as what he *can* do; second, only those who take the examination can, of course, be ranked. Both these aspects of the examination system are of concern to everyone who needs paper qualifications for the work he wants to do. A well set examination paper, which is neither too easy nor too difficult, should reflect as closely as possible what a candidate *can* do. If the paper is too difficult, a number of candidates may find that they cannot answer any of the questions and be unable to display what they know about the subject. This will mean that the examination will not distinguish between the weaker candidates, indicating which individuals have some, if an inadequate knowledge of the subject, and which have no knowledge of the subject at all. If the paper is too easy, it will not differentiate the ablest candidates from the rest, since the ablest will have no opportunity to show the extent of their knowledge, and many candidates may submit correct answers to the entire question paper.

The examination system assumes that candidates will endeavour to answer the question papers set to the best of their ability. To the extent that examinees do not *always* do this, the examination will *not always* indicate those individuals with the most ability in the area of knowledge being tested. Nonetheless, extensive use of examinations for measuring youngsters' levels of ability has shown that, although they are rough and ready tools, most boys and girls do do their best and so the results reflect *approximately* the extent of candidates' knowledge and their order of merit. At least to date no one has devised a better method of performing these functions on a mass scale.

For the gifted and very bright, the examination system can operate quite differently from the way it normally does in indicating the extent and limitations of the average candidate.

All through their years in infant and then junior school, many gifted and very bright pupils have found what they were asked to do to be elementary. As a result, far from being stimulated by school, they have learnt to conceal the extent of their intellectual ability for fear of being unpopular with the other children, and perhaps with the class teacher too. Frequently they will develop the habit of underfunctioning. Such children find it difficult to appreciate that, after having for six of their most impressionable school years adapted to a, for them, unnaturally slow pace of work, upon entering secondary school the time has come for a change in attitude. In any case, since most comprehensive schools have mixed-ability classes for the first two years, very bright pupils will still find the pace slow. There will be nothing to indicate to them that their future prospects will be prejudiced if they do not make some effort with their day-to-day schoolwork, until they are in the third year when it may be too late.

It is quite common for gifted pupils to score higher marks in school examinations than their teachers had expected. This is partly because the class's general atmosphere of anxiety about passing the exam communicates itself to the brightest who, as a result, exert themselves to make some effort during the last few pre-examination days – like everyone else, they do not want to fail. It is partly, too, because intellectually gifted children usually like a challenge, and an examination is seen as such. The very able, then, are likely to come out with *fairly* high examination marks compared with the others in the class. What the examination has not shown is that they would have been capable of scoring an equivalent mark in a more advanced examination! If these boys and girls had been presented with more stimulating work during term time, in many cases they would have made a consistent effort with their academic studies. Their examination marks would then have reflected their high IQ and superior intellectual abilities.

Unfortunately for the very bright, the general practice has grown up in schools of judging pupils' abilities as much on their term work as on their examination results. There is a tendency on the part of teachers, where there is a marked discrepancy between a child's everyday performance and his examination results, to judge the first as being the more reliable indicator and the high examination mark as being the result of good luck! Consequently, when the pupils are grouped at the end of a school year, many of the very bright and gifted youngsters may be put into the lower 'sets' for mathematics, French and so on, and into the lower 'bands' or 'streams', too, if the school has these. Recent research that I carried out among over five thousand comprehensive school pupils revealed that over 8 per cent were gifted in some way, but that two thirds of these went unrecognised by their teachers. Once, of course, the very able children are placed in the lower subject sets, they tend to adjust to the lower level of school expectations. The degree of underfunctioning by gifted pupils may increase, and the whole process outlined above may repeat itself with lower and lower levels of academic performance as they move up the school.

It is on the basis of children's academic records, usually for the first three years during which they are in a secondary school, that teachers decide which youngsters will be entered for GCE O level and CSE examinations, and how many and which subjects each individual pupil will be allowed to take. If parents protest at the small number of subjects for which their child is being entered, a senior member of staff will merely show them the youngster's work record, making it extremely difficult for parents to do anything other than accept it. A child's number of O level passes (which will, of course, depend in part upon the number of subjects for which he has been entered) will be the basis upon which it is decided how many and which subjects the youngster should study for A level. Acceptance on a university course or some other form of higher education depends, in its turn, very largely on an applicant's O and A level GCE passes and grades.

There are several GCE examination boards, and the regulations as regards entry requirements vary. It is expected that candidates will be aged sixteen when they sit O level examinations, but it is not unusual for youngsters to take two or three subjects at the age of fourteen or fifteen *providing* the school they attend will sign the entry form. Although the staff of some schools are under the impression that children must be sixteen before they may take these examinations, this is not the case with several of the boards. Independent schools frequently, and maintained schools occasionally, enter their brightest pupils for two or three subjects when they are fourteen and, on very rare occasions, at even younger ages. The London

University GCE Examination Board has no lower or upper age limits.

Where a boy or girl of school age is not attending school but is being educated at home, parents should approach one or more of the examining boards to find out what special arrangements are made for children under the age of sixteen, or for that matter at sixteen if the youngster has reached that age, to take GCE O or A level examinations. Special arrangements have been made in a number of instances for a child to sit one or more of these examinations at a very young age. The most exceptional case in recent years has been that of Ruth Lawrence, mentioned earlier, who passed GCE A level mathematics when she was nine.

8 Career Prospects

By the time they are in their teens, most boys and girls have some idea of what they would like to do when they are adults. There are very few youngsters who do not want to do anything with their lives, and the proportion is almost certainly smaller still for intellectually gifted and talented children.

When young people say they do not know what sort of job they would like to do when they are older, this may be either because they just have not thought about it or because, consciously or unconsciously, they feel there is no chance of achieving their ambition and so they do not want to talk about it. This attitude has become more general with the current reduction of places in higher education and the greater competition for those which remain. Among many youngsters, too, there is a feeling of desolation and hopelessness on account of the high unemployment rate, which is particularly severe among young people. But although it is understandable that boys and girls should feel like this, to adopt such an attitude is, of course, the worst thing to do. Even if their secret wish is a childish fantasy, it is quite likely to indicate the sort of job in which they would be likely to find the most satisfaction. If they follow up their natural bent with private study, and part-time or voluntary work, they will gain knowledge and practical experience which will increase the likelihood of obtaining a job. In any case, very bright youngsters have a greater possibility than the majority of doing so in the more sought-after occupations.

There are several points to bear in mind which are particularly relevant to the future careers of exceptionally able boys and girls. First, the options as to what their subsequent career may be should be kept open as long as possible in order that, when the time comes, they should have a maximum degree of choice. Second, they should be encouraged to think and talk about their futures at a comparatively early age, that is, once they enter adolescence. Third, they should be given as many opportunities as possible to learn about different occupations and what it is like to work in them. Intellectually gifted children usually see the importance of this approach, and are able to adopt it.

As for talented youngsters, it is frequently necessary for them to be committed from early childhood to their future profession, on account of the particular physical skills they must develop. This applies to gymnasts, acrobats and other circus artists, and to some musicians, such as violinists, who aim to become concert performers. Of course, a number of these youngsters may develop different ambitions as they reach adolescence, so it is desirable to keep their options open as far as possible too, so that they will be able to follow an alternative career should they wish to do so.

The importance of GCE O and A level qualifications
Most exceptionally able teenagers are all-rounders. My research into the characteristics of gifted pupils in six comprehensive schools showed this to be the case, and other researchers in the United States have found the same.

So although exceptionally able pupils are individually more interested in, and better at, one school subject rather than another, they are often found to be good at all the academic subjects and at sport as well. This means that they are capable of obtaining GCE O level passes in a wide range of subjects, say, mathematics, the three sciences, chemistry, physics and biology, English language and literature, French, German, history, geography, art and music – a total of twelve subjects. Most schools send parents a list of options at the end of the third year, from which they are asked to choose the subjects their child will be taking the following year, when he or she enters the fourth year and begins serious work leading up to the GCE O level exams at the end of the fifth. As we have said, intellectually gifted pupils are often quite capable of taking all twelve subjects, particularly if they are allowed to take three of them, say, mathematics, English language and one other at the end of the fourth year, leaving the rest until the end of their fifth.

Unfortunately, in many maintained schools the time-tabling and staffing arrangements will not allow pupils to do this. If, as is often the case in comprehensive schools, pupils cannot take GCE O levels until their fifth year when the maximum is eight subjects, it is probably best for youngsters to choose those subjects which need laboratory equipment, the sciences, and mathematics. Few facilities are required for studying English literature and history, and so it is not difficult to study such subjects privately. Although this is so, there can be an advantage if a young-ster chooses a mixture of science and arts subjects, en-abling him or her to remain free to specialise in either the sciences, mathematics or arts subjects when it comes to choosing which GCE 'A' Levels to take in the sixth form. The choice of a future career will also remain open for as long as possible. Which alternative will benefit a boy or girl most will depend upon individual circumstances.

The long-term value of taking ten or twelve O levels is twofold. First, it ensures that the youngster receives a broad education and is introduced into a large number of different subject disciplines. While, of course, academic learning is not limited by whether an individual is entered for an examination – there is nothing to stop anyone learning history by themselves and no need to enter for a GCE O level in order to obtain a good knowledge of the subject – there is no doubt that having a specific aim and syllabus does help to ensure that a course of study is carried out. Providing a boy or girl is really very bright or gifted, so that taking ten or more O levels is well within his or her capabilities, being entered for public examina-tions rather than just being allowed to study from interest gives the youngster a desirable target. Furthermore, once having passed the examinations – and there is no reason to doubt that those who are genuinely very able will do so – boys and girls will gain a sense of achievement which will increase their self-confidence. At the pre-O level stage the prospect of a broad spectrum of examinations looming ahead will serve to prevent time being wasted in just watching TV or listening to pop music for hours on end. At the other extreme, it will serve to prevent over-specialisation on a narrow subject of study or hobby such as chess, wiring electric circuits, computer technology, bird-watching, military strategies, and so on.

The second reason for obtaining good grades in as many O level examinations as possible is the one that is usually given – the results are nearly always the basis on which pupils are admitted to GCE A level courses. These in their turn are main routes to obtaining a university degree or correspondingly high qualification, with a view to entering one of the professions or industrial or commercial management, or to becoming an expert in one of the more advanced branches of technology. It is still just possible to avoid this well trodden path to obtaining an intellectually satisfying job, but it is safe to say that all the other routes are more difficult to follow and are less reliable.

Choosing a career

I suggested earlier that gifted youngsters should be encouraged to discuss possible future careers at a comparatively young age. Many young people reach the end of their university degree courses without being sure as to the career they wish to follow, so it is certainly not a case of *expecting* a teenager to *know* what he wants to do when he has finished his education. It will, though, help him if he has some idea of what he wants to do when the time comes to decide. It is useful, for instance, for a child to think about whether he would prefer to work in the open air or in a building, and whether the prospect of working with things, machines, perhaps computers, or dealing with people as in personnel management appeals to him most. Even though he may change his ideas completely about even these broad categories of work, when he has to make choices later he will be better placed for making the right one if, over a period of time, he has given some thought to and talked over the various alternatives. If it is advantageous for most youngsters to give thought to their futures, it is particularly important for the very bright and gifted to do so, since their greater ability opens up more alternatives to them.

If youngsters are to think usefully about the sort of jobs they would like to do as young adults, they will need to know as much as possible about the sort of work the job entails, conditions, promotion prospects, rates of pay and the likely competition to be met in obtaining employment of the kind they are contemplating. This brings us to the last of the three points listed at the beginning of the chapter – that adolescents should be given as many opportunities as possible to learn about various occupations.

The first way of doing this is to obtain books about different jobs from the school careers department and the public library. Most books that describe the different jobs that people do will be found in the library section under 'Careers'. A different view of a job can be obtained by reading a novel that gives a picture of what it is like to work in the sort of job in question. For instance, there are novels set in hospitals which will give an idea of the lives of doctors and nurses; others are set on farms, and particularly well known are the books by James Herriot about his life as a Yorkshire vet. A word of caution is necessary here: novels are likely to give a romanticised view of what it is like to follow the occupations in question. The non-fictional careers booklets usually give a better idea about what a job is really like, though they too may give insufficient emphasis to the less pleasant aspects.

Work experience

A boy or girl will be greatly helped in obtaining a realistic view of a job if he or she has an opportunity of working in a firm. The Government's Youth Training Scheme, which is operated by the Manpower Services Commission, gives youngsters an opportunity for practical experience of working in a firm, as well as course-work at a college. Even though they are trainees and only work in a firm for a few weeks, in addition to the actual training given, they will gain from contact with the people doing the job that they would like to do. 'Work experience', as this is called, enables youngsters to learn something about the adult world and about the disciplines and routine of working life.

Teenagers will probably find that if they take part in a work experience scheme in a factory or office they will be given unskilled, routine work to do, and not the kind that they hope and expect to do at a later date. This can hardly be avoided as they will, after all, be inexperienced school-leavers – albeit gifted ones! Nevertheless, they will learn a great deal from being with adults in an industrial or commercial setting. They may learn something about the job they think they would like to do when they have finished their education, and the experience may either confirm them in their desire or make them realise it is not really what they want.

With gifted youngsters, it is likely that after they have completed their education at a university or polytechnic they will enter one of the more prestigious occupations. Participation in a work experience scheme may be the only time in their lives when they will do the work normally performed by the lower paid sections of our society, and the experience may give them a view of an aspect of society with which they are unfamiliar.

There are a number of ways in which teenagers can obtain work experience. First, the careers teachers in secondary schools often make arrangements for older pupils to spend a few weeks in a firm, a hospital or a factory. If nothing suitable is forthcoming from this source, youngsters who are over sixteen can go along to their local careers office and ask for help there.

In addition, many parents may be able to arrange for their son or daughter to spend a few weeks at their own place of work, or may have a friend or relative who can arrange it. If none of these suggestions are of any avail, a youngster might find an opening by writing to the personnel officers of local firms.

Part-time work
Another way of obtaining working experience is by finding a part-time job. For those over sixteen it is worth watching the small ads in the local newspapers, although temporary jobs are rather rare and competition for them considerable. Another way of seeking work is to telephone or call on shops, garages, garden centres and so on, as these firms sometimes employ youngsters on Saturdays or on both days of the weekend.

Taking a part-time job is usually frowned on by parents, but here again the position is different for the very bright and gifted. They should not, of course, be overloaded, for there is a limit to the amount of work, academic or otherwise, that they can do. At the same time, it is probable that the capabilities of an individual with an IQ of 130+ are not being used to full advantage in school. For example, if a gifted sixteen-year-old is taking seven or eight O levels, which is probably the most he or she will have the opportunity of doing in the majority of comprehensive schools, having a part-time job for seven or eight hours at weekends – serving in a shop or perhaps spending two or three weeks during holidays serving petrol or as a waitress – may have the effect of making the boy or girl feel more interested in academic work when he or she returns to it. The youngster will derive greater benefit, too, by doing several short periods with various employers, which will enable him to appreciate something of the vast differences between firms and give him an opportunity to meet more people from different walks of life. Experiences of this sort are education too, in a broader and perhaps truer sense of the word!

Higher education
Once a young person has taken his GCE O levels it is time to decide which subjects, and how many, he will take at A level. If he has been allowed to do so, he may have taken one or two O levels when he was fourteen or fifteen, or he may have sat one or more of the A/O GCE papers in English or mathematics, which are of a standard about one year beyond O level. In some independent schools a gifted boy or girl will already have taken an A level examination before entering the sixth form. Where a youngster in a comprehensive school was accelerated into a higher age group during his primary schooling, he will enter the sixth form at fifteen plus. This will make no difference to the two-year A level course which, under normal circumstances, he will begin the September following his O level examinations.

It is at this stage that the individual must choose those subjects that he will study during the next two years. Apart from having to spend many hours on the subjects he selects, his choice will determine which courses he will be eligible for when he leaves school and proceeds to university or other institution of higher education. For this reason it is vital to consider most carefully at this point what career he or she wishes to follow, and how he or she intends to obtain the necessary qualifications.

Once a young person has some idea of what he wants to do in life, it is advisable to have a talk (or perhaps a further talk) with the careers teacher, who should be able to advise him as to the sort of course he will need to take after he has left school, and where such a course is available. There will be prospectuses from various universities and other institutions of higher education in the school's careers room, which the careers teacher will probably encourage him to look through. Near the end of the summer term, after the O level examinations are finished, the careers teacher will probably interview individually each of those pupils who were candidates and make suggestions about what he or she should do the following session. As we have said, greater benefit will be gained from this interview if the youngster has prepared for it in advance by thinking over what he wants to do and by discussing it with his parents.

Most sixth-formers who are aiming to enter a university or take a course at a polytechnic need three A level subjects, although two, and occasionally one, will be acceptable for some university and polytechnic courses. The higher the grades an applicant has, the more likely it is that he will be offered a place, but it is wrong to assume that this is the only factor taken into consideration by admissions tutors. Enthusiasm on the part of a prospective student is also very important. A course of study in four A level subjects spread over two years should provide intellectually gifted pupils with about the right amount of work. A highly gifted youngster would probably be able to handle more than this in his stride, but the number of A levels which can be comfortably managed depends partly on the extent to which the subjects chosen are related to each other.

One gifted girl I know took over the course of two years, without any apparent undue effort, five A level subjects and one A/O examination, spread as follows: first-year sixth – A/O level in English and A level in combined mathematics; second-year sixth – four A levels: in pure mathematics, applied mathematics, physics and chemistry. In this girl's case, the school advised that she should have examinations to work for at the end of her first year in the sixth so as to ensure that she gave some attention to her work.

Parents will probably find that most schools advise against a boy or girl taking more than three A level subjects. The probable reasons for this are, first, that three subjects have been found sufficient for the majority of pupils proceeding to university and, second, merely because this is the accepted number, school timetables have generally been drawn up with a view to pupils taking three or less A levels. To accommodate one or two individuals taking four, faces most maintained and some independent schools with serious difficulties.

It is to the advantage of gifted boys and girls to take the right number of A level examinations *for them*. There are two main reasons for this. First, as a general rule the more A level passes with good grades a young person has, the wider the choice later on. This means that the better his or her A level results, the more likely a youngster is to be accepted by whichever institution of higher education he chooses and for whatever course he wants. An illustration will make this point clearer.

If there are two boys, one of whom has four A levels and the other only two, and both want to go on a particular course which is oversubscribed at a well recognised university, the boy with the four A levels has a good chance of being accepted and the one with two is most unlikely to be offered a place. If, on the other hand, both boys wanted to go to one of the lesser known universities to take a course for which there were few applicants, the probability is that both would be offered a place. So it can be seen that the choices open to the boy with four A levels are greater than those for the boy with only two.

Apart from the practical points that have just been described, there are other reasons why a gifted youngster capable of taking four or more A levels should do so. For those like the girl described on p. 233, the lesson is clear. If she had been allotted only three A levels which she would have taken at the end of her second year, she might have felt, probably correctly, that there was no need for her to make any effort for at least the first nine months. If in fact she had done this, the chances are that when the nine months ended she would have put off making a serious start with her academic work for even longer and, quite possibly, when the examinations eventually came along, she would have been insufficiently prepared and so would have gained indifferent results with perhaps three C grades. In fact, this girl gained three As and two Bs in the five A level papers she sat.

Also, if a gifted youngster studies the number of A level subjects that give him a reasonable amount of work to do, he will be making more profitable use of two of the limited number of years available for education. As a result, the breadth of knowledge gained will be greater than it would have been had his studies been restricted to fewer subjects. Some will say that this reason is the more important of the two offered here, and should have been placed first. But the fact of the matter is that, with our present system of selection by examination for entrance to courses leading to a career, the most important consideration for youngsters must be the acquisition of the qualifications. It is only in this way that they can proceed with the studies that will enable them eventually to obtain the sort of job they want and for which they have the requisite capabilities.

Oxford and Cambridge university entrance

Oxford and Cambridge Universities are the oldest in the UK and are often considered to be the most prestigious. As a general rule, schools only enter those they consider to be their best pupils, yet only about one in three of the applicants receives the offer of a place. These universities also receive a large number of requests for admission for both undergraduate and postgraduate courses from students all over the world.

These two factors make Oxford and Cambridge centres of international scholarship. Students are assembled without regard to age, colour, race, religion or cultural background. Gifted boys and girls will find brilliant minds with whom to enjoy the cut and thrust of intellectual argument. They will be able to debate their own particular subject or topics of national or international importance and other issues of public debate. Academic excellence is matched by similar standards in music, art, drama and sport.

Of the generations of students that have passed through these universities, large numbers have subsequently made major contributions elsewhere – in the academic field, in government, industry, commerce and culture. The records of the many outstanding young men and women who have graduated from these two universities encourage employers to look first among the new Oxbridge graduates for new entrants at management level to their firms. Although there is no guarantee that an Oxford or Cambridge degree will automatically lead to a boy or girl subsequently obtaining a good job, the likelihood is usually greater than if he or she attended one of the other universities. By Christmas 1982 less than one in thirteen new graduates from Brunel, Cambridge and Oxford Universities had failed to find a job (*Times Educational Supplement* 9.9.1983 p. 11) but one in four from Lancaster, Coleraine, St David's and Lampeter had failed to do so. For the other universities the proportions were in between these two extremes. Young people and their parents should not be put off applying for admission to Oxford or Cambridge because of the usually very traditional style of the courses described in the college prospectuses. The degree course work is only a part of what the university has to offer, only one of the opportunities that may lead to an exciting and satisfying career.

Oxford and Cambridge Universities are made up of a number of autonomous member colleges. Intending applicants should apply to the university itself for an application form for the entrance examination. There are *no set academic requirements* which a prospective student must have *before* taking this examination – O or A levels are not necessary at this point. Information requested on the form includes the names of the colleges, in order of preference, to which the candidate wishes to apply, and the form should be completed and returned to the university, together with the registration fee, by the beginning of October in the year before which entrance is required. Intending students should also obtain a form from the Universities Central Council on Admissions (UCCA) and complete and return it to the council.

Once a candidate has taken the entrance examination, his papers will be marked by the tutors at the college he has named as his first choice. Prospective students who reach an acceptable standard *for that college* will be asked to attend for an interview. The college then selects those students it wishes to admit and offers them a place. The basis on which choices are made varies according to the policy of the individual colleges. In general, although merit is probably an important factor, it is not the only one; for instance, past benefactors may have left endowments for the sons of the clergy, of officers in the armed services and other particular groups. The marked examination scripts and other papers relating to a candidate to whom a college has not offered a place are forwarded to the second college on his list, where he may, in due course, be called for an interview. This procedure is repeated rapidly until all the colleges have filled all their undergraduate places for the forthcoming academic year.

Prospective students may take the entrance examination on more than one occasion (but they must usually be under the age of twenty-one). It is quite common for schools to enter pupils before they have taken their A level examinations, in which case they sit the exam during their fourth term in the sixth form (the exam is held during the Autumn term). Even when a student passes the college entrance examination, before he can take his place he must, unless he has won a scholarship, have satisfied the university's minimum entrance requirements, which are the equivalent of five O levels plus two A level passes. If, before he has passed his A level exams, a candidate satisfies the tutors of a college as to his probable suitability to become an undergraduate, the college will offer a 'conditional acceptance' – that is, he is offered a place providing he passes his A level exams with specified grades in the sixth term. Sitting the university entrance examination during their fourth term is an advantage to most students since, if they are not successful in obtaining a place then they will be able, if they wish, to take it again in the seventh term, when they have finished studying for their A levels. On the second occasion they will be helped by the experience gained from having taken the examination before and will be better prepared than if they sit for the first time in their seventh term.

Other universities and institutions of higher education

There are forty-two other universities in Britain (including Ireland) which are enabled under a Royal Charter to award their own degrees, and between them they offer a large number of different courses. In addition, there are about thirty polytechnics and a considerable number of other colleges that offer degree courses. These are awarded under the auspices of the Council for National Academic Awards (CNAA). This body sets the standard to be achieved for the award of a degree and monitors the academic level reached in the various institutions. It also awards the largest number of degrees (nearly a third of those given in the UK), since it is responsible for doing so for all those institutions of higher education which have degree courses but which are not part of one of the universities.

Useful information on degree courses will be found in 'Guide for Applicants' published by the Advisory Centre for Education in 1979. Many of these universities and polytechnics provide courses of the highest academic standard. Certain universities are leaders in particular fields, for instance Brunel for technology, St Andrew's University is particularly famous for marine biology, Queen Elizabeth College, London University for work in microbiology, Warwick for mathematics, Bristol for drama, and so on.

The various universities have their own regulations with regard to entrance requirements and other matters. Students enrolling for the degree courses conducted at polytechnics or other colleges for CNAA awards must have passed two subjects at A level and three others at O level. There are a number of reference books, some of which are given in the 'Guide for Applicants', which give information about the entrance requirements of particular universities and of the courses available. Similar details are available for the polytechnics and other colleges. Most public libraries will have some reference books, but they are not always up-to-date and the regulations may have changed. Once it has been decided which subject, what sort of course and where your son or daughter would like to study, write to the institution for details of their entrance requirements and courses.

The chief difference between the universities and the other institutions is that the former tend to offer courses with a rather more academic or theoretical approach, whereas the polytechnics and the colleges which prepare students for CNAA degrees often run courses which are more vocational in character. The distinction between the universities and the other institutions, though, is not clear-cut.

The number of subjects in which students may take degrees has widened during recent years and now includes various branches of commerce and business studies. Degrees may be taken in speech therapy and nursing, and in subjects connected with electrical and mechanical engineering and metallurgy as well as in many other subjects. 'Sandwich degrees' are available at various institutions, mainly for technical or vocational courses. A period of academic study at the institution is followed by a period of practical work in the relevant industry, and then the course finishes with another period of academic work. Another method of obtaining either an honours or a pass degree is through the Open University.

Alternative routes to satisfying careers

There is no doubt that the easiest way of obtaining an intellectually stimulating and satisfying job is along the recognised route through school to university, but it is not the only route. For those able young people for whom school has been a disaster for one reason or another, there are other ways of achieving a successful career. The possibilities are of two types – those which enable individuals to obtain GCE qualifications other than through school, and, more limited, those which provide a way of avoiding formal examinations altogether.

Teenagers are free to leave school when they are sixteen. They can then apply to take a course at a college of further education, where they will usually be treated as young adult students. The atmosphere is quite different from that found in most schools, and the students are at least partly responsible for organising their own work. A youngster can obtain qualifications at these colleges for entrance to a university or polytechnic quite as easily, and probably more easily, than if he stays at school, provided he is well motivated and does not need a teacher to make sure he is doing his work.

These colleges provide a wide variety of full- and part-time courses. The range of subjects offered varies from place to place but is likely to include O and A level GCE courses with a choice of science or arts subjects, electrical and mechanical engineering, commerce and other vocational subjects, in all of which students can obtain qualifications at various levels below degree level. The tuition in these colleges is usually of a high standard and by well qualified staff, and the choice of subjects is very much wider than in ordinary schools.

The second method of obtaining GCEs other than at school is through correspondence colleges (the addresses of a few of the best known are given in the back of this book). The advantage of these courses is that they can be arranged to meet individual requirements. A gifted youngster may not need to spend two years working for passes in three A level subjects, but can probably do them in a year or fifteen months, studying at his own pace. The correspondence college will send 'units' of the course to the student at intervals of his choosing; he then works through the unit and sends his work to a tutor who marks it and returns it to him, usually with a model answer. The student (or his parents) enters himself for whichever GCE subjects he wishes to take when he feels ready to sit the examinations.

The Open University provides degree courses which are made up of a number of alternative courses. *No entrance qualification is required* in order to become an Open University student, but places are given to young applicants only in special circumstances. The regulations change from time to time, so for anyone who is interested, it is worth writing for details to find out what courses are available and the current situation as regards enrolments.

One way in which a bright or gifted youngster who, in spite of his ability, is unable to pass examinations, may be able to find a satisfying job is through one of the Manpower Services' Youth Training Schemes. These are part of a government-sponsored project to help unemployed school-leavers find a job. Details are available through your local careers office. Under the YTS arrangements are made with selected firms, in practice usually fairly large ones, to take an agreed number of school-leavers and to give them a practical commercial or industrial training. The trainees also attend at a local college of further education to cover other aspects of the training. The schemes provide an opportunity for bright youngsters to choose the type of industry in which they would like to be employed, to work in a firm and to show keenness, aptitude and ability on the job. From a start of this sort, an able and hard-working individual might be able to establish himself within the firm or obtain a job in another firm in the same industry, with a reasonable prospect of a satisfying career ahead of him.

One of these schemes may be of particular interest to able teenagers who have no paper qualifications. Recently, Information Technology Centres (ITeC) have been set up in a number of towns in the UK where youngsters are taught about the technical side of computers, microprocessors, electronic circuitry, Prestel, Viewdata, electronic office equipment, word processors, etc. No qualifications are necessary, but applicants must be school-leavers aged sixteen (in some cases seventeen-year-olds are accepted) and be unemployed. To date nearly all applicants are from the ranks of the less able rather than from among the able and gifted, so the courses have been designed primarily to cover elementary work for school-leavers of limited academic ability. But these Information Technology Centres are staffed with well-qualified instructors so that advanced courses could probably be provided if there was a demand for them.

Self-Employment
Another avenue for very bright or gifted individuals is to become self-employed and to start their own businesses. No formal qualifications are necessary to do this. The formalities are minimal, and until a business becomes established the only essential steps are to register the

name, to inform the Collector of Taxes (though no taxes will be due until a profit is made) and the Department of Health and Social Security, as the self-employed must pay their own national insurance contributions.

The first essential for anyone contemplating this course of action is to know what they can produce that is saleable – that is, what other people will want sufficiently to pay money for. The product can either be actual objects such as toys which the young person has made from wood or plants which have been grown from seed, or a service, such as gardening for those who cannot or do not want to do it themselves or something requiring more expertise such as repairing typewriters and other office equipment. And whatever an aspiring businessman intends to produce, his very first consideration must be 'Who will buy it?' Until it has been established that there is a market for the product, it is most unwise to invest much capital. The way to test the market is to go out and ask prospective customers if they would like gardening done, typewriters repaired or whatever service is being offered. If it is a case of producing actual articles, then it is necessary to make a few samples of the product to take round to show to the 'buyer' in suitable shops.

This is only an outline of a few avenues worth investigating, and there are certainly many very real opportunities for young people with ability and initiative who want to start their own businesses. But profits may not be made easily and a small businessman who cannot sell his product will suffer a loss. Free booklets on how to proceed when starting a business are available from the local or London offices of the Department of Trade and Industry, who will also provide information on new government schemes to give financial and other aid to small business-people.

9   Conclusion

I hope this book has helped the parents of very bright and gifted children to gain a better understanding of their offspring. I have tried to make it easier to appreciate how difficult are the situations which so many of them face, particularly when they are at school. I have attempted to analyse the causes of these problems and to show how most of them stem from the greater speed with which gifted children learn and the rapid rate at which their mental development takes place. As we have seen, the gifted, although physically children in the same way as others of similar age, are different mentally – and it is this which, so often unexpected, can be so difficult to recognise when it happens.

A test has been provided with this book to give parents some idea of their child's level of ability. Parents should bear in mind that a high score on an intelligence test – that is, a high IQ – is the commonest but not the only indicator that a child is gifted. For those who have come to the conclusion that their youngster probably is intellectually gifted, it is hoped that a better understanding of the causes of the problems which arise will assist them in deciding in which way they can best help their boy or girl. I have attempted to present the child's point of view, in showing the sort of frustrations with which a gifted youngster has to contend when at school.

The second part of the book has concentrated on setting out the possibilities for improving the situation in which a gifted, very bright or talented child is placed. The options facing parents, of course, change at different stages: from the pre-school period, through the primary and secondary stages, to the point when the boy or girl is ready to consider the alternative possibilities for a future career. It is hoped that by making the issues and choices clearer parents will be better able to face difficult decisions, and, above all, that the children themselves will benefit.

The state educational system has evolved over little more than a hundred years, and the network of free primary and secondary schools caters fairly adequately for the majority of pupils. As has been explained in an earlier chapter, the 1981 Education Act made it the legal duty of LEAs to identify and provide special facilities for those children under their jurisdiction who have learning difficulties. The report of the Warnock Committee made to the Secretary of State for Education and Science in 1978 on 'special educational needs' states* that the committee did not regard the problem of highly gifted children as being relevant to their enquiry, yet later† they say that up to 'one in five children is likely to require special educational provision at some time during his school career . . .', and they go on to say that most of these special educational needs will have to be met in ordinary schools. Then the 1981 Education Act defines a child as having a 'learning difficulty' if he has 'a significantly greater difficulty in learning than the majority of children of his age'. It appears, then, that official policy is not concerned with bright and gifted children making full use of their intellectual abilities.

Only when a boy or girl has become psychologically maladjusted or has developed a physical ailment are public funds made available to provide the special educational facilities required in order to repair the damage. Letters addressed to Dr Lowenstein (who runs the therapeutic community at Allington Manor School) show how anxious and distressed some parents are about their children. One parent writes:

> . . . my son is four years and five months old. He has now begun attending a third nursery school as the first two said they could not manage him. He becomes very disruptive if he is not kept busy all the time. Our doctor referred us to the psychiatric wing of our local hospital but the doctors there said they could find nothing wrong

* 'Special Educational Needs', op. cit. p. 4.
† Ibid., p. 95.

with him. Robin does not like mixing with other children of his own age and becomes very frustrated and irritable when he has to do so.

Robin is very intelligent and advanced for his age. He can read and does so continuously, hardly ever having his nose out of a book. He is extremely interested in anything mechanical like cars, trains, etc. and will sit and listen carefully when their workings are being explained to him.

I am very worried indeed about what will happen when he is five and has to start going to school. Can you tell me where I could send him to school? I am a single parent and cannot afford to pay fees at a private school. Can you tell me where I can get some help because I just do not know what to do about Robin.

Here is part of a letter from another parent:

. . . when I spoke to you on the 'phone recently I think you said that the authorities would agree for a child to have special education if it was shown that he had problems at school. My son is ten and has been seeing a doctor in the psychiatric department of the children's hospital. I do hope Jeremy can come to you. He is so very unhappy at the present time. I have read so much about your work and I have absolute faith in what you can do. I do hope you will help Jeremy.

And a third parent writes:

. . . our son Peter is now eight years old and he has been a problem ever since he was a small baby. We tried to understand him but he has not fitted in with friends and always prefers his own company. He will concentrate for hours on the detailed design and working of Lego models.

For the last three years he has been at a small private school where all the children were allowed to learn at their own pace with a teacher teaching one-to-one if necessary. Now at eight he is too old to stay there any longer and we don't know where to send him.

Before going to school Peter was at a playgroup. He

was always asking questions and when he wasn't given a proper answer he went into a tantrum. He was left on his own after that and was very frustrated. Things were no better when he went to the local primary school. We were told that Peter disrupted the whole infant section while they were in the hall. The head teacher then said that she would see to it that he was made to do as he was told. That was when we took him away and sent him to the small private school where he has been since. I went to work so as to have money for the fees.

Peter is very keen to learn. He loves going round museums and asks constant questions. We would like you to assess Peter for us and to give us some advice about what to do about school.

Dr Lowenstein has been able to help many parents whose children do not fit into ordinary LEA schools. His wide experience in psychology and education as well as his particular interest in gifted children has enabled him to help rehabilitate many youngsters and restore family and other social relationships. It was in 1977 that he set up the day and boarding school in Hampshire called the Lowenstein Therapeutic Community. The school is small and there is a family atmosphere. The needs of every individual attending the school are assessed, and a separate programme of work is planned for each boy or girl according to their particular requirements. Although often doing different things from each other, the children work together in small groups of about five. At other times there are group discussions. The school has its own farm and there are all the usual facilities for physical and recreational activities. All this is possible because of the very high teacher-pupil ratio. The school specialises in providing a therapeutic environment and children who are experiencing all sorts of learning difficulties are accepted. Where a child can be shown to come into this category, the fees will be paid if necessary by the LEA. Pupils are also accepted from parents privately.

The centre is particularly valuable for gifted children who have suffered, for some reason or other, psychological damage. For those gifted boys and girls whose only real problem is that they possess such brilliant minds that ordinary schools cannot cater for their needs, Allington Manor provides a setting within which they can progress at their own pace. Dr Lowenstein makes a point of ensuring that no individual is held back however fast he or she learns. Special arrangements are made to encourage a child's particular interests, whatever these may be.

The main aim of this book is to help the parents of gifted and talented children. It tries to do this, first, by showing them that they are not alone with their problems, but that there are other families with similar difficulties. Second, it provides parents with information about the various possibilities open to them and will thus, I hope, help to prevent the difficulties often associated with bringing up and educating gifted children from building up to a crisis. Even in those cases where a child has been faced with severe setbacks at home or at school, there will be someone who can help and the probability that at least a partial remedy can be found. If this book has succeeded in helping gifted children in any way, then it will have been successful in its purpose.

Score Sheet

A Picture Vocabulary   *Total*

No.	Ans.	Score	No.	Ans.	Score	No.	Ans.	Score
1	b	——	8	b	——	15	d	——
2	c	——	9	d	——	16	c	——
3	c	——	10	a	——	17	a	——
4	c	——	11	c	——	18	c	——
5	b	——	12	d	——	19	d	——
6	a	——	13	a	——	20	b	——
7	a	——	14	b	——			——

B Vocabulary

1 ——	5 ——	9 ——	13 ——	17 ——	
2 ——	6 ——	10 ——	14 ——	18 ——	
3 ——	7 ——	11 ——	15 ——	19 ——	
4 ——	8 ——	12 ——	16 ——	20 ——	——

C Absurdities

1 —— 2 —— 3 —— 4 —— 5 ——   ——

D Rhymes

1 —— 2 —— 3 —— 4 —— 5 ——
6 —— 7 —— 8 —— 9 —— 10 ——   ——

E Picture Oddities

missing bench leg   lorry wrong side of road
missing pram handle   gate opens across pavement
missing bicycle saddle   lamp wrong way round
missing chimney (1st house)   only one child on seesaw
missing windows (2nd house)   car door handle on front   ——

F Circles

No.	Ans.	Score	No.	Ans.	Score	No.	Ans.	Score
1.	6	——	4.	2	——	7.	4	——
2.	6	——	5.	6	——	8.	2	——
3.	4	——	6.	5	——	9.	4	——

                                                            ══

Score Levels for the Gifted and Bright

Your child is almost certainly gifted or very bright if he or she gains a test score in line with that shown on the table below for his or her age.

If his or her score is high in any section or combination of sections as shown below, then he or she may be gifted in one area and should be fully assessed.

The test has been devised for very bright children, and those of average ability will find it exceedingly difficult, possibly only achieving a score on a par with a gifted child as much as six years younger.

The test is most reliable between the ages of seven and twelve.

| Age | Total Score | | Section Scores | | |
	Probably gifted (IQ 130+)	*Bright (approx. IQ 125+)*	A	B	E + F
adult	64	55	20	19	15
12–16	57	49	18	15	12
11	45	40	15	12	12
10	41	35	12	10	10
9	36	30	10	8	10
8	31	25	10	6	5
7	26	20	8	5	5
6	22	15	8	5	5
5	17	10	—	—	—
4	12	7	—	—	—
3	8	5	—	—	—

Useful Addresses

Able Children (Pullen Publications) Ltd for Thinking Skills Booklets), Park Lane, Knebworth, Herts SG3 6PF. (0438 812320)

Advisory Centre for Education (ACE), 18 Victoria Park Square, London E2 9PB. (01-980 4596)

BBC Schools' Broadcasting, The Langham, Portland Place, London W1A 1AA. (01-935 2801)

Blandford Press, Link House, West Street, Poole, Dorset BH15 1LL. (0202 671171)

Career Analysts, Career House, 90 Gloucester Place, London W1. (01-935 5452)

Careers Consultants Limited, Freepost, 12–14 Hill Rise, Richmond, Surrey TW10 5BR. (01-940 5668)

Early Learning Centre, 25 Kings Road, Reading, Berks. (0734 595451)

Education Otherwise, 18 Eynham Road, London W12. (01-749 2199)

Independent Schools' Information Service, 56 Buckingham Gate, London SW1E 6A9. (01-630 8793/4)

Independent Television Schools' Programmes, Knighton House, 52–66 Mortimer Street, London W1N 8AN. (01-636 6866)

Invicta Plastics Limited, Oadby, Leicester. (0533 717211)

Learning Development Aids, Duke Street, Wisbech, Cambs. (0945 63441)

Lego UK Limited, Wrexham, Clwyd LL13 7TQ. (0978 266949)

Dr L. F. Lowenstein, Lowenstein Therapeutic Community, Allington Manor School, Fair Oak, Eastleigh, Nr. Southampton, Hampshire. (0703 692621)

Mercers College (Correspondence), Ware, Herts. (0920 5926)

National Extension (Correspondence) College, 18 Brooklands Avenue, Cambridge. (0223 316644)

Nottingham Educational Supplies (NES), 17 Ludlow Hill Road, West Bridgford, Nottingham, NG2 6HD. (0602 234251)

'Offspring', E. J. Arnold & Son Limited, Butterley Street, Leeds LS10 1AX. (0532 432333)

The Pre-School Playgroups Assn., Alford House, Aveline Street, London SE11 5DH. (01-582 8871)

The Publishers Association, 19 Bedford Square, London WC1B 3HJ. (01-580 6321)

Purnell Publishers Limited (for THREE FOUR FIVE COURSES), Poulton, Bristol, BS18 5LQ. (0761 413301)

Auditions Secretary, Junior Associates, Royal Ballet School, 155 Talgarth Road,
London W14 9DE. (Contact by letter only)

Secretary of State for Education, Department of Education and Science, Elizabeth House, London SE1 7PH. (01-928 9222)

The Administrator, Shell-London Symphony Orchestra, Barbican Centre, London EC2Y 8DS. (01-638 4141)

Taskmaster Limited, Morris Road, Clarendon Park, Leicester, LE2 6BR. (Leicester 704286)

Wolsley Hall Correspondence College, 99 Banbury Road, Oxford. (0865 54231)

World Education Service, Murray House, Vanden Street, London SW1. (01-222 7181)

Index